Strategic Power
and Soviet Foreign Policy

STRATEGIC POWER AND SOVIET FOREIGN POLICY

ARNOLD L. HORELICK AND MYRON RUSH

The University of Chicago Press / Chicago & London

Library of Congress Catalog Card Number: 66–13874

THE UNIVERSITY OF CHICAGO PRESS, CHICAGO & LONDON
The University of Toronto Press, Toronto 5, Canada

© *1965, 1966 by The* RAND *Corporation*

Printed in the United States of America

To Vivian and Theresa

PREFACE

THIS BOOK IS about the interrelation of Soviet strategic military power and foreign policy. It deals with the years since the advent of nuclear weapons made strategic power seem too destructive to employ militarily and yet too dangerous to ignore in political calculations. The novel question of international relations in our time is the political effect in peacetime of mankind's concern over the consequences of thermonuclear war. The foreign policies of the major powers have manifestly been affected by this unprecedented peril but in diverse ways that are the subject of controversy among statesmen, military thinkers, and scholars. We shall be concerned with its effects on Soviet foreign policy.

The present Soviet leaders rose to power under Khrushchev at a time when the Soviet Union first began to acquire the new weapons. They, no less than their former leader, have been attracted by the political potentialities of the new situation created by nuclear weapons as well as sobered by its dangers. In Part 1, this new situation is presented as it emerged after Stalin's death, when the U.S.S.R. first acquired the means to wage intercontinental nuclear warfare and when the Soviet leaders' military and political understanding of these weapons began to take form.

Part 2 examines in detail the boldest attempt yet made to exploit strategic weapons politically, an attempt made possible by Soviet development and test-firing of an intercontinental ballistic missile in advance of the United States. This led to a remarkable effort, sustained over four years, to deceive the West regarding the pace and scope of the Soviet Union's program for building and deploying ICBM's. The myth of the "missile gap," which this Soviet effort helped to create, dominated the strategic dialogue between the United States and the Soviet Union from the launching of the first Sputnik in the fall of 1957 to the building of the Berlin wall in the second half of 1961. The Soviet attempt to deceive the Western powers regarding the U.S.S.R.'s ICBM capabilities will therefore be discussed here in considerable detail.

Part 3 consists in a reappraisal of Soviet foreign policy during this period in the light of what became known only several years later about Soviet military capabilities. In retrospect, it attempts to distinguish the military-political actions that Soviet leaders were prepared to take from those they merely threatened. The clearest exposition and the decisive test of Soviet political strategy in those years was the campaign against Berlin from 1958 to 1962. When the myth of Soviet missile superiority was exposed late in 1961, thus frustrating the Soviet political offensive in Berlin and elsewhere, the Soviet leaders attempted to give it new impetus by clandestinely deploying missiles in Cuba. Their failure revealed even more starkly the limitations imposed on Soviet foreign policy by United States strategic preponderance. It compelled the Soviet leaders to reconsider the potentialities of the political use of strategic power in the light of military policies that would be feasible in the foreseeable future.

Part 4 examines three alternative Soviet military policies that will most likely be considered by the post-Khrushchev leadership and that could conceivably give rise to one of the following strategic states: continued Soviet inferiority, some form of parity, or Soviet superiority of a marginal kind. These strategic states could provide the basis for divergent political strategies, which are considered here in terms of their feasibility and possible consequences. The book concludes by considering the role that strategic power may play in the future in relation to other instruments of Soviet foreign policy.

This study presents the conclusions of its authors on the subject of the political use of Soviet nuclear strategic power down to mid-1965, when the research was terminated. However, additional evidence that became available in the interval before publication has been examined and found to be consistent with the analyses and conclusions contained in the book. This study is a contribution to The RAND Corporation's continuing program of research undertaken for United States Air Force Project RAND.

A. L. H.

M. R.

ACKNOWLEDGMENTS

THIS BOOK IS the product of research on the Soviet Union's political use of strategic power conducted by the authors, jointly and individually, over a period of several years. During this time, numerous colleagues contributed to the shaping of our views and particularly to our understanding of the difficult military problems that are examined. Among these colleagues, we are especially indebted to Bernard Brodie, Herbert S. Dinerstein, Daniel Ellsberg, Alexander L. George, and Hans Speier. Of course, the authors alone are responsible for the views and conclusions expressed in the book. Our responsibility for this study, the whole as well as the separate parts, is indivisible. Each chapter was first discussed jointly, then drafted by one author and revised by the other; when substantive differences arose, they were resolved by intellectual exchanges, either oral or written. Many of the ideas expressed in these pages originated as by-products of these exchanges and constitute the reward of our collaborative intellectual labor. We or our research assistants made our own translations of the Russian materials cited in this book. Interested readers may find translations of most of them in *The Current Digest of the Soviet Press*.

The authors wish to express their gratitude to Janet Zagoria and Lilita Dzirkals, who, at different times, provided extensive and conscientious research assistance.

Finally, Myron Rush wishes to take this opportunity of thanking his coauthor, Arnold Horelick, for generously contributing a disproportionate amount of effort to the completion of the work after he (Rush) went on leave of absence from The RAND Corporation in 1963.

CONTENTS

PART THREE

STRATEGIC POWER AND SOVIET
FOREIGN POLICY

PART FOUR

SOVIET STRATEGIC CHOICES AND
THEIR POLITICAL IMPLICATIONS

PART 1

NUCLEAR UNCERTAINTY:
ARENA OF THE COLD WAR

INTRODUCTION

RULERS HAVE ALWAYS FACED the problem of how to employ military force politically to achieve objectives that might otherwise not be achieved at all or only by engaging in hostilities. They have sought to solve the problem by employing military threats and demonstrations in support of their diplomacy. The development of thermonuclear weapons, however, has made the political use of strategic power an acute problem, for the military use of these weapons might entail terrible destruction even to the victor. The requirements, risks, and costs for the political use of strategic power are much lower than for its military use. Hence, the political use of strategic power has never been so attractive.

Since the first demonstration of the military power of the atomic bomb, statesmen have expected the acquisition of nuclear weapons to be politically valuable. Today, leaders of countries aspiring to possess nuclear weapons are more likely to be motivated in their quest by political rather than strictly military considerations. Events of the past decade, however, have also revealed something of the difficulties encountered in trying to make political capital of strategic power. The destructive capacity of the new weapons is so great that even a state which has achieved a measure of strategic superiority may nonetheless so fear the other side's inferior strategic forces as to make resort to general war a last and desperate expedient. To the extent that the weaker side has knowledge of this fear, the stronger side's efforts to extract political advantage from its superiority may be obstructed.

Awareness of these difficulties has convinced many observers that the political worth of nuclear forces has been greatly overrated and that the only purpose they can serve is to defend a state's most "vital interests."[1] Some students of the problem have questioned whether the strategic forces possessed by the United States and the Soviet Union can do much more in time of peace than neutralize the political and diplomatic value of the opposing strategic forces.

No one doubts that the advent of thermonuclear weapons and

---

[1] Louis J. Halle, for example, contends that "the diplomatic uses of a nuclear panoply are limited largely to situations in which one is defending, against external attack, a *status quo* considered vital" ("Peace in Our Time," *New Republic*, December 25, 1963, p. 17).

3

modern delivery vehicles and their availability to both sides have radically altered the international situation and that even a thermonuclear stalemate may bring some advantage to one side or the other. Nor is there much doubt that if the forces of one side were manifestly capable of launching a highly effective first strike, one that was virtually retaliation-proof, they could be used directly to achieve major political objectives. What is chiefly at issue is the political significance of real or alleged disparities in strategic forces when neither side possesses a manifestly overpowering superiority.

This book considers the use of strategic power for political ends chiefly from the perspective of Soviet foreign policy. To do so, however, it must first illuminate the general problem of the political use of nuclear forces.

Political use of strategic power does not directly depend on the objective capabilities of the two sides. It depends in the first instance on their beliefs about the strategic balance and on the beliefs of one side about the beliefs of the other and of third parties. Since it involves beliefs, and beliefs about beliefs, it is a highly subjective undertaking, once or twice removed from actual military capabilities.

Of course, it is true that the relevant beliefs are inevitably conditioned by the objective capabilities of the two sides; numerous facts regarding the strategic balance are known to the protagonists and they cannot disregard them in forming their estimates. But there are also great uncertainties in calculating the relative capabilities of revolutionary new strategic weapon systems that have never been employed in combat; these uncertainties may be compounded by incomplete information on the opponent's force structure, by doubt as to the tactics he would employ in the event of hostilities, and especially by the opponent's efforts to widen the area of uncertainty and to manipulate it to his own advantage.

To this inevitable uncertainty, which even the most rigorous analyst or military planner cannot wholly penetrate, is added the imprecision of the statesman's notions regarding strategic matters, which, being influenced by many non-technical factors, may diverge widely from the military planner's refined estimate. Yet the beliefs of statesmen are the stuff of political conflict that rests on strategic forces.

Much of the political struggle involving strategic forces takes place within the limits of this area of uncertainty. Both the calculated "resolution" whereby an inferior power defends its outposts and the bluffs or deceptions that make it possible to win positions from an equal or more powerful opponent are facilitated by the uncertainty that encompasses modern strategic capabilities.

In the era of thermonuclear weapons, uncertainty pervades all military calculations of the strategic balance. Uncertainty, however, may be substantially greater on one side than on the other; moreover, the effects of a given degree of uncertainty on both sides need not always be symmetrical. The successful political employment of strategic power does not require that one's own uncertainties be wholly overcome; it requires that the relevant uncertainties of the opponent be maximized and that the situation be so manipulated as to make the outcome of a given confrontation turn on the opponent's uncertainties rather than on one's own.

In employing their strategic forces for political ends, then, the Soviet leaders must seek to deepen their opponent's uncertainties and anxieties about the strategic balance and to conceal their own; if the required beliefs about Soviet military capabilities do not already exist, the Soviet leaders must try to induce them. This can be an exceedingly difficult undertaking. It is no mere preliminary to the political exploitation of strategic power but lies close to the heart of the enterprise. Various means are available for this purpose:

a) Soviet leaders might *assert* that they possess such capabilities or that they have the military forces that entail them.

b) Soviet leaders might *make threats* that presuppose such capabilities.

c) Soviet leaders might *demonstrate* something of their military capability to induce opponents to credit the U.S.S.R. with the requisite additional capabilities.

d) Soviet leaders might *take actions*, violent or non-violent, that imply they are confident their strategic capabilities are what they claim them to be; acquiescence or ineffectual resistance by opponents would suggest that they shared the Soviet estimate of the strategic balance.

The first two methods have this limitation: The assertions and threats must themselves be credible. Demonstrations, on the other hand, are often persuasive only to the extent that they reveal secrets; thus they may achieve their object only at the cost of surrendering advantages that secrecy confers. The most effective means available to the U.S.S.R. to induce in an opponent the desired beliefs about the strategic balance is to take actions, backed by strategic threats, that impinge on important interests of that opponent. Such actions might include non-violent measures; for example, the unilateral rescinding of rights, privileges, or immunities created by prior agreements (closing the access routes from West Germany to West Berlin), aggression against countries allied with the United States, and even limited military attacks on the opponent himself. However, if the party whose interests are to be harmed by such actions does not already have the required beliefs regarding Soviet capabilities, the actions may be extremely risky. On the other hand, less risky, more ambiguous actions that only impinge on peripheral interests of the opponent may not significantly influence his beliefs about the strategic balance. Thus far in the cold war, the Soviet leaders have relied chiefly on assertions, threats, demonstrations, and peripheral actions to achieve their ends; they have been reluctant to risk direct action against major Western interests. As we shall see, this reluctance, grounded in the Soviet leaders' sober appraisal of the strategic balance, has had far-reaching effects on the conduct of Soviet foreign policy.

The political use of strategic power poses further requirements. To employ strategic power effectively on behalf of a *specific* political objective, Soviet leaders also have to make their opponents believe that the alleged correlation of strategic power necessitates conciliation of the Soviet Union *on the question at issue*. It is a little like bringing a queen to bear in chess in order to reconcile one's opponent to defeat in an engagement between pawns. The threat to employ strategic forces militarily in some contingency can be varied as required from a mere rumor of doubtful origin to veiled or implicit threats in the middle range and on upward toward—though it may always fall well short of—the classical ultimatum. For all its flexibility, the threat of strategic attack with nuclear weapons is a dangerous game, pervaded by uncertainty, in which both sides take risks.

The political use of strategic force by the Soviet Union in pursuit of major gains entails major costs and risks. It tends to increase hostility toward and suspicion of the U.S.S.R. in the West and can also lessen Soviet influence among unaligned countries. In such circumstances, policies that are most fruitful in a relatively relaxed international atmosphere may suffer and even have to be abandoned. Moreover, the uncertainty in any direct confrontation between the two chief powers, when intensified by the threatened employment of strategic forces, creates risks that cannot reasonably be assumed in order to achieve a small object and that are greatly amplified if the object sought is weighty.

The difficulties, costs, and risks involved in the political use of strategic forces are formidable; yet, as we shall see, the Soviet leaders have not always been deterred by them. They have tested the efficacy of this political tool in the nuclear age, experiencing some of the benefits as well as the hazards. Now, after a period of comparative quiescence in the cold war, they must again decide what political role to assign to their strategic forces in the future. The fate of mankind may depend on their choice.

ONE

THE POLITICAL USE
OF STRATEGIC POWER:
SOVIET AND WESTERN ATTITUDES

UNLIKE THE PHYSICAL EFFECTS of nuclear weapons, which can be calculated without reference to the politics of those who might be destroyed by them, their political effects cannot be analyzed apart from the political character and objectives of the parties possessing them. Few would argue with this statement. Yet many write as if nuclear weapons, which in war "would not distinguish between Communists and non-Communists, between atheists and believers, between Catholics and Protestants," [1] also reduced to insignificance the political differences between the powers possessing them. This view manifests itself in diverse ways in Western literature on the cold war, military strategy, arms control, and disarmament. The advent of nuclear weapons and the idea of indiscriminate, universal destruction that is associated with them have contributed to the widespread popularity of the thesis of the "mirror image" as the principal cause of international tension: The Soviet leaders perceive (falsely) in the United States a threat to their country's security that is a mirror-image of the threat to American security that we perceive (falsely) in the Soviet Union.[2] In this view, the cold war is chiefly the product of dangerous mutual misperceptions. Some have carried the argument to the point of denying that there are any essential differences in the political character or the goals of the two great powers.[3]

This particular interpretation of the behavior of the parties engaged in the cold war, which emphasizes its symmetrical character, originated for the most part among psychologists. But some strategic analysts, too, are inclined to approach international relations as if the powers contending in the real world were the faceless "Reds" and

---

[1] N. S. Khrushchev, *Sovetsko-frantsuzskaia druzhba: zalog mira* ("Franco-Soviet Friendship: Pledge of Peace") (Moscow: Gosudarstvennoe Izdatel'stvo Politicheskoi Literatury, 1960), p. 35.

[2] See, especially, Urie Bronfenbrenner, "The Mirror Image in Soviet-American Relations: A Social Psychologist's Report," *Journal of Social Issues*, XVII (1961), No. 3, 45–56.

[3] See, for example, Erich Fromm, *May Man Prevail* (Garden City, N.Y.: Doubleday & Co., 1961), *passim*.

"Blues" of the war-game room, where each side is equally motivated to maximize its "payoffs," which are defined according to certain objective, hence mutually shared, criteria. In the burgeoning field of arms control and disarmament studies, the assumption, usually implicit, that the political objectives of both sides engaged in the cold war are equally dominated by a desire to avoid thermonuclear war often leads to a preoccupation with technical schemes for breaking the deadlock that fail to cope adequately with the large and crucial area of political disagreement between the two sides, which extends beyond their shared concern over sheer survival.

But the powers confronting one another are not faceless, nor are they simply suffering from hallucinations reciprocally induced by staring at one another through a distorting pane they have mistaken for plate glass. The differences between the two sides are real and substantial, and they intrude themselves into virtually every facet of the interplay between them. To acknowledge this is not necessarily to make moral judgments regarding these differences. Certainly, it does not follow from their existence that they can be resolved only by the annihilation of one side by the other or by their mutual destruction. But to live with these differences in an age of thermonuclear weapons, it is first necessary to recognize that they exist and to understand their implications.

The differences that concern us in this study are those that bear most directly on the political use of strategic power by the two sides. They arise between

1. the foreign policy objectives of the contending powers;
2. the means available to them for pursuing their objectives;
3. the principles that guide their employment of these means and their distinctive styles of political warfare; and
4. the constraints under which they operate in conducting the struggle.

Differences in these areas strongly condition the attitudes of the leaders of the two sides toward the political use of strategic power and, specifically, toward ways of coping with the uncertainties inherent in calculations of the strategic balance.

The political employment of strategic nuclear threats by both the Soviet Union and the United States has become a well-established phenomenon of international life in recent years. There is, however, a fundamental distinction between the purposes for which these threats have been used by the two sides: the Soviet Union has issued such threats principally in support of its efforts to extend Soviet power or influence into non-Communist areas of the world; the United States has resorted to strategic threats for defensive purposes, to preserve allied or friendly non-Communist countries from Communist domination. In other words, United States strategic power has not been brought to bear politically to overthrow Communist regimes. The battlefronts of the cold war have been almost exclusively in non-Communist areas, although military operations, once begun, have sometimes extended to Communist territory, as in North Korea and North Vietnam. In neither instance, however, did the United States even threaten to employ its full military power in order to bring about the elimination of Communist regimes in these countries. During the Cuban crisis of October, 1962, United States strategic power was brought to bear politically but only in pursuit of a limited objective—the removal of Soviet offensive weapons from the island—and not to secure the removal of the Castro regime.

The Soviet Union, on the other hand, has made broad and differentiated use of strategic threats in support of a wide range of offensive foreign policy objectives. "Strategic threats" is used here as a broad term for the expression by one government, verbally or by other means, of an intention to employ its strategic forces against another in certain circumstances. The nature of Soviet strategic threats has varied with the particular situation, the political interest to be served, and the audience to be influenced. Typically, Soviet strategic threats have fallen far short of being ultimatums; often they have been no more than warnings, menacing insinuations, vague predictions of dire consequences, or merely claims of Soviet strategic strength placed in suggestive contexts. Usually the employment of Soviet strategic power was threatened as the *possible ultimate consequence*, not as the *certain and immediate consequence*, of an opponent's failure to satisfy a Soviet demand.

The demands have also varied greatly in kind and in degree as well as in the time period allowed for their satisfaction. Most frequently, the Soviet leaders have required that an opponent refrain from some action that he was allegedly contemplating (for example, a Turkish attack on Syria, 1957; United States attacks on Iraq, 1958, and on Cuba, 1960). Threats covering such demands may be considered "empty threats" if the party threatened is in any case disinclined to carry out the forbidden action. But such threats are not without political value since third parties, or even the threatening side, may interpret failure to act as evidence that the threatened party has yielded to the threat.

On other occasions, the Soviet Union has demanded that an

opponent cease activities in which he was already engaged (for example, the Anglo-French-Israeli attack on Egypt, 1956; American U-2 flights over the Soviet Union, 1960). Still other threats have been designed to coerce the opponent into initiating some positive action (for example, withdrawal of allied troops from West Berlin, 1958–62). Since non-compliance is immediately apparent following demands of the last two types, the time period specified for compliance is particularly important.

All these threats, warnings, and menaces emanating from the Soviet leaders have had one thing in common: they have invoked the image of thermonuclear war in support of Soviet political interests. This image has been present in one form or another even though the immediate and direct employment of Soviet strategic forces has rarely been threatened explicitly except in response to a strategic attack on the U.S.S.R. or its allies. Although the sanction threatened is thermonuclear war, precisely when, how, and even by whom such a war might actually be initiated is frequently not spelled out. Only the danger that such a war may occur and the conditions for averting it are specified: if the West fails to acquiesce in Soviet demands war may occur; acquiescence will avert war.

The Soviet *Juridical Dictionary* provides a useful definition of the term "threat" in the broad sense in which it is employed in this book:

A threat is a special form of influencing a victim psychologically so as to compel him to commit some action or other, or to refrain from committing it, in the interests of the threatener. This type of threat in certain circumstances . . . may paralyze the will of the victim and lead to the result desired. . . .[4]

The Soviet Union has not attempted to secure changes in the status quo directly by the use of strategic threats. Non-strategic means have been employed as the direct instruments: the use of or threat to use Soviet conventional military strength (as in Eastern Europe, 1945–48; in Iran, 1946; in Berlin since 1948); proxy armies (as in Korea, 1950–53); the export of weapons (as to Egypt and Syria in 1955); support of subversion and guerilla warfare (as in Greece, 1947–48, and Laos, 1960–61). Strategic threats have typically been employed to enhance the effect of these non-strategic instruments and to limit the West's freedom of action in opposing them.

In their use of strategic threats the Soviet leaders have sought to

---

[4] *Juridical Dictionary* [*Iuridicheskii slovar'*] (2d ed.; Moscow: Gosudarstvennoe Izdatel'stvo Iuridicheskoi Literatury, 1956), Vol. II, p. 550.

plant in non-Communist audiences an impression of the great discrepancy between the universally destructive character of thermonuclear war and the seemingly narrow and remote character of the issue of the moment. In effect, they argue: Who wants to die to prevent an East German instead of a Russian from checking Allied documents? Since the West has not pressed for similar "small" changes in the Communist status quo for their own advantage, it has often been made to appear that the danger of thermonuclear war arises from Western intransigence and bellicosity on behalf of a myopic, reactionary defense of the non-Communist status quo. To prevent armed conflict the status quo in the non-Communist world must be adjusted by negotiations and mutual concessions; the status quo in the Communist world need not be changed because it poses no threat to world peace.

In contemporary circumstances, use of strategic threats for offensive political purposes is tantamount to nuclear blackmail. It is calculated to capitalize on mankind's fear of thermonuclear war and on uncertainties regarding Soviet strategic intentions and capabilities, which are fostered by Soviet secrecy. By indulging in this practice, the Soviet leaders have artificially raised international tension in order to advance their political interests. They have relied on the restraint, responsibility, and forbearance of the West, particularly the United States, to prevent the arms race from getting out of control. The evident contrast between the Soviet penchant for using strategic threats and the restraint and responsibility of the American response has at times served Western interests; but it can have this effect only if Soviet threats fail to produce their intended effects. If Soviet threats succeed, United States restraint may be perceived by others as aloofness or fear of commitment.

In taking political advantage of mankind's concern over the danger of thermonuclear war, the Soviet leaders have relied heavily on the great uncertainties that attend calculations of the strategic balance and of the intentions of the powers possessing nuclear weapons. Western leaders have tended to regard the possibility of miscalculations of the strategic balance as a source of great danger; Soviet leaders, on the other hand, have sought to capitalize on such miscalculations. In the past these divergent attitudes toward uncertainty significantly influenced military planning on both sides.

Whereas the United States tended to insure against its own uncertainty or against Soviet miscalculation by acquiring larger strategic forces than might otherwise have been deemed necessary, the U.S.S.R. procured only a limited capability to attack the United States, relying heavily on its ability to convey exaggerated impressions of this capability. Although it is true that the United States is better able than the Soviet Union to pay for "insurance," the difference in attitudes is only partially explicable by the difference in the sizes of the United States and Soviet economies. More fundamental are differences between the *functions* of strategic forces as seen by the two sides and differences in the extent of reliance on *non-strategic means* for deterrence and for the achievement of positive objectives.

The United States strategic force has been designed to deter a Soviet attack on the United States and, in addition, to deter local Soviet military aggression and political aggrandizement. The Soviet strategic force also serves as a deterrent, but essentially as a deterrent to United States and Western responses to its own military and political offensives. From the Soviet point of view, the threat posed by the American strategic force at any given moment is the product of American capabilities multiplied by the provocation offered by Soviet behavior. The former is only partially amenable to Soviet influence, but the latter is essentially under the control of the Soviet leaders, who, enjoying the initiative, may either intensify or moderate their behavior as circumstances require. The United States, on the other hand, tends to see the immediate danger as the product of the relative military capabilities of the rival strategic force coupled with the extent of Western resistance to Soviet pressures. The Soviet leaders can avoid being provocative when circumstances are not favorable; they can always resume the offensive at some later time. But the West feels it must permanently maintain on a high level its capacity to resist encroachment lest temporary slackness be exploited—politically, if not militarily—by the vigilant opponent. Thus, strategic insurance seems necessary because control of tension is judged to reside in Soviet hands. The political yield from Western weapons always seems to lag behind their objective military capabilities. Uncertainty is viewed as tending to work in the opponent's favor, with the result that larger forces recommend themselves as means to reduce potentially dangerous uncertainties, one's own as well as the opponent's.

The Soviet leaders, on the other hand, apparently regard themselves as the beneficiaries of the non-linear relationship between the political and military value of strategic weapons. The advantage they derive is not simply the opportunity to cut costs for strategic forces but also the wider range of options open to Soviet decision-makers and strategic planners. Increments in Soviet strategic power, even if they are not large enough to alter significantly the real strategic balance, may have disproportionately large political consequences, because the Soviet leadership is often able to magnify their effects by playing on the anxieties and uncertainties of its opponents.

Western uncertainty regarding Soviet strategic capabilities and intentions has been a prime asset of the Soviet Union throughout most of the cold war. Soviet secrecy, effective in varying degrees over the years, has greatly facilitated the efforts of Soviet leaders to manipulateWestern uncertainty. In recent years, technological innovations have greatly improved the West's ability to penetrate Soviet secrecy, and the Soviet leaders have lifted the veil somewhat themselves, but the relative lack of information about Soviet capabilities continues to be an important fact of life in the cold war.

Soviet secrecy embraces not only denial to foreigners of access to facilities in the U.S.S.R. deemed to be of strategic significance but also tight control over the output of Soviet media of communication. It is true that the content of Soviet communications has changed in many significant ways since Joseph Stalin's death, but the ability of Soviet leaders to control what is communicated has not lessened appreciably. The West, by contrast, not only speaks with many voices but listens with many ears. The significance of this difference for the conduct of the cold war by the two sides can hardly be exaggerated. For the cold war, on a day-by-day basis, is to a remarkable extent a war of words. It is largely by verbal means that the intentions, will, and resolution of the adversaries—as well as something of their capabilities—are communicated to one another and to third parties. Warnings, threats, counterthreats, and ultimatums are the characteristic language of the cold war. Clearly, it is what is believed to be behind the words—the power and will to use it—that determines their credibility. But the West has frequently been highly uncertain in its beliefs about Soviet strategic intentions and capabilities and this uncertainty has often compelled it to weigh carefully the words of the Soviet leaders.

The Soviet leaders are both more strongly inclined and better able to convey exaggerated impressions of their strategic power than are their opponents. They have in fact engaged in deliberate, systematic, and sustained strategic deception against the West. We shall treat this practice in detail elsewhere in this book. But here it is pertinent to identify another fundamental difference between the two systems that are engaged in the cold war, a difference that makes deceptive practices more feasible for the Soviet Union and vulnerability to their effects more likely in the West.

Governments disposing of nuclear weapons bring them to bear politically in order to influence the policies of other governments in ways that favor their interests. To influence Communist policy in the cold war means to influence the small circle of rulers in Moscow and in Peking, and perhaps the ruling groups in some other Communist capitals; but given the nature of the political process in Western societies and within the Western alliance as a whole, to influence the West's policies means to influence the governments, parties, or peoples allied to the United States as well as important private groups in America itself. The Communists can bring pressure and propaganda to bear at many more points than the West, since all the groups mentioned, as well as articulate opinion in neutral countries, can make their influence felt in Washington. Of course, the most far-reaching and rapid results can be achieved by directly influencing the estimates and beliefs of the top United States and Soviet decision-makers themselves, and both sides have tried repeatedly to do this, with varying degrees of success. But this is far more difficult to accomplish than to exert indirect pressure on them by influencing groups whose opinions they consider important. The top decision-makers, though they lack important information about the capabilities and intentions of their opponents and are therefore uncertain regarding certain crucial strategic matters, are nevertheless far better informed than any other group or party and less vulnerable to the adversary's attempts to mislead. For this reason the strongest Soviet pressures and threats have usually been directed against governments and peoples allied to the United States.

The ability of the Soviet Union to invoke, for self-serving political purposes, the image of a thermonuclear war that would imperil the peoples of distant lands has provided the Soviet leaders with a powerful new instrument of foreign policy. With the aid of this instrument the Soviet Union has become a truly global power, as it was not during Stalin's rule. To exert Soviet influence in distant places, Stalin had at his disposal a world-wide network of disciplined Communist parties and front organizations, but at the time of his death they were largely discredited and increasingly ineffective as instruments of Soviet foreign policy. The chief military means at Stalin's disposal—the large conventional Soviet ground forces—made it necessary for him to limit his active foreign policy interventions to countries in contiguous areas that could be threatened by Soviet bayonets. Of course, Stalin had become so rigid in his strategic thought and so Byzantine in his style of political action that he might have proved incapable of fashioning political strategies and tactics appropriate for exploiting intercontinental nuclear weapons even had he possessed them. In any case, it was left for his successors, and particularly Nikita Khrushchev, who came to power when the U.S.S.R. began to acquire the new weapons, to develop and to test such strategies and tactics. The emergence of Soviet strategic nuclear power, and the initial phases of evolving Soviet policy concerning its political use are the subjects of the next chapter.

TWO

THE EMERGENCE OF SOVIET
STRATEGIC NUCLEAR POWER

THE SPECTACULAR DEVELOPMENT of Soviet strategic offensive systems since 1953 tends to obscure in our minds the situation that existed in that year. When Stalin died in March, 1953, the U.S.S.R. had but a limited stock of atomic bombs and only obsolescent bombers of limited range (TU-4) to deliver them.[1] The range of the TU-4, which was modeled on the United States wartime bomber, the B-29, was inadequate for flying missions against the United States and returning to the U.S.S.R. Some Western observers believed that the U.S.S.R. could employ these planes in one-way missions against the United States, but this view was disputed.

Within a few years the destructive capabilities of both sides in the cold war were greatly magnified by the availability of thermonuclear weapons. In August, 1953, the U.S.S.R. surprised the world by exploding a thermonuclear device a few months after the United States had done so.

Moreover, in the next two years the U.S.S.R. acquired a new twin-turbojet medium bomber, the Badger, and two modern types of heavy bomber with an intercontinental range, the four-turbojet Bison and the multi-turboprop Bear. By 1955 the number of Bisons may already have been sufficient to provide a small initial operational capability against the United States.[2] Although it may have appeared that the Soviet program for modern intercontinental bombers had drawn almost abreast of the United States, the Soviet Union remained far inferior to the United States in over-all strategic offensive power.[3] The United States already possessed a large force of medium jet bombers (B-47) and the overseas bases and means for aerial refueling required to make them devastatingly effective against the U.S.S.R. By contrast, the U.S.S.R. lacked a comparable number of their own medium jet bombers (Badger), as well as the capacity to base them outside the

---

[1] Robert A. Kilmarx, *A History of Soviet Air Power* (New York: Frederick A. Praeger, Inc., 1962), pp. 250–51.

[2] See Raymond L. Garthoff, *Soviet Strategy in the Nuclear Age* (New York: Frederick A. Praeger, Inc., 1958), p. 178.

[3] The Bison evidently did not prove entirely satisfactory. According to Kilmarx, "By 1956 it was evident that although this aircraft had been put into production after a remarkably short lead time it was inferior to the United States B-52 in speed, combat radius, and combat ceiling" (*op. cit.*, p. 253).

country. Moreover, the Soviet Union had not yet demonstrated that it possessed an aerial refueling capability for its force.[4] By 1955 the Soviet Union probably had the means to inflict substantial casualties on American cities in a first strike, but only at the cost of having the U.S.S.R. destroyed in retaliation. It also had a limited capacity to retaliate against a United States first strike, but only if the American attack failed to wipe out the small Soviet intercontinental force. From the Soviet point of view, the strategic balance had probably not improved since 1953, but the world was impressed by Soviet technical achievements and the U.S.S.R. seemed capable of procuring an effective intercontinental force within a few years, if it so desired.

For several years afterward there was concern in some quarters in the West that a "bomber gap" might be developing to the advantage of the Soviet Union.[5] Actually, the Soviet force of intercontinental bombers increased far more slowly after 1955 than the West had expected. Since the United States heavy bomber (B-52) force increased very rapidly during these years, the margin of numerical superiority shifted markedly in favor of the West. This advantage was partly offset, however, by a substantial increase in the Soviet capacity to destroy Western Europe in an initial nuclear attack from the air. During the period from 1953 to 1957 the Soviet leaders managed to convey to the world a new conception of the strategic balance. Instead of disparaging nuclear weapons and threatening to "rebuff" the aggressor, as they had done previously, they now began to claim that they too had the means to inflict great destruction on the countries of their enemies.

The U.S.S.R.'s acquisition by 1955 of a relatively weak intercontinental nuclear capability served to reinforce the earlier political and moral constraints against a United States nuclear attack on the Soviet Union. Given the absence of any inclination on the part of the United States to initiate a preventive nuclear war, the level of threatened Soviet retaliatory damage that was sufficient to deter an *unprovoked* United States first strike was small; consequently, it was not difficult for the Russians to gain credit for possessing the strategic forces necessary to inflict such damage.

Remarkably, some United States leaders began publicly to speak of nuclear war as mutual annihilation even before the Soviet leaders

---

[4] The Soviet Union reportedly revealed an aerial refueling capability for their turbojet bombers during 1956 and 1957 (Kilmarx, *loc. cit.*).

[5] On the rise and decline of the "bomber gap," see Allen Dulles, *The Craft of Intelligence* (New York: Harper & Row, 1963), pp. 162–63; and also Kilmarx, *op. cit.*, pp. 253–54.

explicitly claimed a capacity to attack the United States with nuclear weapons. President Dwight D. Eisenhower predicted on December 8, 1953, that civilization would probably be destroyed in a nuclear war.[6] A Soviet "retired general" expressed complete agreement with this "appraisal of the danger involved in present-day atomic weapons." In support of this view, however, even he spoke only of the *potentialities* of aircraft, missiles, and submarines and said nothing of existing Soviet intercontinental capabilities.[7] Several weeks later a top Soviet leader, Anastas Mikoyan, spoke of the salutary effect on the United States government of Soviet possession of the thermonuclear bomb and observed that American newspapers had begun to discuss the destruction of American cities in the event of war. But he, too, said nothing directly of Soviet intercontinental delivery capabilities.[8]

Some of Stalin's successors, notably Premier Georgi Malenkov, apparently shared the President's estimate of the consequences of a future nuclear war, or at least believed it useful to subscribe publicly to the mutual destruction thesis. On March 12, 1954, seven months after he had announced that the United States had no monopoly on the thermonuclear bomb, Malenkov told the Soviet people that a new world war fought with the terrible new weapons meant "the destruction of world civilization." [9] Malenkov's unprecedented statement was welcomed in some Western circles as an indication that the new rulers of the Soviet Union might be prepared to abate the cold war and accept the constraints of a peace induced by mutual deterrence. Previously, Soviet spokesmen had clung stubbornly to the militant, Stalinist prediction that only capitalism would be destroyed in a new world war.

Malenkov appeared to be ruling out a military resolution of the East-West conflict as no longer feasible for either side. Moreover, he did so just as the Soviet Union had achieved the technological breakthroughs that seemed to place it, for the first time, in a position to compete with the United States for ascendancy in the means of intercontinental warfare. Instead of proposing an intensified arms effort, Malenkov and his supporters advocated a reduction in military expenditures. He and his closest associates in the Presidium, Mikhail Pervukhin and Maxim Saburov, omitted the standard formula about "strengthening" Soviet defense forces from their Supreme Soviet

---

[6] *New York Times*, December 9, 1953.
[7] *Izvestiia*, January 19, 1954.
[8] *Kommunist* (Erevan, Armenia), March 12, 1954.
[9] *Pravda*, March 13, 1954.

election speeches in March, 1954, although other Presidium members voiced it. At the same time, Malenkov sought to divert Soviet resources into the stepped-up production of consumer goods. His foreign and domestic political strategy may have been based on what later came to be known in the West as "minimum deterrence," that is, reliance on a relatively small nuclear capability to deter the principal opponent from initiating war.

Malenkov's economic and defense proposals, however, and the estimate of the international situation on which they were based, met with stiff opposition from other members of the Party Central Committee Presidium. Involved in the dispute were two closely related questions: (1) What is needed to deter a United States attack against the U.S.S.R.? (2) What are the military requirements of Soviet political strategy? In 1954 the first question was debated publicly, but in muted language, between the Malenkov faction and the opposition led by Nikita Khrushchev; the second question was not publicized at all until the Khrushchev faction had succeeded in ousting Malenkov from the premiership. Since the dispute illuminates the range and character of Soviet thinking, in a crucial period of its formation, on the political consequences of nuclear weapons, it merits detailed consideration here.

Malenkov's advocacy of a "minimal" nuclear strategic capability for deterring a United States attack was countered by his opponents with warnings against complacency and relaxation of the military effort. It was still true, they emphasized, that so long as capitalism existed the possibility of an attack on the U.S.S.R. was ever present. Soviet Defense Minister Nikolai Bulganin's statement on Armed Forces Day (February 22, 1954) that the Soviet government was trying to maintain peace "as long as possible" implied that war would eventually come.[10] A hapless theorist who dared suggest that it had now become possible to "paralyze" the operation of Lenin's law on the inevitability of war so long as imperialism existed was sharply reminded that laws of history can neither be destroyed nor paralyzed.[11] Shortly afterward Bulganin rebutted the notion that the West might be deterred from war by concern over humanity's destruction:

---

[10] *Krasnaia zvezda* ("Red Star"), February 23, 1954. On March 26, 1955, this idea was repeated by Kliment Voroshilov in the phrase, "if the aggressors have not *so far* succeeded in launching a new war . . ." (*Pravda*, March 27, 1955 [italics added]).

[11] V. Tereshkin, "The Great Mass Movement of the Present Day," *Zvezda* (Leningrad), February, 1954, pp. 139–40, as cited in H. S. Dinerstein, *War and the Soviet Union* (New York: Frederick A. Praeger, Inc., 1959), p. 68.

We cannot assume that the imperialists are spending enormous material resources and vast sums of money on armaments merely to frighten us. Nor can we reckon on the humaneness of the imperialists who, as life has shown, are capable of using any weapons of mass destruction.[12]

When the Supreme Soviet met in late April, it was clear that the issue had been decided in favor of those who thought as Bulganin did and that Malenkov had been compelled to retreat. Malenkov now asserted that a Western attack on the Soviet Union "would inevitably lead to the ruin of the capitalist system" and that the West would be crushed in an atomic war.[13] A statement on "strengthening the defensive capability of the Soviet Union" was apparently enjoined upon him, for he stated this policy in the name of both the Central Committee and the government, although previously, in speeches since becoming premier, he had consistently slighted the Central Committee, of which Khrushchev had been appointed first secretary in September, 1953. Malenkov went on to say:

The Soviet Armed Forces have at their disposal and *will have at their disposal* everything that is necessary for carrying out their lofty mission—to stand guard over the defense of the motherland and be ready always to deliver a crushing rebuff to an aggressor who would want to disrupt the peaceful toil of the peoples of our country!

This statement also bears the mark of a forced retreat, for Malenkov's commitment to provide the armed forces with all necessary means in the future was without precedent in that period. Pervukhin, like Malenkov, remedied his error of the previous month by calling for strengthened Soviet defenses.[14]

Having established the ascendancy of their estimate of the international situation and consequent views on defense policy, the opponents of the Malenkov group continued to press their attack. This suggests that a full resolution had not been achieved. Khrushchev and Bulganin publicized their concern about defense policy in speeches delivered in Eastern European satellite countries, where Presidium control over their utterances may have been less stringent. Khrushchev, in an impromptu speech broadcast in Prague (June 15, 1954), called for "daily strengthening of our armed forces," softened in the published version into an exhortation to "consolidate the defensive capability of our countries."[15] Bulganin used the occasion of his Warsaw speech (July 21) to repeat and spell out his warning of the

---

[12] *Pravda*, March 11, 1954.
[13] *Izvestiia*, April 27, 1954.
[14] *Pravda*, April 27, 1954 [italics added]. Saburov did not address this meeting of the Supreme Soviet.
[15] *Pravda*, June 16, 1954.

danger of an atomic attack on the U.S.S.R. In a statement having at that time no close parallel in Soviet history, he carried a step farther his March warning against reliance "on the humaneness of the imperialists" to deter them from the use of atomic weapons, pointing now to the danger of a surprise attack on the U.S.S.R. and specifying the United States as the potential aggressor:

It is obvious that until the United States renounces the use of atomic and hydrogen weapons, the Soviet Union is forced to possess these weapons so as not to be left without weapons in case of a surprise [*neozhidannost'*].[16]

It would appear, then, that the international implications of the invention of the hydrogen bomb and its possession by both the United States and the U.S.S.R. were interpreted in radically different ways by Malenkov and Mikoyan on one side and by Bulganin on the other. Mikoyan explicitly stated, and Malenkov seemed to imply, that the possession of thermonuclear weapons by both sides made war less likely. Bulganin argued in March that "we cannot assume that the imperialists" will be deterred from the use of weapons of mass destruction and two months later specifically warned against the threat of a surprise United States attack with nuclear weapons. In the interval between Bulganin's two speeches, Khrushchev seemed to move toward Bulganin's position while Malenkov and Mikoyan retreated from theirs. Bulganin's Warsaw statement, like his earlier remarks bearing on defense policy, may have been in response to representations from certain top military leaders.

The post-Stalin debate in military circles on the revision of Soviet military doctrine, centering on the role of strategic surprise in nuclear war, coincided with the struggle between Malenkov and his Presidium opponents and reached its culminating point precisely at the time of Malenkov's defeat. There was good reason for this, for, while Malenkov emphasized the deterrent effect of thermonuclear weapons, others in the Soviet Union perceived that their effect might be ambivalent. As one Soviet writer later put it, nuclear weapons have the double-edged effect of sobering the capitalists and simultaneously arousing in them hopes for a new blitzkrieg.[17] In mid-1954, Soviet political and military leaders for the first time began referring publicly to the increased danger of surprise nuclear attack. In May, Marshal A. M. Vasilevsky warned of the need to maintain fighting preparedness

---

[16] *Izvestiia*, July 22, 1954.
[17] E. G. Panfilov, "Has War Ceased To Be the Continuation of Politics?" *Voprosy filosofii*, 1957, No. 1, p. 246.

"so that nothing unexpected can catch us unawares," [18] and a few days after Bulganin's Warsaw speech Admiral N. G. Kuznetsov stated that "our people will not permit the imperialists to catch us unawares and unprepared in case of aggression." [19]

Late in December, after the NATO Council authorized the use of nuclear weapons to resist aggression in Europe, there were further allusions by Soviet leaders to the need for preparations to meet a surprise attack. In the last days of 1954, when the controversy over heavy versus light industry was being resolved in favor of the traditionalist heavy-industry school, Kliment Voroshilov told "a large group of generals, admirals and officers" of his concern about a surprise attack. In his speech on the presentation of medals, reported very briefly by Radio Moscow (December 31, 1954), he said:

Contrary to the will of their peoples, the reactionary circles of certain states are organizing an arms race, building aggressive blocs and restoring German militarism. Under these conditions we must show great vigilance and always be on guard so that no unexpected events could take us unawares.

At the February, 1955, meeting of the Supreme Soviet, at which Malenkov was deposed from the premiership, Bulganin added: "The capitalist camp will not catch our people unawares." [20] In his foreign policy statement V. M. Molotov went even farther, recalling Bulganin's language in July:

This measure [the creation of a unified military command for the Soviet Bloc] arises from the necessity to strengthen the defense capability . . . having in view any accidents or surprises. [21]

Voroshilov warned twice more against being caught "unawares" in an address to the R.S.F.S.R. Supreme Soviet on March 26, 1955. [22]

Thus Bulganin's contention that existence of the hydrogen bomb lessened Soviet security by increasing the danger of a surprise attack was echoed in three major speeches by Soviet leaders after the Supreme Soviet convened. Mikoyan and Malenkov, as we have said,

---

[18] *Krasnaia zvezda*, May 7, 1954.
[19] *Pravda*, July 25, 1954.
[20] He continued: "The aggressors seem to believe seriously that the more they threaten the more they frighten us" (*Izvestiia*, February 10, 1955). Khrushchev had earlier voiced a related idea—that Western leaders had actually interpreted Soviet protestations of peace as evidence of Soviet weakness (Prague Radio, June 15, 1954). This evident jibe at Malenkov's "error" of March, 1954, was excised from the version of Khrushchev's speech published by *Pravda* (June 16, 1954).
[21] *Pravda*, February 8, 1955.
[22] *Pravda*, March 27, 1955.

had implied that the hydrogen bomb would improve Soviet security once the U.S.S.R. had it. The Bulganin view was also reflected in the abandonment of the old Stalinist thesis, to which the U.S.S.R. had clung dogmatically since World War II, that strategic surprise is an unreliable, "temporary" factor that cannot under any circumstances play a decisive role in war. The new doctrine held that postwar advances in military technology, notably the advent of nuclear weapons and jet aviation, greatly enhanced the role of surprise in war and rendered surprise attack "particularly dangerous." [23]

The forceful statements by Khrushchev and Bulganin during the summer of 1954 implied that the question of defense policy had not yet been fully resolved. Substantial evidence that differences persisted among the elite emerged during celebrations on the anniversary of the October Revolution. The main speaker, Saburov, as in his March Supreme Soviet election speech, failed to call for strengthening defense.[24] Saburov's unusually mild speech was greeted coolly by his audience, and the published version—most unusually—contained no applause markings.[25] The following day, in his Red Square parade address, Bulganin pointedly remarked that

in the international situation so far *no such changes have taken place* as would give us grounds to lessen in any measure our attention to questions of strengthening our defense capability.[26]

Hence it would appear that the Malenkov group, after being forced to retreat publicly on the question of defense policy at the April meeting of the Supreme Soviet, made a further effort to publicize its views, through the medium of Saburov's anniversary speech, which was immediately countered by Bulganin. Defense policy, still a subject of public controversy in early November, was probably linked with the dispute over priority for heavy industry in late December and in January, 1955. Khrushchev's January report to the Central Committee, which was echoed in *Pravda* on the day Malenkov resigned, attacked the views of rightist "theoreticians" on priorities for con-

---

[23] The revised doctrine was expounded in greatest detail by Marshal of Tank Troops P. A. Rotmistrov, in *Krasnaia zvezda*, March 24, 1955, and in "On the Role of Surprise in Contemporary War," *Voennaia mysl'*, 1955, No. 2. For detailed treatments of the post-Stalin revision of Soviet military doctrine, see Dinerstein, *op. cit.*, pp. 28–63, and Garthoff, *op. cit.*, pp. 61–91.

[24] The significance of the omission in both instances is evident from the fact that the speakers on the three previous October Revolution anniversaries—Lavrenti Beria, Pervukhin, and Voroshilov—had enjoined the strengthening of defense, just as the majority of the Presidium did in the election campaign.

[25] *Pravda*, November 7, 1954.

[26] *Pravda*, November 8, 1954 [italics added].

sumer goods as "particularly intolerable . . . at a time when the imperialist powers are stepping up wild preparations for war." [27] The stress on the danger of being caught unawares suggests that Bulganin's view of the insecurity of the Soviet position even when both sides possessed thermonuclear weapons had won out over the belief that the advent of the hydrogen bomb presented a new opportunity for lessening the likelihood of war.

Malenkov had juxtaposed his statement that a new world war would mean the destruction of civilization with a call for "firm and lasting peace" and against continuation of the "cold war policy." Although it was presumably the West that Malenkov had in mind when he spoke of the "cold war policy," he warned both sides of the danger they faced if that policy continued. His speeches do not reveal any underlying notion that the U.S.S.R. could conduct its cold war policies with greater abandon because the new weapons had automatically eliminated the danger of a world war:

It is not true that humanity has the choice only between two possibilities: either a new world war or the so-called cold war. The peoples are vitally interested in the firm consolidation of peace. The Soviet Government stands for the further easing of international tension, for a firm and lasting peace, and resolutely opposes the cold war policy because that policy is one of preparing a new world war which, with modern means of warfare, means the destruction of world civilization.[28]

His opponents, once they had succeeded in ousting him from the premiership, complained that the views he expressed would paralyze Soviet policy.

After Malenkov's defeat in February, 1955, the dangerous implications of his belief in mutual deterrence were subjected to pointed criticism. The authoritative party journal, *Kommunist*, argued that emphasis on the mutually destructive consequences of nuclear war played into the hands of the imperialists; it created the false impression that "the atomic threat is such that the instigators of war will not dare to use their own bombs, since they will not decide to commit suicide." Such a concept, the journal said, blunts the vigilance of the people toward those "who in the preparation of nuclear war would like to take the people by surprise." [29]

Malenkov's opponents, as we just observed, feared that his ex-

---

[27] *Izvestiia*, February 3, 1955.
[28] *Pravda*, March 13, 1954.
[29] "The Peoples Decide the Fate of the World and Civilization," *Kommunist*, 1955, No. 4, p. 16.

pressed belief that nuclear world war would destroy world civilization implied the need for a more cautious and conciliatory foreign policy and created a situation in which opportunities for Soviet political gains would be severely limited. But Malenkov, as we also have seen, was at pains to direct attention to the dangers of continuing the cold war. In another formulation, peculiar to him at the time, Malenkov argued that peaceful coexistence was both "necessary and possible": [30] possible, presumably, because Soviet acquisition of the hydrogen bomb strengthened what had previously been a weak Soviet bargaining position; but also necessary, because recourse to war could result only in mutual annihilation.

The implications of Malenkov's emphasis on the "necessity" of peaceful coexistence and the dangers of the cold war rankled his opponents. As Voroshilov stated shortly after Malenkov was deposed: "We cannot be *intimidated by fables* that in the event of a new world war civilization will perish." [31] A journal of the Party Central Committee later spelled out the Party's objection to the thesis of a balance of terror: it was an "effort to *intimidate the working class with atomic weapons, to compel the proletariat to give up the struggle for power and for socialism.*" It branded those within the socialist camp who predicted mutual annihilation as "frightened Philistines, fawning before their [imperialistic] masters"; they were "trying to *sow terror* in the world and to push the toilers on to the *path of capitulation to imperialism,* allegedly in the interests of 'self-preservation' of socialism . . . from the atomic bomb." [32] As we shall have occasion to observe later, the leader of the victorious faction, Khrushchev, subsequently found reason to emphasize publicly the destructiveness of nuclear war and thus brought his Chinese Communist critics to charge him, as he had done Malenkov, with capitulating to the imperialists out of fear. Like Stalin before him, who adopted his rivals' policies after purging them, Khrushchev was to take over many of Malenkov's views on war and peace, but he placed them at the service of a radically different strategy.

Malenkov's opponents charged him with propagating two harmful opinions about the political consequences of thermonuclear weapons —opinions that superficially seem contradictory but really are not: first, they charged Malenkov with false confidence that nuclear war

[30] *Pravda,* January 1, 1955.

[31] *Pravda,* March 27, 1955 [italics added].

[32] V. Platovskii, "The Marxist-Leninist Teaching on the Party and Contemporary Revisionism," *V pomoshch' politicheskomu samoobrazovaniiu,* 1958, No. 6 [italics added].

would not be initiated by an "imperialist" surprise attack aimed at wiping out communism; second, they objected to his stated belief that a continuation of the cold war was likely to issue in a nuclear war that would destroy civilization. Distinctive foreign and defense policies follow from the views expressed by Malenkov: maintain a small deterrent nuclear force while seeking to end the cold war and "firmly consolidate peace." These policies were evidently unacceptable to Malenkov's opponents.

During the period of debate on defense policy, Malenkov's rivals emphasized the dangers facing the U.S.S.R. if it should fail to strengthen its military posture. They avoided boasting of Soviet strategic power to an extent that might foster the complacency for which they had criticized Malenkov. As a consequence, the impression conveyed by the debate on defense spending in 1954 and early 1955 was less of Soviet strategic capacities than of Soviet vulnerability. Once they had purged Malenkov, however, and defeated his effort to reduce military spending—the Supreme Soviet *increased* the military budget by 12 per cent—the successful faction, headed by Khrushchev and the new premier, Bulganin, quickly took steps to remedy the disadvantageous impression of the strategic balance that had been created by the intra-Party dispute. In the first major foreign policy statement of the new Bulganin government, Foreign Minister Molotov claimed that the U.S.S.R. had not only caught up with the United States in the field of thermonuclear weapons but had even surpassed it. Moreover, he directly contradicted Malenkov's previous statement that "world civilization would perish in a new war" by saying that this would be the fate only of the capitalist system.[33] On Aviation Day in July, 1955, the new Soviet leaders made a striking display of their strategic air power. A sufficient number of Bison heavy bombers appeared in the fly-by to persuade Western observers that the U.S.S.R. had achieved an initial operational capability to attack the United States with intercontinental jet bombers. According to former Central Intelligence Agency Director Allen Dulles, the number "far exceeded what was thought to be available" and created the impression that the U.S.S.R. had embarked upon a large-scale buildup of heavy bombers.[34] In addition, the Soviet Union displayed a new turboprop-driven heavy bomber, the Bear, estimated to have an even longer range than the Bison.[35] The July, 1955, Soviet air show

---

[33] *Pravda*, February 8, 1955.
[34] Dulles, *op. cit.*, p. 149.
[35] Kilmarx, *op. cit.*, pp. 252–53.

was probably one of the most successful peacetime military demonstrations of modern times. It significantly influenced Western estimates of the strategic balance in the two-year period before the Soviet Union test-fired its first intercontinental ballistic missile. In 1956, according to the testimony of former Defense Secretary Neil H. McElroy, it was estimated in the United States that by 1959 the Soviet Union could have about six to seven hundred Bison long-range jet bombers in operational units.[36] Actually, the U.S.S.R. procured only a fraction of that number. The impression created by the fly-by of Bison bombers in Moscow in July, 1955, was deliberately misleading. According to Allen Dulles, it was later surmised that the same squadron of Bisons had been flying around in circles, reappearing every few minutes.[37]

The success of this military demonstration was the more remarkable in view of the fact that it received so little support from Soviet military claims. The demonstration was not preceded by authoritative boasts of the Soviet bomber capability against the United States, and boasts were rare even afterward.

In the entire period from the spring of 1954, when the U.S.S.R. first displayed a heavy (that is, intercontinental) jet bomber, until the advent of Sputnik inaugurated a new period of missile claims, the bomber played a subordinate role in Soviet strategic claims. What was emphasized was Soviet possession of nuclear means of mass destruction; the means of delivering them were generally left out of account or referred to allusively. Military aviation was discussed, of course, particularly by airmen on appropriate military occasions, but the progress they claimed was usually in such areas as speed and altitude of flight rather than range. Explicit mention of "bombers" was infrequent.

Two expedients served in place of the missing claim of a bomber capability: (1) unspecified claims to possess "reliable means for delivering atomic and hydrogen bombs to any point on earth"; [38] (2) the verbal association of "rockets" (or "long-range rockets") with nuclear weapons. The second of these expedients was employed much more frequently than the first. The unusual reference to strategic rockets in the period 1955–57 reflected actual progress in *developing* such delivery vehicles, but this does not explain verbal neglect of Soviet bombers: the Badger medium jet bomber, which could be effectively employed against Europe, was already operational in

---

[36] Cited in Kilmarx, *op. cit.*, p. 325, n. 27.
[37] Dulles, *op. cit.*, p. 149.
[38] See, for example, Marshal V. D. Sokolovsky, *Pravda*, February 23, 1956.

substantial numbers at a time when the medium-range missile was still in the flight-testing stage. As regards the Soviet capability against the United States, in 1956 the U.S.S.R. was not credited with even having *developed* an intercontinental missile for use against the United States, but it was credited with having an operational bomber capability against the United States. The priority given missiles over bombers in Soviet strategic claims in the period from 1955 to 1957 is striking. As early as 1955 Khrushchev said Western refusal to ban nuclear weapons compelled the U.S.S.R. "also to produce such means of destruction," but for their delivery he mentioned only rocket equipment, not bombers.[39] Marshal G. K. Zhukov also specified rockets, not bombers, when he spoke of the available means of delivery for Soviet thermonuclear weapons in his speech on defense policy to the Communist Party Congress in February, 1956.[40] The chief of the general staff, Marshal Sokolovsky, did the same in his article on Armed Forces Day a few days later.[41] Khrushchev, speaking in England several months after this, again paired thermonuclear weapons with rockets and added: "I am quite sure that we will have a guided missile with a hydrogen bomb that can fall anywhere in the world." [42]

In retrospect, the preference of the Soviet leaders in their military claims for emphasis on strategic missiles, which were still under development, rather than jet bombers, which were already in operational units of the Soviet Long-Range Air Force, is not surprising. The Soviet leaders were then already banking on priority in the development of a technologically new type of strategic weapon to provide the basis for future claims. They preferred not to base such claims upon the development and procurement of weapons such as the United States already possessed and in the operation of which the United States enjoyed great advantages by virtue of its longer experience in strategic bombing and its far-flung network of air bases around the periphery of the U.S.S.R. Yet the lessons of the "bomber gap" were doubtless not lost upon the Soviet leaders. The great political success achieved by the July, 1955, Bison fly-by, even in the absence of Soviet efforts to follow up with extravagant claims and new demonstrations, must have impressed the Soviet leaders with the strong tendency of the West to exaggerate the U.S.S.R.'s strategic capabilities and to incline toward pessimism in estimating the strategic balance. As we

---

[39] Speech in Bangalore, India, *Pravda*, November 28, 1955.
[40] *Pravda*, February 20, 1956.
[41] *Pravda*, February 23, 1956.
[42] *New York Times*, April 24, 1956. The quoted passage was not included, however, in *Pravda*'s text of this speech.

shall see, two years later these lessons were put to use in spectacular fashion when the Soviet leaders began to demonstrate their ICBM and related space capabilities.

By that time the leadership of the Soviet Union was firmly in the hands of Khrushchev, whose views on some questions of military and foreign policy evidently underwent change in the intervening years. At some point after deposing Malenkov from the premiership early in 1955, Khrushchev must have drastically reduced his estimate of the threat to Soviet security posed by superior United States strategic power, for the foreign and military policies that evolved under his leadership were to be grounded in the assumption that the mere existence of such American superiority did *not* gravely threaten the Soviet Union. The intra-Party debate on military and foreign policy that had erupted after Stalin's death coincided with and was in part a reaction to the "new look" defense posture adopted by the new United States administration in 1953 and the related doctrine of "massive retaliation" enunciated by the new United States secretary of state the following year. The concern felt by some Soviet leaders at the time was made explicit years later by Khrushchev in a revealing reminiscence:

There was a time when American Secretary of State Dulles brandished thermonuclear bombs and followed a "positions of strength" policy with regard to the socialist countries. . . . That was barefaced atomic blackmail, *but it had to be reckoned with at the time* because we did not possess sufficient means of retaliation, and, if we did, they were not as many and not of the same power as those of our opponents.[43]

However, in the months and years that followed, it became apparent to the Soviet leaders that United States foreign policy remained essentially committed to defensive "containment," despite occasional bold words about "rollback." The Geneva summit conference of July, 1955, almost certainly marked a turning point in Khrushchev's strategic thinking. His face-to-face meeting with the leaders of the West reassured him that they were not fundamentally bellicose, and the warm enthusiasm for the summit meeting throughout the non-Communist world ("spirit of Geneva") probably added to Khrushchev's confidence that, when necessary, he could quickly change the international atmosphere and relax tensions by offering the West small concessions or even by merely hinting that he might be prepared to do so.

---

[43] *Pravda*, August 12, 1961 [italics added].

A year later the failure of the United States to intervene in Hungary was probably taken by the Soviet leaders as decisive confirmation that the West meant to employ its strategic preponderance defensively and would not make it the basis for a far-reaching political or military offensive against the Soviet Union. At the same time, the Suez crisis demonstrated that the emergent Soviet nuclear capability, though still far inferior to that of the United States, could be fashioned into a potent instrument of Soviet foreign policy. The Soviet attempt to intimidate Britain and France by alluding to the possibility of a rocket attack against them proved to be the forerunner of a series of more direct efforts to exploit Soviet strategic power politically in the later years.[44] It is difficult to determine whether the Soviet rocket threats had any significant direct effects on the governments of Britain, France, and the United States, but there is no doubt that large segments of public opinion in the West, particularly in England, were influenced by these threats and that they in turn brought great pressure to bear on their governments. Certainly, the Soviet hint of a rocket attack on Britain and France gained for the U.S.S.R., in Cairo and throughout the Arab world, a great deal of politically valuable credit for turning back the Anglo-French-Israeli invasion of Egypt.

By June, 1957, Khrushchev had purged his chief rivals in the Party leadership—some of his former associates of the anti-Malenkov faction as well as Malenkov himself and several of his lieutenants—and brought the conduct of Soviet foreign and domestic policies under his personal direction. Several months later he removed Marshal Zhukov, his erstwhile ally in the struggle against the "anti-Party group," from his post as minister of defense and member of the Central Committee Presidium, thereby enlarging his personal control over military policy and its implementation. Khrushchev was now in a position to apply the lessons of the "bomber gap," the Geneva summit conference, and Suez to the shaping of a new political offensive against the West. In August, 1957, Soviet science and technology provided him with a powerful new vehicle for launching this offensive: the intercontinental ballistic missile.

---

[44] For a contemporary analysis of Soviet threats during the Suez crisis, see Hans Speier, *Soviet Atomic Blackmail and the North Atlantic Alliance* (RM-1837; Santa Monica, Calif.: The RAND Corporation, December 10, 1956), esp. pp. 23–42. A number of strategies and tactics later employed by the Soviet leaders to exploit their strategic power for political purposes were anticipated by Speier in this memorandum.

PART 2

THE POLITICS OF SOVIET MISSILE DECEPTION, 1957–61

INTRODUCTION

BEGINNING IN THE LATE SUMMER of 1957, the Soviet leaders, and chiefly Khrushchev, undertook to deceive the West regarding their strategic capabilities. The maneuver is remarkable for its deliberate and systematic character and for the relative consistency with which it was executed over a period of four years.

This deception served as the basis for the boldest attempt yet made to exploit Soviet strategic power politically and played a central role in Soviet foreign policy during this four-year period. The episode helps to lay bare the Soviet leadership's true estimate of American strategy in the cold war; and it also sheds important light on the political character of the Soviet leadership. For these reasons, the Soviet effort to deceive the West regarding its ICBM capabilities will be discussed here in considerable detail.

First, there is a brief account of the Soviet ICBM program in the period 1957–61 as it has subsequently been reconstructed and publicized by responsible United States officials and informed observers. This is followed by a systematic presentation of Soviet ICBM and related claims in distinctive phases of this period and a rough assessment of these claims in the light of present knowledge. Particular Soviet political moves are considered in conjunction with the characteristic claims and demonstrations of each phase. Finally, there is an examination of the public Soviet response to American exposure of the "missile gap" myth in the fall of 1961.

In the aftermath of Sputnik I, which was launched from the U.S.S.R. in October, 1957, there was general acknowledgment that the U.S.S.R. had successfully developed the rocket engines required for an ICBM, and it was widely supposed that the U.S.S.R. would have an acceptable military vehicle in the relatively near future. Yet four years later the American press reported that, according to current intelligence estimates, only a small number of these weapons had been deployed.[1] In September, 1961, according to Senator Stuart

---

[1] Jack Raymond, *New York Times*, November 19, 1961; Hanson Baldwin, *New York Times*, November 26, 1961; Joseph Alsop, *Washington Post*, September 25, 1961. See also "United States Defense Policies in 1961," Library of Congress Legislative Reference Service, June 7, 1962; "U.S. Secret Service Counters Soviet Missile Threat," *Interavia*, XVI (1961), No. 12, 1618. Press reports of that time most frequently cited estimates of between 35 and 75 Soviet ICBM launchers. However, as will be shown, even these estimates exaggerated the actual size of the Soviet ICBM force in 1961. See pp. 36–37.

Symington, Soviet ICBM strength was officially estimated to be only 3.5 per cent of the number that had been estimated in 1959 for mid-1961.[2] According to Senator Symington's figures, the official estimate of operational ICBM's in September, 1961, was only a quarter of what had been supposed three months previously and only one-eighth of the 1960 estimate for mid-1961.

The original intelligence projections were based on the estimated capacity of the Soviet Union to acquire rapidly a substantial force of first-generation ICBM's. The question confronting the United States intelligence community, according to Allen Dulles, director of CIA during those years, was whether the Soviet leaders "would use their bulky and somewhat awkward 'first generation' ICBM, effective though it was, as the missile to deploy, or . . . wait for a second or third generation? Were they in such a hurry to capitalize on a moment of possible missile superiority that they would sacrifice this to a more orderly program?"[3] For four years, Khrushchev and other Soviet leaders gave every indication in their public statements that they were indeed in a hurry to capitalize on their initial advantage and that they were bent on acquiring a large force of first-generation ICBM's. In fact, according to Dulles, writing in 1963, they chose the orderly program, relying on the next generation of improved ICBM's to provide them with their basic ICBM capability.[4] But this became known to the West only much later. The possibility that the Soviet Union might be engaging in a crash program to build and deploy a large force of first-generation ICBM's was not rejected by the United States government until early 1960.[5] Intelligence estimates of the Soviet ICBM program were reduced accordingly, but they still projected a far larger Soviet force for 1961 than was actually credited to the U.S.S.R. in that year.[6] In 1964, the Department of Defense

[2] United States, Senate, *Hearings before the Committee on Armed Services on Department of Defense Programs and Authorization of Appropriations for Procurement of Aircraft, Missiles, and Naval Vessels by the Armed Forces* (S. 2734), 87th Cong., 2d sess., p. 49 [hereinafter referred to as *Hearings before the Committee on Armed Services*]. See also Senator Symington's article in *Reporter*, February 16, 1962.

[3] Allen Dulles, *The Craft of Intelligence* (New York: Harper & Row, 1963), p. 165.

[4] *Ibid.*

[5] Testimony by Defense Secretary Thomas S. Gates, Jr., in United States, Senate, *Hearings before the Preparedness Investigating Subcommittee of the Committee on Armed Services, in Conjunction with the Committee on Aeronautical and Space Sciences, on Missiles, Space, and Other Major Defense Matters*, 86th Cong., 2d sess., p. 442.

[6] Testimony by Secretary Robert S. McNamara, *Hearings before the Committee on Armed Services*, January 19, 1962, p. 50.

revealed that the Soviet Union had by 1961 deployed only "a handful" of ICBM's.[7]

The miniscule scope of the first-generation ICBM deployment program must have reflected decisions made by the Soviet leaders at a relatively early stage. The time required to transform a complicated and radically new weapon system like the ICBM into an operational military capability is considerable. Test vehicles must be produced and flight-tested; operational missiles must be produced and crews trained to operate them; finally, bases must be constructed for launching the missiles. Even if all these things were done concurrently—an expensive and risky procedure—many months would be required. Thus, the decisions that by 1961 led to the procurement of only a token-strength operational ICBM force had probably been made long before it became apparent to the United States that the Soviets were not engaged in a crash program, and therefore, the Soviet leaders probably knew well before the end of 1959 that relatively few Soviet ICBM's would be operational in 1961. Nevertheless, although United States estimates far outran the pace and scope of the Soviet ICBM program, Soviet claims substantially exceeded the inflated American estimates. The great disparity between claims and reality was obscured during much of this period by the difficulty in penetrating Soviet security. Therefore, the progressive Soviet claims, presented consistently and systematically, could be plausibly interpreted as corresponding to real progress in the Soviet ICBM program. The object of this elaborate deception was probably to conceal the very modest scope of the program for the first-generation ICBM and to create politically exploitable uncertainty in the West regarding the emergent strategic balance.

In the chapters that follow, the missile claims and related strategic threats expressed by Soviet leaders in the years 1957–61 are analyzed in considerable detail in order to expose the pattern of Soviet deception as it unfolded and to relate it to the broader political and military context in which it evolved. Before proceeding to the detailed analysis, it may be helpful to set forth some of the general characteristics of the body of Soviet statements that the reader will encounter in this book.

Soviet strategic threats and claims are meant to serve a variety of purposes and to influence the beliefs and behavior of a whole range of

---

[7] "Department of Defense Statement on U.S. Military Strength," April 14, 1964. See also New York Times, April 15, 1964.

audiences. In general, the target of such Soviet assertions is world opinion at large, including certain groups in the Soviet Union itself. Although the Soviet leaders might prefer to convey certain impressions to particular audiences and not to others, or to convey different impressions to different audiences, the requirements of internal logic and systematic exposition in an age of world-wide communications place severe limitations on their freedom to tailor claims to achieve such diversified effects. Although the Soviet leaders have effective control over the contents of Soviet communications, they cannot control the dissemination of statements outside the U.S.S.R. and the countries subservient to it, nor can they limit their impact exclusively to preferred audiences. Thus, the price for attempting to achieve the desired effect on one audience is the risk that the same message may have an undesirable effect elsewhere. To achieve the desired political effect on Western and neutral audiences, for example, the Soviet leaders made ICBM claims that encouraged their restless Chinese allies to press for new Soviet commitments that the U.S.S.R. was evidently reluctant to give. Similarly, the effects on a single audience or on influential groups within a single society may be ambivalent. Thus the Soviet leaders discovered that in addition to the favorable political consequences that flowed from their success in misleading Western opinion regarding the pace and scope of the Soviet ICBM program there were also undesirable consequences, namely, stimulation of United States arms programs. Some unfavorable consequences may have been anticipated; others may not have been, or their extent may have been underestimated. The Soviet leaders may also have had exaggerated expectations regarding the political benefits that would accrue from successful deception. At any rate, in undertaking to engage in deception, the Soviet leaders calculated, rightly or wrongly, that the costs and risks were warranted by the expected gains.

In the period 1957–61, conditions favored the Soviet attempts to deceive the West regarding strategic capabilities. The extent and effectiveness of Soviet capabilities were matters of vital concern in the West, but uncertainty surrounded even the best estimates available to Western leaders. Because the West was uncertain regarding the Soviet program for deploying first-generation ICBM's, it was compelled to treat seriously what the Soviet leaders chose to reveal. The West's predicament was certainly known in Moscow. Persistent Western attacks on Soviet secrecy after 1957, however valuable their political effects on neutral third parties, demonstrated the Western thirst for intelligence. Being aware of this need, the Soviet leaders could make a probing assertion about their ICBM program, observe the West's reaction to it, comment on this reaction, and reinforce the original claim by new assertions. A whole range of verbal tricks was employed to mislead Western opinion by playing on its uncertainty. At the same time, enough of what the Soviet leaders claimed was in accord with what was known or believed in the West that it was not possible simply to discount their claims. They had to be examined in the light of what was known, but because so much was unknown, they were difficult to disprove.

The aura of mystery that surrounded the question of Soviet strategic capabilities in the West was beneficial to Soviet design, and the Soviet leaders sought to maintain it even while lifting the veil from time to time. Khrushchev constantly referred to Soviet "secrets," occasionally revealing something of their substance in private audiences with Westerners or in public speeches. At other times he merely hinted at their existence, as when he alluded to designs for "fantastic new weapons" in the portfolios of the scientists.[8]

Faced with large uncertainties regarding questions of vital concern, many in the West were predisposed to expect the worst, namely, that the Soviet Union would rapidly acquire a substantial intercontinental strategic force. This expectation was based on an understanding of Soviet intentions then current among Western leaders and their advisers, on the strategic requirements that were believed to guide Soviet military policy, and on a new appreciation of Soviet technical capabilities. The last was largely the product of the unexpectedly rapid progress of Soviet rocket technology, as demonstrated by the U.S.S.R.'s highly successful space program. The space program afforded Soviet leaders an opportunity to stage a sustained and non-provocative military demonstration, which was an integral part of the ICBM deception. To the West it seemed to confirm some of Khrushchev's key ICBM claims and, together with information on the Soviet research and development programs, provided the basis for estimates of Soviet technological capability in the field of strategic missiles.

The reputation acquired as a result of their space program provided Soviet leaders with a reservoir of credibility on which to draw for purposes of strategic deception. The reservoir was regularly replenished by new and more spectacular space ventures. A reputation for credibility is not simply something to enjoy but something to use.

---

[8] *Pravda*, January 16, 1960.

The Soviet leaders sought to use their credit to secure political advantage. Because credibility is a fragile asset, easily dissipated, caution is called for in exploiting it. A military claim by one side will be measured by the other against what it already knows and believes; if the discrepancy is too great, the claim will be discounted. Thus to persuade the opponent that one's forces are greater than he supposes requires that the margin not be excessive. Generally, but not always, the Soviet leaders observed this maxim.

Caution was enjoined for another reason. The Soviet leaders faced the risk, however they estimated it, that ultimately their deception would be exposed, either wholly or in part. Exposure might seriously discredit them and thus diminish their future capacity not only to deceive their opponents but even perhaps to communicate crucial information. This risk did not deter them from engaging in strategic deception on a large scale, but it conditioned their choice of deceptive technique. They generally avoided explicit statements of a kind that, even if not susceptible to immediate refutation, might be proved false in the near future. Acceptance of this restraint, in order to minimize future losses in credibility, prevented the full exploitation of opportunities for exaggerating capabilities.

The most inflated claims of the Soviet leaders pertained to questions that were largely matters of judgment, such as the consequences of thermonuclear war and the over-all strategic balance defined grossly. These claims implied the possession of very large operational strategic forces without actually asserting it. It was left to Western observers to make the logically correct, but factually false, inference.

As a rule when a claim lent itself to generalized and vague expression (for example, one concerning "the balance of forces"), the advantage claimed for the Soviet Union tended to be pronounced and stated explicitly. On the other hand, deceptive claims regarding more concrete and specific subjects (for example, weapon systems) were expressed ambiguously. Qualitative claims were preferred, quantitative ones usually avoided. Repetition was employed frequently both to emphasize claims and to gain their acceptance by conditioning the target audiences. If the reiterated claims went unchallenged, silence was interpreted as assent, and soon the strategic advantage claimed for the U.S.S.R. was said to be one that was "well known" or "admitted in the West." Statements of Western authorities, both officials and private citizens, were employed as supporting evidence.

The Soviet leaders sometimes quoted Western sources that credited the U.S.S.R. with even more than they themselves had claimed.

The logical progression of Soviet claims, particularly those regarding the production status of the ICBM, as well as the internal consistency of the claims made possible by tight official control of Soviet communications media, was also helpful in inducing credibility. All of these characteristics of the Soviet claims combined to produce a deceptive image of growing Soviet strategic power that dominated the international political dialogue for four years beginning in the summer of 1957.

THREE

ICBM DEVELOPMENT CLAIMS
AUGUST, 1957–OCTOBER, 1958

ON AUGUST 26, 1957, the official Soviet news agency, TASS, announced that a "super-long-range multistage intercontinental ballistic rocket"[1] had recently been successfully tested and that the results indicated "it is now possible to send missiles to any part of the world." TASS stated that the U.S.S.R. had solved the problem of creating ICBM's.[2] After this initial revelation, there were no public announcements of non-orbital rocket launchings until the extended-range firings into the Pacific Ocean of what were officially termed "scientific rockets" in 1960.

In the six-week period between the TASS ICBM announcement and the launching of Sputnik I (October 4, 1957), the Soviet press published several articles on the technical characteristics of ballistic missiles, emphasizing their speed of flight, high altitude, long range, relative accuracy, and ability to hit distant targets with little or no warning; but the articles did *not* claim that the vehicle actually tested by the U.S.S.R. possessed these attributes.[3] Khrushchev himself did not comment on the Soviet ICBM during these weeks, though he later revealed to former Vice-President Richard M. Nixon that he was the author of the very widely publicized statement on the strategic implications of new weapons developments that was published in *Pravda* on September 8, 1957, as an interview with Air Marshal K. Vershinin.[4]

Only after the launching of Sputnik I did Khrushchev publicly assume the role of leading Soviet spokesman on the progress of the Soviet ICBM program and interpreter of its military-political significance. Under his influence, Soviet ICBM claims immediately took on a political color. Whereas the August test announcement claimed

---

[1] The Russian expression "intercontinental ballistic rocket" is equivalent to "ICBM." In directly quoting the Russian, the closest English equivalent of Soviet terminology is given; elsewhere the more familiar terms—for example, "ICBM"—are employed.

[2] *Pravda*, August 27, 1957.

[3] See *Sovetskaia aviatsiia*, August 31, 1957; *Sovetskaia Rossiia*, September 14, 1957; *Sovetskii patriot*, September 16, 1957.

[4] See the article by Earl Mazo on Nixon's 1959 trip to the U.S.S.R., *New York Herald Tribune*, September 14, 1960.

only that "the problem of creating ICBM's had been solved" and did not even assert that a complete weapon system had been developed, after the Sputniks Khrushchev spoke of the Soviet ICBM as "fully perfected." [5] Khrushchev told James Reston of the *New York Times* three days after the Sputnik I launching: "We *now have* [*u nas seichas est'*] all the rockets we need: long-range rockets, intermediate-range rockets and short-range rockets." [6] He said in November, following Sputnik II: "I think that it is no secret that *there now exists* a range of missiles with the aid of which it is possible to fulfill any assignment of operational and strategic importance." [7] Later that month Khrushchev boasted to William R. Hearst, Jr., that "the Soviet Union has [*imeet*] intercontinental ballistic rockets with hydrogen warheads." [8]

Khrushchev's early comments on the Soviet space successes and their implications for Soviet weaponry were expressed with exuberance, but it was a controlled exuberance. Generally choosing his words with care, he employed such ambiguous expressions as "there now exists" and "we now possess." The claim to "possess" ICBM's and the related claims of this initial period were to evolve in logical sequence, successive claims building on their predecessors and laying the foundation for those to come. [9] This gradually emerging pattern argues that Khrushchev's early assertions on the ICBM were not merely spontaneous expressions of elation or powerful emotion but were meant to communicate misleading hints about the state of Soviet armaments.

That the West was the prime target of this deception may be deduced from Khrushchev's introduction and frequent repetition of his claims, during the fall of 1957, in four interviews with prominent Western correspondents who were sure to publicize them in the West, and from his omission of them from his key address to a Soviet audience on the fortieth anniversary of the Communist Revolution.

From the time of the first Sputnik launching, Khrushchev tried to

---

[5] *Pravda*, November 29, 1957.
[6] *Pravda*, October 11, 1957 [italics added]. Khrushchev's reference here to sufficiency applies clearly to types of missiles rather than to numbers of any specific type.
[7] Khrushchev's replies to P. Dampson, correspondent of the *Toronto Telegram*, in *International Affairs*, 1957, No. 11, p. 15 [italics added].
[8] *Pravda*, November 29, 1957.
[9] An exception to this pattern is Khrushchev's assertion during his interview with Hearst that "we now possess the *absolute* weapon," a characterization of the ICBM that Khrushchev was never to repeat (*Pravda*, November 29, 1957).

make it appear that the ICBM capabilities of the two sides were proportional to their space exploits. Thus, three days after the launching of Sputnik I, he told James Reston:

When we announced the successful testing of an intercontinental rocket some American statesmen did not believe us. The Soviet Union, they claimed, was saying it had something it did not really have. Now that we have successfully launched an earth satellite, only technically ignorant people can doubt this. The United States does not have an intercontinental ballistic rocket, otherwise it would also easily have launched a satellite of its own. We can launch satellites, because we have a carrier for them, namely—the ballistic rocket.[10]

In addition to primacy in launching a satellite, Khrushchev sought at once to establish satellite weight as a criterion for estimating the power of the missiles available to the two sides. After the U.S.S.R. launched its half-ton Sputnik II, he stated in reply to a question by United Press correspondent Henry Shapiro:

I am absolutely certain [that the United States does not have the ICBM]. If they had, they would have launched their own sputnik, as we did. We launched our sputniks on the basis of our intercontinental ballistic rocket. The United States intends to send up a sputnik weighing 11 kilograms. Is that a ballistic rocket? Further, nobody knows when the United States will launch this satellite. Our first sputnik, on the other hand, weighed 83.6 kilograms, while the second had a useful weight of 508 kilograms. If necessary, we can double the weight of the satellite.[11]

And again later:

We can double and more than double the weight of the satellite, because the Soviet intercontinental rocket has tremendous power, which makes it possible to launch an even heavier satellite to an even greater height.[12]

In seeking to squeeze as much ICBM credit from Soviet space accomplishments as he could, Khrushchev went so far at the end of November, 1957, as to claim in effect that the U.S.S.R. already had a stockpile of up to twenty ICBM boosters. (This was almost a full year before he spoke directly of Soviet ICBM *production*.) He told the Hearst party on November 29, 1957:

The fact that the Soviet Union was the first to launch an artificial earth satellite, which within a month was followed by another, says a lot. If necessary, tomorrow we can launch 10, 20 satellites. All that is required for

---

[10] Reported in *Pravda*, October 11, 1957.

[11] *Pravda*, November 19, 1957.

[12] *Pravda*, January 26, 1958. Sputnik III, launched in May, 1958, reportedly had a mass of 2,925 pounds, that is, 2.6 times that of Sputnik II.

this is to replace the warhead of an intercontinental ballistic rocket with the necessary instruments. There is a satellite for you.[13]

The major Soviet claim of this initial period, that the U.S.S.R. had won the race to create an intercontinental ballistic missile, readily lent itself to dramatic demonstrations that gained for it a high degree of credibility. The Sputnik launches in October and November, 1957, and May, 1958, were quickly and widely accepted as confirming the U.S.S.R.'s August, 1957, claim. The *New York Times* sounded the alarm three days after the launching of Sputnik I:

There has been some tendency in this country these past six weeks to doubt or to minimize the significance of last August's Soviet claim to have intercontinental ballistic missiles. In the light of the new evidence, it is the better part of wisdom to assume that the Soviet Union does have such missile capability, and that it is now engaged in a major effort to provide itself as soon as possible with large numbers of such weapons. It is clear we do not have such missiles now, and the time when we may have them is uncertain.[14]

In this early period, although United States government officials tacitly acknowledged the validity of the Soviet claim to have developed an ICBM, they disputed the Soviet contention that a "real" change had already occurred in the strategic balance. Thus Secretary of State John Foster Dulles stated at a press conference on August 27 that the existence of a Soviet ICBM did not "initially" affect the present military balance between the two countries.[15] President Eisenhower, in a television-radio address after the second Soviet satellite launching in November, reassured the country that "although the Soviets are quite likely ahead in some missile and special areas, and are obviously ahead of us in satellite development, as of today the over-all military strength of the free world is distinctly greater than that of the Communist countries."[16] At various times in

---

[13] *Pravda*, November 29, 1957. Taken literally, "tomorrow we can launch" implies the existence of a substantial number of launchers, whereas probably no more than a single ICBM-type launcher was then in operation for flight tests and space launchings.

[14] *New York Times*, October 7, 1957.

[15] *New York Times*, August 27, 1957.

[16] *New York Times*, November 8, 1957. Anticipating concern over the "missile gap," which became a national issue some years later, scientists both in and out of government offered estimates at that time of how many years the United Stated lagged behind the Soviet Union in space. The most widely quoted, by Soviet as well as American media, was Wernher von Braun's estimate of "well over five years." The *New York Times* referred specifically to *space* activities; publicists in this country and abroad usually did not distinguish between space and missile capabilities, a practice that was vigorously encouraged and exploited by Soviet propaganda. See

this period both President Eisenhower and Dulles asserted that manned bombers would continue "for some years to come" to be a more accurate and more reliable means for delivering nuclear bombs.[17] Although United States spokesmen frequently drew a distinction between test-firings of new weapons and the acquisition of operational weapons in quantity, the main American response was directed at refuting the Soviet contention that ICBM's had rendered manned bombers obsolete. This tended indirectly to support Soviet efforts to depict the strategic balance as a confrontation of Soviet ICBM's and United States manned bombers.

Moreover, although administration leaders denied that Soviet ICBM progress had adversely affected the present United States strategic posture, operational measures were soon taken to strengthen *current* defenses against Soviet surprise attack. On November 11, the *New York Times* reported that, as of October 1, the Strategic Air Command was being raised to higher levels of alertness to ensure that one-third of the force could be airborne within fifteen minutes after notice. On November 13, the President announced a speedup in the dispersal of SAC to additional bases and in the provision of facilities for quicker response.[18] On January 7, 1958, the White House announced that it would request an additional 1.26 billion dollars in defense funds to provide for acceleration of the ballistic missile program, ballistic missile detection, and SAC alert and dispersal.[19]

When the TASS announcement of the first Soviet ICBM test was issued on August 26, 1957, the five-power United Nations Disarmament Subcommittee was in its fifth month of sessions in London. Despite some progress in the spring, by late summer the negotiators had reached an impasse. Nevertheless, the atmosphere remained remarkably free of propagandistic vituperation and recrimination until the meeting of August 27, the day following the TASS announcement. On that day, the Soviet delegate, Valerian Zorin delivered a violent and unexpected attack on the Western powers that signaled the collapse of the negotiations. Two days later, Zorin peremptorily declared the most recent Western proposals to be entirely unacceptable to the Soviet Union, and on September 6 the subcommittee recessed without even an agreement to reconvene.

Arnold L. Horelick, "The Soviet Union and the Political Uses of Space," in Joseph M. Goldsen (ed.), *Outer Space and World Politics* (New York: Frederick A. Praeger, Inc., 1963), pp. 43–70.

[17] *New York Times*, October 3, 16; November 7, 13, 18, 1957.

[18] *New York Times*, November 13, 1957.

[19] *New York Times*, January 7, 1958.

President Eisenhower, in expressing his disappointment over Zorin's attack on the latest Western proposal, observed:

It is noteworthy that this attack coincides with the boastful statement by the Soviet Union that they have made advances in the development of means for bringing mass destruction to any part of the world. . . ."[20]

Although the coincidence of the ICBM-test announcement and the hard Soviet turn in London raised Western concern regarding Soviet intentions in the disarmament field, the Soviet leaders did not at that time attempt to use their ICBM progress directly to secure particular concessions from the West. The high points of Soviet belligerence in the Syrian-Turkish crisis, in late August and early October, 1957, coincided with the ICBM announcement and the launching of Sputnik I, but the ICBM played only a marginal role in Soviet speeches, notes, and letters during the crisis. This remained true the following year in the Middle East and Quemoy crises. During this period, however, Soviet ICBM development was used prominently to support broad Soviet assertions of the changed character of the international situation.

In their public assessments of the effects on international relations of Soviet progress in rocket technology, the Soviet leaders distinguished between its impact on the over-all "correlation of world forces" (a Communist concept embracing political, social, and economic, as well as military, factors), on the one hand, and on the strategic balance, more narrowly defined, on the other. Far more attention was devoted to the former than to the latter. The Soviet leaders quickly proclaimed that a shift in the world correlation of forces in favor of the socialist camp had occurred; but they attributed the shift to Soviet breakthroughs in science and technology, as evidenced by the Sputniks, rather than specifically to the Soviet ICBM. The key formulation of this period, which was raised to a programmatic level by its inclusion in the Moscow Declaration of November, 1957, stopped short of an explicit proclamation of superiority, stating only that a favorable shift was occurring.[21]

---

[20] Statement by President Eisenhower, White House Press Release, August 28, 1957, cited in Bernhard G. Bechhoefer, *Postwar Negotiations for Arms Control* (Washington, D. C.: Brookings Institution 1961), p. 399.

[21] *Pravda*, November 22, 1957. This restraint contrasts with the practice of the Chinese Communists, who claimed shortly after the Sputnik launchings that a new turning point in international affairs had been reached, that the "East wind" now prevailed over the "West wind," and, explicitly, that the U.S.S.R. had achieved military superiority over the United States. See Donald S. Zagoria, *The Sino-Soviet Conflict, 1956–1961* (Princeton, N.J.: Princeton University Press, 1965), pp. 152–65. These

Nor was Soviet superiority in the military realm claimed at this time. Instead, attention was centered on denying the military superiority of the United States. Soviet publicists stressed that the advent of strategic rockets nullified strategic advantages formerly possessed by the United States: (1) the United States had lost its traditional advantage of relative invulnerability to direct attack; (2) the importance of strategic aviation, on which the United States was said to rely, was sharply reduced by the advent of ICBM's, which could deliver nuclear weapons to distant targets more efficiently and were invulnerable to existing means of defense; and (3) United States overseas bases, which could now be destroyed quickly and easily by Soviet rockets, had lost their former military value.[22]

Of these three strategic changes, it was the last two, and particularly the third, that were spelled out most concretely. Soviet retaliation against United States territory in the event of war was said to be certain, but the level of damage that could be inflicted was left vague. United States vulnerability was usually implied in frequent assertions that the creation of ICBM's had "solved the problem of delivering a hydrogen warhead to any point on the globe" and that "distance is now no obstacle." [23] The most extreme statements of that period were made by Khrushchev, as when he told Henry Shapiro: "If war is not averted, the Americans will experience the most devastating war ever known by mankind. It will rage not only in Europe and Asia, but, with no less fury, in the United States." [24] Yet, in citing the means available to the U.S.S.R. for striking American targets, Khrushchev was careful not to speak only of ICBM's.[25] He conveyed the impression of an existing Soviet operational ICBM capability without, however, explicitly claiming it. Thus, he told Shapiro that "modern military techniques *make it possible* with submarines and with the help of ballistic rockets to keep all of America's vital centers under fire,

Chinese claims anticipated by more than two years analogous ones by Khrushchev and other Soviet leaders.

The divergent Soviet and Chinese assessments of the strategic balance in 1957 were involved in the dispute over global strategy that developed in the Communist camp.

[22] See, for example, "A Policy from Positions of Folly," *International Affairs*, 1957, No. 12; M. Rubinstein, "Science and International Relations," *Mirovaia ekonomika i mezhdunarodnye otnosheniia*, 1958, No. 6; N. Inozemtsev, "Atomic Diplomacy of the U.S.A.: Projects and Reality," *Mirovaia ekonomika i mezhdunarodnye otnosheniia*, 1958, No. 3.

[23] See, for example, Andrei Gromyko's United Nations speech of September 30, 1957; Khrushchev's replies to *Toronto Telegram* questions, in *International Affairs*, 1957, No. 11.

[24] *Pravda*, November 19, 1957.

[25] *Pravda*, November 19, 29, 1957.

to blockade U.S. ports." [26] In his interview with the Hearst group, he said that a new war, unlike past wars, would be immediately carried to the United States, "because intercontinental ballistic missiles *now make it possible* to hit a target in any area of the globe." [27] Remarkably, Khrushchev said almost nothing of Soviet manned bombers, although they were probably the only means the Soviet Union then had for an intercontinental strike. Only twice in the period did he mention Soviet strategic air power, and then merely as an indication that new and better delivery means were now available to the U.S.S.R. He wrote to Bertrand Russell, for example, that the U.S.S.R. "now possesses the means of fighting against the United States if the latter should unleash war against us. The Soviet Union had these means previously also, in the form of intercontinental bombers, but the ballistic rocket is of course an improved weapon." [28]

Not only was the level of damage that the U.S.S.R. could inflict upon the United States left vague, but the American targets that Soviet strategic power could destroy were not specified in greater detail than is conveyed by such terms as "territory" and "vital centers." By contrast, statements about both the level of damage and the target system in Western Europe were quite specific and frequently reiterated. If war were unleashed, "the logic of struggle" would require the U.S.S.R. to strike the network of United States bases rimming the Soviet Union. The destructive power of such blows would be so great that the Western European NATO countries would be "put out of commission" or "wiped from the face of the earth."

It was during this period that Khrushchev introduced the concept of "country-busting" into Soviet discussions of modern war. Repeatedly, he pointed out that the Soviet Union possessed means to destroy entire countries of the NATO alliance. Official government notes and letters during this period warned, for example, that West Germany would have "no chance of survival" and that "the very existence" of Great Britain would be threatened in the event of war. [29] Delivery means were not usually specified, but as Khrushchev pointed out in the "interview" published in Marshal Vershinin's name: "One needs no ICBM's to shoot at military bases in Western Europe and also in Turkey, Iran and some other countries." [30]

[26] *Pravda*, November 19, 1957 [italics added].
[27] *Pravda*, November 29, 1957 [italics added].
[28] *Kommunist*, 1958, No. 5.
[29] *Pravda*, March 31, 1958; December 7, 1957,
[30] *Pravda*, September 8, 1957.

FOUR

PRODUCTION CLAIMS
NOVEMBER, 1958–OCTOBER, 1959

IN THE FIFTEEN MONTHS prior to November, 1958, Soviet leaders claimed to have successfully tested the ICBM and to possess a stock of vehicles but said nothing directly of their production. In that month, however, in a speech on the seven-year plan, Khrushchev announced: "The production of the intercontinental ballistic rocket has been successfully set up."[1] Early in January, 1959, he distinguished between "creation" and "production" of the ICBM and affirmed Soviet pre-eminence in both.[2] When presenting the draft plan to the Twenty-first Party Congress several weeks later, Khrushchev implied that further progress had been made by announcing: "*Serial* production of the intercontinental ballistic rocket has been successfully organized."[3] Later, toward the end of 1959, Khrushchev characterized Soviet ICBM production so as to imply that the highest stage of production had been achieved; he said the Soviet ICBM was "on the assembly line."[4] And shortly afterward he announced to the Supreme Soviet that the U.S.S.R. led "in the creation and mass production of intercontinental ballistic rockets of various types."[5]

Khrushchev first spoke of the production of Soviet ICBM's just a few days after precipitating the Berlin crisis by his demand, on November 10, 1958, that allied occupation of West Berlin be terminated within a short time.[6] His follow-up statements on ICBM production to the Supreme Soviet were made in January and February, 1959, during the period of rising Soviet pressure on the allied governments as they attempted to co-ordinate their responses to the new Soviet challenge. Meanwhile, in the United States the "missile gap" controversy had been born. Two weeks before Khrushchev made his claim regarding serial production of the ICBM, reports of a secret briefing by Defense Secretary McElroy to the Senate Foreign Relations Committee had touched off a sharp controversy in the United

---

[1] Control figures for the development of the national economy of the U.S.S.R. for 1959 to 1965, *Pravda*, November 14, 1958.

[2] Speech at a meeting of the Belorussian Supreme Soviet, *Pravda*, January 4, 1959.

[3] *Pravda*, January 28, 1959 [italics added].

[4] *Pravda*, November 18, 1959.

[5] *Pravda*, January 15, 1960 [italics added].

[6] The relationship between Soviet missile deception and the U.S.S.R.'s Berlin strategy is analyzed in chapters ix and x, pp. 105–25.

States regarding the magnitude of the Soviet ICBM threat faced by the United States and the measures required to cope with it.[7] The day after Khrushchev made his serial production claim, Secretary McElroy told the Senate Preparedness Subcommittee that the United States had no intention of matching the Soviet Union "missile for missile" in the ICBM field but would rely on its diversified arsenal of heavy bombers and intercontinental and shorter-range missiles to gain superiority.[8]

The ICBM claims that Khrushchev chiefly sought to make credible in this period were those having to do with production. He relied chiefly on logical progression and on repetition and verbal reinforcement of the claim. For example, he announced the organization of serial production in his initial speech to the Twenty-first Party Congress and simply reaffirmed it with emphasis in his concluding speech: "When we say that we have organized the serial production of intercontinental ballistic rockets, it is not just to hear ourselves talk." [9] A week later he said that at first "some leaders of the West automatically expressed doubts, but on second thought promptly stated that if the Russians said so, it means that serial production of missiles has certainly been organized. This is really so." [10] The following year Khrushchev spoke of "mass production" of the ICBM.

Although Khrushchev's claim that the Soviet ICBM was in serial production did not lend itself to direct demonstration, some measure of support appeared to be provided for it indirectly by the expenditure of ICBM vehicles in flight tests and space activities. It was reported in the United States press that by 1960 some thirty Soviet ICBM test-firings had taken place.[11] In addition, at least six vehicles were expended in space shots by the end of 1959 (three Sputniks and three Luniks). Since only a handful of Soviet ICBM's were deployed as late as 1961, however, most of the vehicles produced were evidently for purposes of research and development and space boosters.

[7] New York Times, January 17, 1959. Five days earlier, a New York Times article, reportedly based on interviews with "numerous persons having intimate knowledge of the defense effort," gave the following forecast of Soviet versus American ICBM inventories in the early sixties: 1960, 100 to 30; 1961, 500 to 70; 1962, 1,000 to 130; 1963, 1,500 to 130; 1964, 2,000 to 130. The gap was not expected to be closed until after 1964 when sizable numbers of Polaris and Minuteman missiles were scheduled to enter the United States force.
[8] New York Times, January 30, 1959.
[9] Pravda, February 5, 1959.
[10] Pravda, February 13, 1959.
[11] Robert A. Kilmarx, A History of Soviet Air Power (New York: Frederick A. Praeger, Inc., 1962), p. 260.

It appears, then, that in speaking of serial production of ICBM's Khrushchev deliberately sought to mislead the West. Certainly, his reference to mass production of the ICBM in January, 1960, was meant to persuade the West that Soviet ICBM's were being produced in substantial numbers for early deployment, which was not true.

In this progression of Khrushchev's production claims, nothing was said of an operational capability. Defense Minister Marshal R. Ya. Malinovsky, however, addressing the same congress that heard Khrushchev tell of the organization of serial production of ICBM's, expressed gratitude to the men who had "equipped the armed forces with a whole series of military ballistic missiles, [including] intercontinental." [12] This claim was repeated several weeks later, on Army Day, by Marshals K. S. Moskalenko (later appointed commander of rocket troops) and V. I. Chuikov.[13] And in the Soviet military newspaper *Krasnaia zvezda* ("Red Star"), Marshal A. A. Grechko asserted that the Soviet armed forces had "received" the ICBM.[14]

If there is any uncertainty that Khrushchev's production claims were intended to deceive, the claims of Soviet military leaders in February, 1959, were clearly false insofar as they implied an operational capability. Certainly, the marshals' claims seem designed to create a misleading impression regarding a non-existent operational capability.

United States official spokesmen did not publicly credit the Soviet Union with an operational ICBM capability at that time. In June, Secretary McElroy reportedly told newsmen that the U.S.S.R. was expected to have ten ICBM's by the end of 1959.[15] A month later, however, according to a United Press International dispatch on a filmed television interview of McElroy by Senator Kenneth Keating, the Defense Secretary said the Soviet Union might have beaten the United States in the race to get the first intercontinental ballistic missiles into the hands of combat units.[16] UPI quoted McElroy as saying that the number of operational Soviet long-range missiles was "at the most only a very few—less than ten" and that this was not too important because of countervailing American retaliatory power.

At the Twenty-first Party Congress in January, 1959, Defense Minister Malinovsky described some of the characteristics of the

---

[12] *Krasnaia zvezda*, February 4, 1959.
[13] *Sovetskaia Rossiia*, February 23, 1959; *Izvestiia*, February 22, 1959.
[14] *Krasnaia zvezda*, February 22, 1959.
[15] *New York Times*, June 28, 1959.
[16] *New York Times*, July 27, 1959.

Soviet ICBM: it was very powerful, invulnerable, and had "pinpoint accuracy." The accuracy of the Soviet ICBM had earlier been questioned by United States leaders. President Eisenhower said in October, 1957, that although the Soviets had demonstrated they could fire objects "a very considerable distance" the military value of their missile could not be judged without knowledge of its accuracy.[17] In support of his new claim regarding the Soviet ICBM's accuracy, Malinovsky now cited the success of the Lunik space shot earlier in the month.[18]

In this country, Malinovsky's claim was anticipated on January 29 by Wernher von Braun and Homer Stewart of the National Aeronautics and Space Administration, who testified before a Senate subcommittee that American space experts believed the U.S.S.R. could now pinpoint a city in the United States with a ballistic missile fired more than five thousand miles away. They said this appraisal was based largely on the accuracy of the January 2 Lunik firing.[19] Subsequently, however, President Eisenhower and Secretary McElroy disputed Malinovsky's claim.

In this period, Soviet leaders were apparently setting the stage for later claims of military superiority based on strategic missile forces. For the time being, however, they claimed only a rough equality with the United States. They were quick to dispute Western claims of superiority, especially when such claims were taken to imply a retaliation-proof strategic capability against the Soviet Union. According to Malinovsky, "playing down the effective capacity of the U.S.S.R. to deal a counterblow to the aggressor and exaggeration of their transoceanic capabilities, especially in the field of strategic ballistic rockets, do not testify to the presence of common sense among the U.S. military." [20] That the U.S.S.R. had "no less force and capabilities" than the United States was stressed by Khrushchev as well as Malinovsky.[21]

The claimed achievement of strategic parity with the United States provided the foundation for radical revisions in the Soviet leaders'

[17] New York Times, October 10, 1957.
[18] The lunar rocket launched by the Soviet Union on January 2, 1959, bypassed the moon at a distance claimed to have been around 3,500 miles and then went into heliocentric orbit between the earth and Mars. A second lunar rocket impacted the moon in September. See Arnold L. Horelick, "The Soviet Union and the Political Uses of Space," in Joseph M. Goldsen (ed.), Outer Space and World Politics (New York: Frederick A. Praeger, Inc., 1963), p. 56.
[19] New York Times, January 30, 1959.
[20] Pravda, April 11, 1959.
[21] Pravda, March 19, 1959; April 11, 1959.

public estimates of the effectiveness of Soviet deterrence and the likelihood of war. At the Twenty-first Party Congress in January, 1959, Khrushchev declared that because of favorable shifts in the balance of power the danger of capitalist restoration (imposed by external force) was now finally excluded: in the U.S.S.R. "socialism has triumphed not only fully, but irreversibly." [22] Earlier, the end of "capitalist encirclement" had been officially proclaimed: "At present," Khrushchev stated in 1958, "it is not known who encircles whom, the capitalist countries the socialist states, or vice versa." [23]

Accompanying these claims were increasingly confident assertions about the deterrent effect of Soviet military strength, that is, assertions that the shift in the balance of forces was now understood in the West. Thus, Khrushchev declared in May, 1959:

The imperialists know our strength. To attack us is tantamount to suicide; one would have to be insane for this. I do not believe they are as stupid as all that; they understand the consequences which the unleashing of war against the socialist countries may have for them.[24]

And a few months later, Khrushchev reiterated this estimate, leaving no doubt about its authoritativeness by attributing it to the Party Central Committee and the Soviet government:

Comrades, the Central Committee of our Party and the Soviet Government believe that a situation has at present been created in which the imperialists will hardly dare to launch a war against our motherland or against the countries of socialism. Our forces and those of our socialist allies are colossal and in the West, apparently, this is now understood.[25]

The possibility that a madman, like Hitler, might embark upon a suicidal adventure, was conceded, but Khrushchev expressed confidence that such adventures could be "cut short" or that "a strait jacket can be found" for such a madman.[26] The Soviet leaders no longer emphasized, as they had four years earlier when they deposed Malenkov, the danger of a rational, premeditated attack by the West against the U.S.S.R. They now stressed "the grave danger that even a slight miscalculation by statesmen in one country or another may lead to yet another war." [27] The danger that war might result from a technical accident or from an irrational act by a subordinate officer

---

[22] *Pravda*, January 28, 1959.
[23] *Pravda*, March 27, 1958.
[24] *Pravda*, June 1, 1959.
[25] *Pravda*, July 30, 1959.
[26] *Pravda*, October 15, 1958; January 28, 1959.
[27] *Pravda*, August 31, 1959.

became a standard Soviet theme during this period, spearheading protests against armed SAC training flights and airborne alerts. Even so, war, which until 1956 was still deemed inevitable so long as capitalism existed, was now officially no longer "fatalistically inevitable" and might soon (1965) "be excluded from the life of society." [28]

Khrushchev insisted that the probability of premeditated Western attack on the U.S.S.R. had been reduced "not because the imperialists have become wiser or kinder, but because they have become weaker." He likened the aspiration of the West to destroy the socialist countries to the desire of a hungry wolf with blunt fangs to kill a powerful lion. [29]

Despite these confident assertions about the improved strategic position of the Soviet Union, Khrushchev's disinclination for the time being to claim a large operational ICBM capability was evident. He concentrated instead on gaining credence for his ICBM production claims. The most expansive Soviet missile claims during this period were reserved for the NATO countries of Europe. Khrushchev in particular frequently seized opportunities to boast of the U.S.S.R.'s capability to wipe these countries from the face of the earth with missiles (presumably of medium or intermediate range). In fact, this was sometimes done even in response to United States claims of a capacity to destroy the Soviet Union. [30]

By contrast, Khrushchev employed vague generalizations and other circumlocutions to avoid explicit claims to a large operational ICBM capability. Evidently he did not wish—by making blatantly premature claims that would in any case be disbelieved—to destroy his credibility abroad as an authoritative source of information on the Soviet ICBM. Thus, in responding to Western assertions that NATO's long-range bomber capability conferred strategic superiority

---

[28] *Pravda*, January 28, 1959.

[29] *Pravda*, March 27, 1959.

[30] "These bellicose militarists should ponder about their country and its follies. If such a country as ours, which occupies one-sixth of the globe, can, as they assert, be destroyed in a brief period, how much time is needed to destroy other smaller countries, the allies of the United States, by resorting to the same means with which we are threatened? If the American generals and admirals ignore their allies and write them off, it is their own affair" (Khrushchev press conference, March 19, 1959, *Krasnaia zvezda*, March 20, 1959). And on another occasion, "If we are attacked we shall try first of all to destroy the rocket bases directed against us. And what does destroying these bases mean? They are located not in bare rocky country, but where people live. But the governments of countries which provide territory for rocket bases of a transoceanic power for some reason do not take the vital interest of their peoples into account" (Khrushchev speech in Albania, *Izvestiia*, May 29, 1959).

over the U.S.S.R., Khrushchev sought to nullify this admittedly huge bomber force, not by claiming a large Soviet ICBM capability, as he might have done, but rather by asserting that the West's bombers were vulnerable to modern air defenses.[31] Similarly, when Western leaders said, according to Khrushchev, that the United States would not be menaced in the event of war since the Soviet Union "still has few intercontinental rockets," the Soviet Premier countered their statements, not by explicitly claiming a large ICBM capability, but by asserting that the United States had "long ago" lost its invulnerability to attack. On one occasion, he added, imprecisely, that the Soviet Union now had "the means to deliver a crushing blow against an aggressor at any point on the earth's surface." [32]

The low key in which Khrushchev and other Soviet leaders pitched their ICBM claims during the summer and early fall of 1959 may also have been related to the chain of diplomatic events that led to the short-lived "spirit of Camp David" in the fall. There was a perceptible lull in Soviet boasts regarding the U.S.S.R.'s ICBM program after the announcement in the summer that Khrushchev would visit the United States. Khrushchev himself intimated the reason for this: "I want to go to the U.S. as a man of peace. . . . If during my talks with the President I had a rocket sticking out of one pocket and a second out of another . . . what kind of talk would that be?" [33] Nevertheless, the very eve of Khrushchev's departure for the United States was the moment chosen by the Soviet Union to launch the U.S.S.R.'s second lunar rocket, Lunik II, which impacted the moon on September 12. When he arrived in Washington, the Soviet Premier presented the American President with a replica of the metal Soviet pennant that had been placed in the Lunik payload. Although Khrushchev made much of Soviet space triumphs during his visit to the United States, he apparently resolved not to speak of missiles, for he observed midway: "I have already made many speeches in the United States but have not once resorted to the word 'arms,' let alone 'rockets.' " [34] But he said this just after anger had led him to break his resolve, adding, "If I have spoken about it today, you must understand I had no choice." When he spoke of rockets on this occasion, however, it was less to boast of the size and scope of the Soviet ICBM

---

[31] Interview with West German Social Democratic party editors, *Pravda*, May 9, 1959.
[32] Speech to the Twenty-first Party Congress, February 5, 1959, *Vneocherednoi XXI s"ezd Kommunisticheskoi partii Sovetskogo Soiuza* ["Extraordinary XXI Congress of the CPSU"] (Moscow: Gospolitizdat, 1959), Vol. II, p. 405.
[33] *Pravda*, August 6, 1959.
[34] *Pravda*, September 20, 1959.

program than to warn of what it might become if the United States rejected peaceful coexistence and maintained the cold war:

If you are not ready for disarmament and want to go on with the arms race, we accept that challenge, for we now have the necessary strength and all the possibilities to create modern weapons, and as for the output of our rockets, these are on the assembly line.[35]

In his efforts to intimidate the United States, then, Khrushchev found it useful to suggest two somewhat contradictory theses: that the U.S.S.R. was *rapidly acquiring* a powerful force that could destroy the United States, and that the U.S.S.R. would *take steps to acquire* such a force if the United States was not more conciliatory. The first of these themes, intended to deceive, was dominant; the second, more in accord with the actual Soviet ICBM program and its potentialities for expansion, was only briefly prominent and was discarded almost as soon as Khrushchev returned to the U.S.S.R.

---

[35] This translation was distributed by the Associated Press (see the *New York Times*, September 21, 1959). These words, spoken by Khrushchev extemporaneously at a reception in Los Angeles on September 19, after he had finished reading his prepared text, were softened in the official Soviet version: "If you are not prepared for disarmament and want to continue the arms race, we will have no choice but to go on making rockets, which in our country are being turned out by the assembly-line method" (*World without Arms: World without Wars* [Moscow: Foreign Languages Publishing House, 1960], Vol. II, p. 221).

FIVE

CAPABILITY CLAIMS
NOVEMBER, 1959–APRIL, 1960

EVEN AFTER RETURNING from the United States in October, 1959, Khrushchev continued to claim only that the U.S.S.R. was ahead of all other countries in the production of rockets;[1] he still said nothing of an ICBM operational capability. In an interview earlier in the year, Khrushchev had vaguely asserted, under prodding, that the Soviet Union had "enough rockets for America, too, should war be unleashed against us";[2] but not until November, 1959, did he try to indicate that the U.S.S.R. possessed a substantial operational ICBM capability:

We now have stockpiled so many rockets, so many atomic and hydrogen warheads, that, if we were attacked, we could wipe from the face of the earth all of our probable opponents.

He repeated this statement almost verbatim on December 1, 1959.[3] By leaving bombers out of account and making rockets the vehicles for this terrible blow and by talking of "all of our probable opponents," he gave the impression that the vehicles were in fact ICBM's capable of reaching the United States. It is true that Khrushchev did not then or later single out the United States among the countries that could be "wiped from the face of the earth" by the Soviet Union. But on the basis of no reasonable interpretation could the United States be excluded from the category of the U.S.S.R.'s "probable opponents." The formula employed, however, was imprecise. By straining the meaning of Khrushchev's words, for example, one might suppose that the rockets "now" stockpiled were to supplement bombers previously available. But even this bare possibility, like other similar ones, was subsequently eliminated in a new variation of the formula. In January, 1960, in his authoritative speech on defense policy to the Supreme Soviet, Khrushchev advanced a new form of warning:

I stress once again that we already have enough nuclear weapons—atomic and hydrogen—and the corresponding rockets to deliver this weapon to the

---

[1] *Pravda*, October 8, 1959.
[2] Interview with West German Social Democratic party editors, *Pravda*, May 9, 1959.
[3] *Pravda*, November 15, December 1, 1959.

territory of a possible aggressor, [so] that if some madman stirred up an attack on our state or on other socialist states we could literally wipe from the face of the earth the country or countries that attacked us.[4]

This statement reduced the ambiguity of the earlier one in the following ways: (*a*) The destruction was now to be visited upon any *country* that attacked the U.S.S.R. instead of on any probable *opponent*, thus eliminating the bare possibility that the rulers in their capitals, not the peoples of countries, were the targets. (*b*) The word "literally" was added to the phrase "wipe from the face of the earth," as though to make the threat of annihilation unequivocal. (*c*) It was now made clear that the nuclear weapons were to be delivered on target by rockets, not bombers.

An important ambiguity that remained arose from the retention of the term "rockets." Khrushchev presumably meant land-based rockets, since he made no mention of either bombers or submarines from which rockets might be launched. He had not previously claimed an air-to-surface missile capability, and after 1958 he had dropped his earlier references to a submarine-launched missile capability. The only land-based Soviet rockets at that time, however, were in the U.S.S.R.: to reach the continental United States would require ICBM's. Thus, in asserting that the U.S.S.R. had sufficient rockets to wipe from the face of the earth the countries that might attack it, Khrushchev implicitly claimed a not inconsiderable operational ICBM force. This claim was repeated to the Supreme Soviet by the Minister of Defense, Marshal Malinovsky. Subsequently, it was quoted by several other Soviet military leaders, including the head of the Warsaw Pact forces, Marshal Grechko.[5]

Shortly after Khrushchev's speech, Moscow announced the successful testing over a distance of sixty-five hundred nautical miles of a rocket ostensibly designed to further the Soviet space program, although its military significance was made clear.[6] These tests seemed to confirm Khrushchev's remarks to Senator Hubert H. Humphrey in December, 1958, regarding the Soviet Union's capacity to extend greatly the range of its ICBM.[7] The first rocket was said to have hit

---

[4] *Pravda*, January 15, 1960.
[5] *Pravda*, May 9, 1961. Grechko added, in his own words: "Soviet rocket troops now [are] able to destroy the aggressor at any point on earth."
[6] In an address to the Indian Parliament, Khrushchev stated that "quite recently [January, 1960] we successfully tested powerful intercontinental ballistic rockets which demonstrated new great achievements of Soviet scientists" (*Pravda*, February 12, 1960).
[7] Humphrey, "My Marathon Talk with Russia's Boss," *Life*, January 12, 1959, p. 80.

within two kilometers of its aiming point, and this report provided the first numerical claim as to the accuracy of the Soviet ICBM.[8]

The assertion in early 1960 that the U.S.S.R. had sufficient rockets to destroy the United States was, in its implications, the most far-reaching Soviet ICBM claim. Although the claim, of course, could not reasonably be taken to mean that the Soviet Union was capable of killing the entire population of "any attacking country" (obviously a reference to the United States), it clearly implied the possession of a large number of operational ICBM's. Some notion of what Khrushchev meant to convey by the expression "literally wipe from the face of the earth" is suggested by an earlier "country-busting" threat he had leveled against West Germany. In May, 1959, Khrushchev, agreeing with an earlier estimate, said that not more than eight warheads with yields of from three to five megatons would have to be exploded over West Germany—a country less than one-thirtieth as large as the United States—in order to "put it out of commission." [9]

Marshal Malinovsky, who spoke to the Supreme Soviet immediately after Khrushchev had spoken on defense policy, explicitly referred to calculations of this type made by "both our own and foreign specialists." In an illustrative calculation, he used as a unit of measure a bomb with a yield of two megatons; but the state he used had an area of only three hundred fifty to five hundred thousand square kilometers, far smaller than that of the United States. Malinovsky concluded that if one hundred two-megaton bombs were exploded over such a state the resulting blast damage and lethal radioactivity would transform it into "a lifeless desert." [10]

Even if Khrushchev's claim was not based on such precise numerical calculations, it clearly was made on the basis of informed reflection. It extended previous claims to include the United States and was the culmination of a long sequence of ICBM claims. Khrushchev asserted it three times: twice in an equivocal formulation and finally in a major address on defense policy to the Supreme Soviet, when a number of ambiguities in the earlier formulation were resolved. Moreover, it was repeated by top military leaders, including Defense Minister Malinovsky, who were certainly informed and presumably had reflected on what they were saying. The claim was

---

[8] *Pravda*, January 22, 1960. Subsequently, TASS said of the first test in a new series in the fall of 1961 that the rocket hit within *one* kilometer of the target (*Krasnaia zvezda*, September 15, 1961).

[9] *Pravda*, May 9, 1959.

[10] *Pravda*, January 15, 1960.

deliberate and meaningful, but it was clearly false. Nor was it false merely in being slightly premature: the Soviet leaders had no intention of deploying large numbers of their first-generation ICBM, and this must certainly have been known to Khrushchev at the time. More than a year later, as is now known, the U.S.S.R. had still deployed only "a handful" of ICBM's.[11]

The question arises: Could Khrushchev really have believed that his claim of January 14, 1960, might influence Western beliefs about the strategic balance? Khrushchev must have known from public statements by responsible United States government officials that United States estimates did not credit the U.S.S.R. with having more than ten operational ICBM's at the time he made his claim.[12] But Khrushchev's efforts to deceive Western opinion required only that there be *uncertainty* regarding estimates of Soviet ICBM capabilities, and of this there was ample evidence. Soviet leaders on several occasions publicly questioned the ability of the United States to assess Soviet operational ICBM capabilities.

In mid-1959, several months after military leaders announced that the Soviet armed forces had been supplied with ICBM's, Khrushchev said:

Certain American generals and admirals . . . allege that the Soviet Union has few intercontinental rockets. . . . [Almost certainly it had no operational ICBMs at that time.] But this, after all, is what the American military men assert. It should be said, however, that it is always better to count the money in your own pocket than that in the other fellow's. I might say, incidentally, that we have enough rockets for America, too, should war be unleashed against us. . . .[13]

Khrushchev's confidence that the United States was uncertain about its estimates of Soviet ICBM capability may have been enhanced during his visit to this country, when, in his presence, certain of his American hosts acknowledged their respect for Soviet rocket capabilities on the basis of demonstrated Soviet achievements in space.[14] Moreover, the expressed official United States estimate of the Soviet ICBM program was strongly criticized in some military and political circles, and by journalists, as being too conservative.

---

[11] See p. 37.

[12] Secretary McElroy's December 1, 1959 press conference, *New York Times*, December 2, 1959.

[13] *Izvestiia*, May 5, 1959.

[14] Khrushchev remarked, for example, "When I was in the United States, American leaders told me: 'Yes, we have now become convinced that you can deliver freight to any point on earth' " (*Pravda*, October 10, 1959).

Although the estimates of the future Soviet operational ICBM force were especially criticized, the official estimate of the existing force was also thought to be too low. (It was publicly acknowledged in February, 1960, that parts of the intelligence community had registered dissents from the national intelligence estimates.)[15] This controversy, which was partly conducted in public, accentuated the note of uncertainty in the West's estimates. Publicly announced United States policies sometimes had a similar effect. On December 1, 1959, Defense Secretary McElroy disclosed plans for a possible airborne alert, with nuclear-armed bombers continuously in the air, to make up for any missile gap that might arise.[16] This manifest concern that the U.S.S.R. might rapidly deploy a large ICBM force and thus achieve a first-strike capability may have encouraged Khrushchev to imply that the U.S.S.R. already possessed a missile capability to wipe the United States from the face of the earth.

Whatever its uncertainty about the future, however, in late 1959 the administration credited the U.S.S.R. with only a small operational ICBM capability. According to McElroy, both the United States and the U.S.S.R. had about ten combat-ready ICBM's. A discrepancy having appeared between what the U.S.S.R. claimed and what the United States publicly conceded, the Soviet military newspaper, *Krasnaia zvezda*, hastened to defend the Soviet position:

We declare openly that the "data" at the disposal of A. Dulles are of little interest to us. To calculate in Washington the number of rockets and other types of Soviet arms is of as little use as counting crows on the fence. Why does the master director bother at all? We are prepared to answer his question. How many rockets do we have? Enough! Enough to wipe from the face of the earth any country which dares attack the Soviet Union. N. S. Khrushchev frankly and openly declared this at the January session of the U.S.S.R. Supreme Soviet.[17]

Were these assertions of confidence that the United States could not learn the size of the Soviet ICBM force real or feigned? Could this confidence have survived the Soviet leaders' awareness of the U-2

---

[15] United States, Senate, *Hearings before the Preparedness Investigating Subcommittee of the Committee on Armed Services, in Conjunction with the Committee on Aeronautical and Space Sciences, on Missiles, Space and Other Major Defense Matters*, 86th Cong., 2d sess., *passim.*, esp. 114–21 (hereinafter cited as *Hearings before the Preparedness Investigating Subcommittee*).

[16] Some weeks later, in his budget message (January 18, 1960), President Eisenhower rejected this proposal but authorized the acquisition of a standby alert capability for heavy bombers.

[17] January 31, 1960.

flights? Subsequently, as we shall see, Khrushchev intimated that the U-2's had not flown over areas where the ICBM was deployed, thereby implying that, although they may not have found ICBM sites, this provided no basis for United States confidence that there were none to be found.

Another means employed to heighten American uncertainty in estimating Soviet ICBM capabilities was the assertion by both Khrushchev and Malinovsky that Soviet ballistic missile sites could readily be concealed. Speaking of ballistic rockets, including those of great range, Marshal Malinovsky observed:

The building of large, expensive airfields with complicated equipment is not required for launching rockets. It is far easier to camouflage and even completely conceal rocket-launch positions; this guarantees a higher degree of security and invulnerability for rocket weapons.[18]

Khrushchev also spoke of Soviet ability to conceal the launching sites of *strategic* rockets (that is, rockets having a range of more than one thousand kilometers), though he was probably intentionally vague as to whether ICBM's were to be included in that category. Soviet territory is so immense, he observed, that "we have the possibility of dispersing rocket facilities, of camouflaging them well." [19]

It appears, then, that in early 1960 the Soviet leaders believed that within the United States government and politically important groups in America there was substantial uncertainty regarding the Soviet ICBM force and that this uncertainty could be heightened by misleading statements about the location and concealment of Soviet missile sites and deceptive claims of numbers of missiles. If, in the eyes of the Soviet leaders, American beliefs and opinions regarding Soviet strategic power seemed uncertain and, to some extent, manipulable, this kind of uncertainty may have been even more apparent to them in Western Europe, where the Soviet interest lay in undermining the confidence of America's allies in its capability and will to deter or turn back Soviet encroachments in Europe. Heightening the impression in Western Europe that Soviet strategic power exceeded that of the United States was now particularly important in the light of the negotiations on Berlin and Germany that were scheduled to recommence at the summit in May. And in the early months of 1960 that impression evidently did predominate in Western Europe and to a lesser degree throughout the non-Communist world. A survey by the

---

[18] *Pravda*, January 15, 1960.
[19] *Ibid.*

United States Information Agency in 1960 found that radical changes had taken place in popular assessments of relative United States–Soviet military strength as compared with views held in the years prior to Sputnik and ICBM.[20] In Western Europe, the foreign area of most critical importance to the United States, the survey found that most people "were convinced that the balance of military power no longer favors the United States as it formerly did":

> While sophisticated political and press opinion tends to regard the current military situation as one of nuclear stalemate in which neither of the two super-powers has any material advantage over the other, the more impressionistic popular opinion has seemingly concluded from Soviet boasts of superiority and American admissions of a temporary "missile gap" that the United States is not only currently militarily inferior to the USSR but will continue to be so for the next decade or two as well.[21]

Elsewhere, in the world, according to the USIA report, most opinion was divided on military strength, the predominant belief being that a nuclear stalemate existed. "However, in almost all areas," the report stated, "expectations appear to be that the USSR will achieve military superiority, although there is probably no clear concept of what this superiority will consist of, or what its significance will be." [22]

If, as seems abundantly clear, Khrushchev was engaged in a grand deception of the West, what were the consequences inside the Soviet bloc? The rocket claim served as the chief justification for the one-third reduction in the Soviet armed forces proposed by Khrushchev in January, 1960. Its falsity must have raised a serious problem with widespread ramifications in the Soviet military establishment. The

---

[20] United States Information Agency, Office of Research and Intelligence, *Free World Views of the US–USSR Power Balance* (R-54-60, August 29, 1960).

[21] *Ibid.*, p. 5. The results of opinion surveys concerning relative military strength, conducted in five Western European countries shortly after Soviet ICBM claims reached their culmination in January, 1960, are given below (*ibid.*, p. 22).

	Great Britain February, 1960	West Germany February, 1960	Norway June, 1960	France February, 1960	Italy February, 1960
Number of cases	613	599	1,020	608	591
United States ahead (%)	15	22	15	16	38
U.S.S.R. ahead (%) ...	59	47	45	37	32
Both equal (%)	4	8	17	16	5
No opinion (%)	22	25	23	31	25

[22] *Ibid.*, p. 1.

topmost Soviet commanders, at least, could not readily be deceived in matters affecting the strength of Soviet strategic forces and must therefore have been privy to the deception. Several of them evidently connived at Khrushchev's policy, including Defense Minister Malinovsky and Marshal Moskalenko, later commander of strategic rocket troops for a time.[23] Others among the top commanders, perhaps also aware of the deception, may have resisted the troop cut, for several were removed from their posts in the following months.[24]

In its final form, as noted above, Khrushchev's rocket claim referred to "an attack on our state or on other socialist states," thereby extending the Soviet nuclear umbrella over the other countries of the Communist camp. Although Soviet leaders were doubtless confident that the U.S.S.R. would not soon be called upon to employ its newly asserted rocket capability on behalf of its allies, the assertion was not devoid of risks.[25] Chinese Communist leaders, already at odds with their Soviet comrades on questions of foreign and military policy, might have been emboldened to exploit Khrushchev's claims politically against the West in ways that could prove dangerous if they were not told the truth about Soviet strategic forces. On the other hand, if they were taken into the conspiracy, they could use the information to embarrass Khrushchev in the political hostilities that were already dividing the Communist bloc. One of the most crucial and obscure aspects of the Sino-Soviet dispute involves the Chinese Communist leaders' beliefs during these years regarding Soviet ICBM capabilities. If they believed that Khrushchev was telling the truth in January, 1960, about Soviet rocket capabilities, their resentment must have been increased by his relatively cautious foreign policy, particularly by his refusal to assume risks on behalf of the U.S.S.R.'s Chinese allies. The consequences must have been equally disruptive of the

---

[23] In subscribing to Khrushchev's claim, however, Moskalenko significantly altered it so that "the Soviet armed forces," rather than simply its nuclear missile forces, were credited with the capability of wiping any country from the face of the earth (*Izvestiia*, January 16, 1960). Malinovsky did not subscribe to Khrushchev's claim in his speech to the Supreme Soviet, although he affirmed it in a speech delivered a few days later (*Krasnaia zvezda*, January 20, 1960).

[24] I. S. Konev gave up his post as head of the Warsaw Pact military forces and V. D. Sokolovsky resigned as chief of the general staff. Neither man was reassigned, although Konev later received an important post as commander of Soviet forces in East Germany after the troop cut was rescinded. In an article published a month after Khrushchev's defense policy speech to the Supreme Soviet, Konev seemed to stress Soviet superiority in technology and *over-all* military strength rather than in operational strategic rockets (*Sovetskaia Rossiia*, February 23, 1960).

[25] Malinovsky cautiously amended Khrushchev's formula to read "an attack on our state *and* on other socialist countries" [italics added]. He seemed to imply that only an attack on the U.S.S.R. would bring about a Soviet attack on the United States.

alliance, perhaps more so, if the Chinese leaders were aware that while greatly exaggerating the progress of the Soviet ICBM program Khrushchev was in fact retarding it by diverting funds to satisfy consumer demands and to assist "bourgeois nationalist" regimes in Africa and Asia.

Khrushchev's magnification of the Soviet ICBM capability contrasts with his belittlement of the Soviet bomber capability. He revealed that the Soviet Union had reduced its production of bombers and forecast that bomber production would continue to decline and might even cease.[26] In part, as noted above, this is readily explicable in terms of his political objectives: to make it appear that in strategic weapons the U.S.S.R. was a full generation ahead of the United States, which was still relying on bombers that were vulnerable and hence obsolete. Yet the effect of these statements was to reinforce the West's confidence that the growth of the Soviet bomber capability against the United States had been slow and to downgrade future Soviet claims of intercontinental bomber capabilities.

These tactics are not so paradoxical as they may appear. The Soviet bomber capability against the United States in 1960, although not insignificant, was greatly inferior to the SAC bomber force and to the growing United States missile capability. Since there was by this time little expressed uncertainty in the United States about the size of the Soviet bomber force, it did not lend itself to exaggerated claims. This was not true, however, of the Soviet ICBM force: it was evident that a considerable margin of uncertainty existed in American estimates and that there was wide disagreement regarding the appropriate assumptions that had to be made in lieu of certainty. The Soviet leaders apparently saw an opportunity to exploit this uncertainty at a time when United States preponderance in strategic forces was actually about to reach a new peak.

Khrushchev's January, 1960, claim of a missile capability to wipe any hostile country from the face of the earth was the extreme instance of a series of deceptive claims that were designed to serve several distinct aims of Soviet policy. The relationship between Soviet missile deception and Soviet foreign policy will be discussed in some detail in Part 3. Here we shall briefly list some of the objectives that Soviet claims were probably meant to support:

---

[26] *Pravda*, January 15, 1960. "Almost the entire military air force is being replaced by rocket equipment. We have by now sharply cut, and it seems will continue sharply to cut and even discontinue the manufacture of bombers and other obsolete equipment. . . ."

1. They were designed to conceal from the West the decision of Soviet leaders not to engage in a large-scale deployment of the first-generation ICBM despite their apparent capability to do so. By concealing this decision, the Soviet leaders hoped to reap whatever political benefits might have accrued to them had they actually decided to engage in such a buildup.

2. The deceptive claims, insofar as they could cause United States leaders to doubt the superiority of American strategic forces, were probably also meant to help deter a United States attack on the U.S.S.R. under circumstances in which the Soviet leaders believed the United States might otherwise conceivably contemplate it. In the report on military affairs to the Supreme Soviet in which Khrushchev claimed a missile capability to wipe any country from the face of the earth, Khrushchev for the first time explicitly asserted that the Soviet strategic force could survive a United States attack even if the United States "really succeeded in striking its blow by surprise." Such a surprise attack Khrushchev treated as the most severe test to which the Soviet strategic force could be subjected.[27] Previously, the claimed capacity of the Soviet force to survive surprise attack was based on the expressed assumption that the United States could be denied the advantage of surprise, that a surprise blow could be "averted," "forestalled," or "pre-empted." Khrushchev now went farther to claim that the invulnerability of the Soviet strategic missile force, which was protected by various measures—dispersal, camouflage, and duplicate targeting (Khrushchev subsequently alluded to hardening[28])—assured that a United States surprise attack could not incapacitate the Soviet strategic force and that the attacking countries would have to take into account the certainty of "a due rebuff."

Most importantly, the nature of this rebuff was radically altered. As we have seen, in the first two years after Sputnik, the retaliatory damage that the U.S.S.R. claimed it could inflict on the United States had been left indefinite: the United States could no longer count on its relative invulnerability but would suffer equally with, if not more than, the U.S.S.R. In contrast, the level of damage that could be inflicted by retaliatory blows against American allies in Western

---

[27] *Pravda*, January 15, 1960. For a detailed analysis of Khrushchev's remarks on the question of surprise attack, see Arnold L. Horelick, " 'Deterrence' and Surprise Attack in Soviet Strategic Thought," *Royal Canadian Air Force Staff College Journal*, 1960.

[28] Speech by Khrushchev at the Third Congress of the Rumanian Workers Party, Bucharest, *Pravda*, June 22, 1960.

Europe was made more definite: complete destruction was threatened. Khrushchev repeatedly stated that in the event of war these smaller, less distant countries would be "wiped from the face of the earth." Now Khrushchev collapsed this distinction and threatened *maximum retaliatory damage* against the United States. The distinction that he had formerly made between the vulnerability in nuclear war of small European countries, on the one hand, and the U.S.S.R., on the other, he now made between all hostile countries and the U.S.S.R.

Although this extreme Soviet claim no doubt was meant to contribute to deterrence of an unprovoked United States attack, the capability it implied was excessive for this purpose. In fact, confidence that the United States would not launch such an attack was already sufficient to convince the Soviet leaders that it was safe to prolong the great Soviet inferiority in intercontinental forces by foregoing a "crash" program for production and deployment of the early ICBM.

3. Another important object of the series of missile claims was probably to put the United States on the defensive in the duel of strategic threats. In this attempt the Soviet leaders were perhaps not without success. Secretary Robert S. McNamara was later to say that the ending of the myth of the missile gap "made it possible to take a firm line with our adversaries and at the same time to reassure our friends that we are strong and determined to use our strength if we have to." [29] Even after it was publicly revealed early in 1960 that United States intelligence estimates of the projected size and pace of Soviet ICBM deployment had been scaled down—that the U.S.S.R. was not engaging in a "crash" program [30]—administration leaders conceded that the Soviet Union "might enjoy at times a moderate numerical superiority during the next three years," with the peak probably occurring in 1962 (Secretary Thomas S. Gates, Jr.). [31] The fierce public debate over the extent of projected Soviet ICBM superiority and its implications tended to obscure the fact of current United States strategic superiority and to lessen its political value.

The Soviet missile and space programs succeeded in curbing United States use of strategic threats against the U.S.S.R., a point on which Soviet leaders have shown marked sensitivity. [32] On a number of

---

[29] *Saturday Evening Post*, December 1, 1962, p. 18.
[30] *Hearings before the Preparedness Investigations Subcommittee*, p. 442.
[31] *Ibid.*, p. 457.
[32] A comprehensive and detailed study of United States military claims in recent years has yet to be made. One has the impression, however, that after Sputnik responsible United States officials tempered their claims of strategic superiority, stressing the

occasions, as in his interview with Averell Harriman in July, 1959, Khrushchev countered United States strategic threats, explicit or so interpreted by him, by invoking the specter of Soviet ICBM's.[33] If, as it now appears, Soviet leaders made exaggerated rocket claims in early 1960, their object was probably not so much to force concessions from the West in a direct confrontation on some crucial issue as to deter the West from the political or military exploitation of its superior strategic power and to provide a promising environment for their own offensive political moves when there appeared to be small risk in making them. Certainly, Soviet military leaders would be more willing to exaggerate Soviet ICBM capabilities in order to conceal weakness than to bluff a superior opponent in an open confrontation.

The circumstances in which the extreme claim was publicized may have seemed to mitigate its inherent dangers. Khrushchev had just returned from his visit to America, where he had arranged for a future summit meeting. International tension had declined considerably from the high point of early 1959, and there appeared to be no reason for a new precipitate rise, unless the Soviet leaders embarked on some dangerous course of action. In view of subsequent developments, it appears that this was not their intention.

The question remains, Why did the U.S.S.R. not try to compensate for its great inferiority in intercontinental bomber forces by capitalizing on its capacity to acquire a large ICBM force before the United States could do so? The answer, apparently, is that the Soviet leaders were confident that they could control the danger of general war even without a large intercontinental strike force. The grounds of this confidence were chiefly political. As had been demonstrated during the previous years, United States preponderance in strategic forces was not an active threat to the security of the U.S.S.R. as long as the latter did not take actions that directly menaced vital American interests. Even if a situation seemed likely to arise in which the American incentive to initiate general war might appreciably increase, the Soviet leaders were probably confident that they could readily extricate themselves by political maneuvers. At the same time, the Soviet leaders probably recognized that United States leaders were unlikely to make large concessions under pressure from the U.S.S.R. if they did not credit the Soviet Union with a strong ICBM force. Thus,

---

capability to cause great retaliatory damage to the U.S.S.R. in the event the United States was attacked rather than the capability to destroy the U.S.S.R. if it attacked a United States ally.

[33] See Harriman, "My Alarming Interview with Khrushchev," *Life*, July 13, 1959, pp. 33–34.

the Soviet leaders had strong incentives for seeking to persuade the West that the Soviet Union would rapidly acquire a large ICBM force and little fear that failure of the deception would endanger the immediate security of the U.S.S.R. Not only was deception regarding the Soviet ICBM a useful instrument of an offensive foreign policy, but bold Soviet initiatives tended to make the deceptive claims more credible.

SIX

THE U-2 AFFAIR AND ITS AFTERMATH, MAY–AUGUST, 1960

INTERNATIONAL RELATIONS in the late spring and early summer of 1960 were dominated by the U-2 incident, the collapse of the Paris summit meeting, and the heightened tension in East-West relations associated with these events. The political context was one in which the Soviet leaders might have been expected to repeat the extreme claims regarding Soviet strategic-offensive capabilities that they had asserted only a few months earlier in the more relaxed atmosphere of the period following the Camp David meeting. But despite the grave provocation that Khrushchev said had been offered by the United States and despite his acknowledgment that revelations of past U-2 overflights had been interpreted in some quarters as a sign of Soviet weakness, he and the other Soviet leaders employed new caution in the military claims they now put forward.

Their new claims were strongly conditioned by the U-2 incident and the questions it raised regarding (1) the U.S.S.R.'s past as well as future air defense capabilities; (2) its ability to keep secret the location of its strategic missile bases; and (3) the vulnerability of these bases if their locations were to become known. Although new and categorical claims were made concerning these aspects of the Soviet defensive posture, the Soviet leadership displayed a marked restraint in making new claims for their strategic-offensive capabilities and even in reiterating the most extreme of their old ones.

Soviet caution was most pronounced in the days following Khrushchev's May 5 announcement in the Supreme Soviet that a United States reconnaissance aircraft had been brought down on Soviet territory. The Soviet Premier took pains to deny that the Soviet government regarded the U-2 incursion as a precursor of war. Although he sought to derive maximum political and propaganda advantage from the incident, he reiterated his intention to proceed to the Paris summit meeting as planned. And he told the Supreme Soviet on May 7 that the incident "must not compel us to revise our plans by increasing appropriations for weapons and for the army, must not compel us to halt the process of reducing the army." [1]

---

[1] *Pravda*, May 8, 1960.

In the wake of the U-2 incident, Khrushchev's references to Soviet strategic rocket capabilities fell far short of his extreme claims of late 1959 and early 1960. He seemed more concerned to emphasize the readiness of the Soviet strategic rocket force rather than its size or capabilities. Thus, on May 5, he stated that although the Soviet Union, unlike the United States, had no bombers on alert, "we have rockets on alert which will hit accurately and inevitably their assigned target and will work better and more reliably than aircraft on alert." [2] That this alert rocket force included some ICBM's was implied by Khrushchev in his press conference at the U-2 exhibit several days later, when he said that Soviet rockets would explode on United States territory "in the very first minutes of a war," if the United States were to unleash one.[3]

On May 7 Khrushchev announced that a main command of rocket troops had been established under Marshal M. I. Nedelin, an organizational move said to flow from the conversion of the Soviet armed forces to rocket weapons.[4] Although the announcement was presumably intended to convey the impression that recent progress warranted the creation of a separate command for rocket troops, what Khrushchev said explicitly—that "the Soviet Army and Navy are being converted to rocket weapons"—was merely a repetition of what he had announced four months earlier from the same rostrum.[5]

Following the abortive summit meeting, Khrushchev indicated satisfaction with the state of Soviet missile production by announcing that the U.S.S.R. had already ceased the production of "certain types of rockets and put the brakes on the manufacture of certain other types." Rockets, he observed, "are not cucumbers, you know—you don't eat them—and more than a certain number are not required to repel aggression." [6] Khrushchev had anticipated this announcement a year earlier, when he stated that "perhaps it will not be long before we will begin to curtail the production of rockets." He had then added that rockets could not be stored "like cucumbers"; they were "delicate things" and needed "constant maintenance." [7] On neither occasion did Khrushchev specify the types of rockets involved, and it is possible that by the spring of 1960 the production of certain older types of tactical or surface-to-air missiles had in fact been terminated or curtailed. But the 1960 announcement, coming immediately after a

---

[2] *Pravda*, May 6, 1960.
[3] *Pravda*, May 12, 1960.
[4] *Pravda*, May 8, 1960.
[5] *Pravda*, January, 15, 1960.
[6] *Pravda*, May 29, 1960.
[7] *Pravda*, May 12, 1959.

reference to Soviet ICBM and MRBM (medium-range ballistic missile) capabilities, evidently was meant to convey the impression that production of strategic rockets was being curtailed.

It was only after the extraordinary tension raised by the U-2 affair and the summit collapse had dissipated that Soviet leaders again began to make flat assertions of Soviet missile superiority, though still avoiding the most extreme claims of the period prior to the U-2 flight. In July, Khrushchev spoke once more of the "undoubted" superiority of the U.S.S.R. in modern means of nuclear weapon delivery.[8] Mikoyan had earlier termed this superiority "vast."[9] During his visit to Austria in July, Khrushchev reaffirmed that, militarily, the Soviet Union was the world's most powerful country.[10] This categorical claim, first voiced by Khrushchev at the beginning of his Indian trip in February, 1960, and reiterated frequently by him and by other Soviet leaders, had last been made on March 4 by Khrushchev in Kabul.

Three new claims of the period May–August, 1960, related directly to the U-2 incident and were designed to offset its negative strategic implications. One of these pertained to the intelligence on Soviet missile bases that the United States might have acquired through the U-2 operation and, by implication, to the credibility of past Soviet missile claims.

In his numerous speeches and press conferences in the first seven weeks after the downing of Francis Gary Powers' U-2 near Sverdlovsk, Khrushchev avoided these crucial questions, though he stated that missile bases were among the U-2 intelligence targets. During his Supreme Soviet speech on May 7, he displayed some of the prints allegedly made from film recovered from Powers' aircraft and said they included photographs of airfields, petrol stores, and industrial enterprises; he said nothing of rocket bases. It was not until June 21, when he spoke at the Third Congress of the Rumanian Workers' Party in Bucharest, that Khrushchev attempted to deal with the implications of the U-2 flights for the security of Soviet rocket bases and, indirectly, for the credibility of past Soviet claims regarding Soviet missile strength.

I assert that the data obtained by the spy flights are of no importance to the defense of the United States. We know that the spy flights were carried out precisely over regions which have no rocket bases. We know

---

[8] Television and radio speech, Vienna, July 7, 1960, *Pravda*, July 8, 1960.
[9] Press conference in Oslo, June 29, 1960, TASS radioteletype in English to Europe, Moscow, June 29, 1960.
[10] Television and radio speech, Vienna, July 7, 1960, *Pravda*, July 8, 1960.

that two–three years ago the regions of our proving grounds, where we conduct experimental launchings of our rockets, were photographed. Precisely the proving grounds for testing rocket weapons were photographed, and not military-strategic rocket bases.[11]

As far as operational ICBM bases were concerned, Khrushchev's expressed confidence that none had been photographed may have been well founded: there may not yet have been any to photograph. However, Khrushchev did not rest his case with a denial that the U-2's had acquired the missile-base data they had sought. "Suppose even," he went on, "that rocket bases should be photographed." Such target intelligence, he asserted, could be of value only to a country that is preparing to strike first. But even for such purposes knowledge of the location of an opponent's missile bases would be inadequate since, "given modern means, it is impossible to put a rocket base out of commission by one, two, or even several blows. Rocket technology now ensures the means for dealing a retaliatory blow in any case." If the phrase "rocket technology" referred only to the measures that Soviet leaders had previously claimed were being taken to protect the Soviet missile force—dispersal, camouflage, concealment—the new claim of relative invulnerability would not have been credible; that claim could only be justified if Soviet missiles had been hardened, and no such assertion had previously been made by any Soviet spokesman.

Thus, the most far-reaching Soviet claims of the period stressed the effectiveness of Soviet air defenses. In his initial treatment of the U-2 affair, Khrushchev restricted himself to boasts that Soviet air defenses could now prevent high-altitude low-speed reconnaissance aircraft of the U-2 type from overflying the Soviet Union with impunity. His purpose was evidently both to deter new flights and to counter the negative effects of his revelation that such flights had been conducted in the past without effective opposition.

Soon, however, possibly in reaction to the State Department's unexpected acknowledgment of Presidential responsibility for the overflights, Khrushchev extended his air-defense claim to cover not only U-2's but SAC bombers as well. "If there are still politicians," he said in a speech at the Czechoslovak Embassy on May 9, "who would like to rely on bombers, they are doomed to failure. With contemporary military equipment, bombers will be shot down before they approach the target." [12] Thereafter, he exploited the downing of the

---

[11] *Pravda*, June 22, 1960.
[12] *Pravda*, May 10, 1960.

U-2 as a demonstration of how well Soviet air defenses could perform against SAC bombers. Thus, in a speech on May 28, he stated:

When we shot down the plane flying at 20,000 meters, the American militarists became alarmed. . . . They were alarmed primarily because their whole military concept of attack on the Soviet Union, based on the use of bomber planes, had now fallen to the ground. Modern bombers, after all, fly at an altitude of 12,000 to 15,000 meters, no higher. Consequently, since we downed a plane flying at 20,000 meters, then, of course, not a single bomber could get through to its target. They would be brought down either by rockets, by fighter planes, or by anti-aircraft artillery which can shoot at their altitude.[13]

Though the Soviet leaders' strategic claims in the aftermath of the U-2 period were concerned chiefly with the U.S.S.R's defensive capabilities, the strategic threats they issued against United States allies were remarkably bold. Khrushchev and Malinovsky stated explicitly that the Soviet Union would strike at any overseas base of the United States from which future overflights might be launched.[14] And when questioned at a press conference on the type of weapon they would employ in such a strike, Khrushchev did not deny that it might be nuclear.[15] Thus, for the first time, Soviet leaders threatened to strike allies of the United States, possibly with nuclear weapons, in response to other than a physical attack on the U.S.S.R., one of its allies, or a friendly third power.

The Soviet threat to strike at bases that might be used in future U-2 missions was not issued in the opening days of the U-2 crisis. During the Supreme Soviet session at which the downing of Powers' plane was revealed, Khrushchev stated only that the U.S.S.R. would give "a most serious warning" to those countries harboring United States reconnaissance aircraft. Apparently, the Soviet leaders interpreted the State Department announcement of May 7, Secretary of State Christian A. Herter's elaborations of it on May 9, and President Eisenhower's supporting press conference statement two days later as signifying the intention of the United States to continue the flights. (Khrushchev was not officially informed until May 16 that the President had decided to suspend the flights.) Evidently, the threats were issued in order to bring pressure to bear indirectly on the United States through its allies. President Eisenhower's statement in Paris on May 16 that the U-2 flights had been suspended and would not be

---

[13] *Pravda*, May 29, 1960.
[14] See, for example, *Pravda*, May 10, 12, 29, and 30, June 4, 1960.
[15] *Pravda*, June 4, 1960.

resumed probably reassured the Soviet leaders, despite Khrushchev's complaint that the President's pledge could only bind the United States until the expiration of his term in office. The threat to strike American overseas bases was repeated several times in May and June but gradually dropped out of Soviet statements thereafter. In July, when the Soviets shot down an RB-47 in the Barents Sea, Khrushchev explained the Soviet failure to strike at the Norwegian base from which it was said to have taken off by asserting that since the intrusion was stopped at the very beginning "the Soviet government limited itself to destroying the aircraft." [16]

A concurrent crisis unrelated to the U-2 affair occasioned an unprecedented, though highly ambiguous, Soviet strategic threat against the United States itself. Upon returning to the Soviet Union from his Austrian visit in July, Khrushchev turned his attention to the crisis in United States–Cuban relations. Addressing a Teachers' Congress in Moscow on July 9, the Soviet Premier declared:

> It should not be forgotten that the U.S. is not so inaccessibly distant from the Soviet Union as it used to be. Figuratively speaking, in case of need Soviet artillerymen can support the Cuban people with their rocket fire if the aggressive forces in the Pentagon dare to launch an intervention against Cuba. And let them not forget in the Pentagon that, as the latest tests have shown, we have rockets capable of landing directly in a given square at a distance of 13,000 kilometers. This, if you will, is a warning to those who would like to settle international issues by force and not by reason.[17]

Although this threat was couched as a "figurative" illustration of Soviet missile capabilities, and not directly as a guarantee of assistance to Fidel Castro, the contingency that it covered was unique. Never before had a Soviet leader threatened even vaguely to strike the continental United States in any eventuality other than an American attack on a member of the bloc. (Cuba at that time was not yet a "socialist country," and Castro had not yet declared himself a Marxist-Leninist.) It was also the first Soviet threat to retaliate against a United States move in the Western hemisphere. In October, 1960, under prodding by Cuban journalists who asked him to comment on the "imperialist" contention that his statement was merely "symbolic," Khrushchev replied evasively that he would "like such statements to be really symbolic." But when pressed to say

---

[16] *Pravda*, July 13, 1960.
[17] *Pravda*, July 10, 1960.

whether Soviet rockets were "adequately prepared" to meet the possibility of intervention by the United States, Khrushchev replied affirmatively.[18] Thus he kept the ambiguous Soviet threat in force, while strongly indicating his reluctance to carry it out. Two years later "Soviet artillerymen" were in position, if only briefly, "to support the Cuban people with rocket fire" from Cuba itself.

[18] *Pravda*, October 29, 1960.

SEVEN

RETREAT TO PARITY
SEPTEMBER, 1960–AUGUST, 1961

By the fall of 1960 an important new stage was reached in the regression from Khrushchev's extreme claims of a missile capability that could wipe any opponent from the face of the earth. The two chief elements of this new position had appeared earlier, but it was not until they became more distinct and reinforced each other that they revealed a modification in the declaratory policy of the U.S.S.R.

1. After January, 1960, Khrushchev *no longer asserted that Soviet casualties in nuclear war would be far less than the West's.* In a speech to a foreign audience (in Austria on July 2, 1960), he went so far as to say: "If we start war to settle disputes between States . . . we shall destroy our Noah's Ark, the Earth." [1]

2. After October, 1960, Khrushchev said several times that, in the event of a world war, fatalities would be great on both sides and would amount to "hundreds of millions."

To an extent, this bald statement had been anticipated by Khrushchev's early claims of a capability to destroy the NATO countries in Europe and by his subsequent statement that the U.S.S.R. could wipe from the face of the earth any country that might attack it. Moreover, in his speech to the General Assembly of the United Nations in September, 1959, Khrushchev had explicitly said that if war broke out, "its toll would run not into millions, but into tens and even hundreds of millions of human lives." [2] But three months after that speech he minimized the U.S.S.R.'s share of these casualties when he told the Supreme Soviet that losses to the Western countries would far exceed Soviet losses. [3] However, when Khrushchev began, in the fall of 1960, to stress the general consequences of nuclear war without differentiating between sides, he seemed to acknowledge that Soviet losses, like the West's, would be a large fraction of the country's population. This theme had been introduced into the Communist party's theoretical journal some months earlier by the military publicist, General Nikolai Talensky, who found it "necessary to

---

[1] *Pravda*, July 4, 1960.
[2] *Pravda*, September 19, 1959.
[3] *Pravda*, January 15, 1960: "We would have many losses, but . . . the West would suffer incomparably more."

emphasize that a future war, if the aggressors succeed in unleashing it, will lead to such an increase in human losses *on both sides* that its consequences for mankind might be catastrophic." [4] Several months later, Talensky expanded this theme in a sensational article in the political journal *Mezhdunarodnaia zhizn'* ("International Affairs"), published in Russian and English.[5] He said that according to careful calculations (which he did not specify) casualties in a world war would be no less than five to six hundred million in the probable main theater, presumably the NATO and Warsaw Pact countries, whose total population he estimated at about eight hundred million. This passage, as well as others in the article, tended to confirm the Soviet people's worst fears regarding the consequences of a new war. Talensky even went so far as to jog his readers' memories of their suffering in the war against Nazi Germany:

Men who lived through the last war recall the terrible destruction of cities which were located in the battle zone. If this degree of destruction is magnified a thousand times and extended over whole continents, then it is possible to form some notion approximating the real consequences of a rocket-nuclear war [pp. 34–35].

Nothing like this had been told the Soviet people before. Talensky claimed no special advantages for the U.S.S.R. in limiting casualties, as had been done in the past.

A few weeks after Talensky's article was sent to the printer, Khrushchev stated that a world war "would lead to the deaths of hundreds and hundreds of millions of people." This same phrase was subsequently employed by Defense Minister Malinovsky, who thus gave it the authority of a serious military estimate.[6] Khrushchev offered the Soviet people only this chilling reassurance: "We are convinced that mankind will not perish in the event of war." [7]

The main political reason for this retreat in the Soviet public assessment of the strategic balance is not hard to discover. Khrushchev's disagreement on world Communist strategy with the Chinese Communists, and with Mao Tse-tung personally, had erupted in a violent dispute with the representative of the Chinese People's Republic at the Rumanian Communist Party Congress in June, 1960. Talensky seems to have been continuing this polemic in his article by warning the Chinese Communist party, which had criticized leaders

---

4 *Kommunist*, 1960, No. 7, pp. 31–41 [italics added].
5 *Mezhdunarodnaia zhizn'*, 1960, No. 10, p. 33.
6 *Pravda*, June 22, 1961.
7 *Pravda*, October 21, 1960.

who were fearful of war, that "to depreciate the peril of rocket-nuclear war is criminal." Khrushchev's assertion that hundreds of millions would die in a nuclear war was made in the days preceding the crucial conference of representatives of Communist parties in Moscow and was repeated in his report on the results of the conference on January 6, 1961.

There was an additional reason for Khrushchev's retreat: America no longer provided the same fertile soil as before for exaggerated Soviet ICBM claims. Although many in the United States disputed or doubted the outgoing administration's assurances that the "missile gap" in the early sixties would be smaller than had earlier been anticipated and would produce no "deterrent gap," the Soviet leaders, knowing the truth, knew also that the United States government was moving closer to it. In his farewell State of the Union message to Congress, President Eisenhower said that "the 'missile gap' shows every sign of being a fiction." [8] Shortly after the Kennedy adminis-tration took office, there were newspaper reports that new studies commissioned by the Defense Department had tentatively shown there was no "missile gap," [9] although this was denied by the White House and by Secretary McNamara, who said it would be premature to draw such a conclusion. [10]

By failing in his statements during this period to differentiate the peril to the Soviet people from that faced by other peoples, Khru-shchev seemed to imply that the strategic balance was one of parity. [11] Talensky went even farther toward suggesting this. The United States strategic offensive force was thus accorded a respect that had been denied it only a few months previously. Khrushchev's long-standing boasts, in which he had been joined by Marshal Malinovsky, that the West's bombers were vulnerable to Soviet air defenses had reached their climax in the aftermath of the U-2 incident. He had then asserted that "not a single bomber could get through to its target."

---

[8] *New York Times*, January 12, 1961.

[9] *New York Times*, February 7, 1961.

[10] *New York Times*, February 8, 17, 1961. According to Senator Symington, the na-tional intelligence estimate of Soviet ICBM capabilities in mid-1961 was 50 per cent lower than the number that was projected for that time period in August, 1960; a "missile gap" apparently remained, but a much smaller one than had originally been projected (United States, Senate, *Hearings before the Committee on Armed Services on Department of Defense Programs and Authorization of Appropriations for Pro-curement of Aircraft, Missiles, and Naval Vessels by the Armed Forces* [S. 2734], 87th Cong., 2d sess., p. 49).

[11] The claim that the U.S.S.R. was militarily the world's strongest power, however, continued to be voiced sporadically.

The West's "whole military concept of attack on the Soviet Union, based on the use of bomber planes [has] been shattered." [12]

The confidence expressed earlier by the Soviet leaders in the effectiveness of the U.S.S.R.'s air defenses was undoubtedly a deliberate exaggeration for deterrent purposes. By the end of 1960, however, even if the Soviet claim that the SAC bomber force was vulnerable to Soviet air defenses had been valid, it would not have provided an adequate basis for denying the effectiveness of the United States strategic offensive force. By that time, the Atlas ICBM was operational, as was the first nuclear submarine armed with Polaris missiles; [13] and SAC bombers had begun to be armed with air-to-surface cruise missiles. This was recognized in a key article by Lieutenant General S. Krasilnikov, who spoke of the need for supplementary means of strategic defense:

Anti-air and anti-rocket defense, which are charged with protecting the rear and the troops, acquire extremely great importance. Destruction of the enemy nuclear rocket [that is, missiles carrying nuclear warheads], nuclear-aviation [that is, bombers carrying nuclear bombs], and rocket-carrying forces [presumably bombers and submarines capable of launching missiles with nuclear warheads] will become one of the primary missions. [14]

Soviet leaders' claims for their strategic offensive forces in this period stressed the availability of large numbers of thermonuclear warheads but were strikingly vague and evasive as to the means of delivering them, particularly against the United States. The Soviet Union was still said to be "superior in the most up-to-date and effective means of delivering nuclear weapons, intercontinental ballistic missiles." [15] Khrushchev spoke of a plant from which he saw rockets coming "like sausages from an automatic machine, rocket after rocket," though he did not say that the rockets were ICBM's. But in characterizing the strategic balance, Khrushchev and the Soviet marshals asserted no more than that the United States was no longer invulnerable and must take that into account in its calculations. This was an old theme, which only served to mark the retrogression from Khrushchev's bold claims of the winter of 1960. There was still an echo of them in Khrushchev's speech in Sverdlovsk (March 2, 1961): "The Soviet Union has the world's most powerful

---

[12] *Pravda*, May 29, 1960.
[13] President Eisenhower's State of the Union message, January 12, 1961.
[14] *Krasnaia zvezda*, November 18, 1960.
[15] Khrushchev's speech to the United Nations General Assembly, September 23, 1960.

rocketry and has produced the quantity of atomic and hydrogen bombs necessary to wipe the aggressors from the face of the earth. . . ." [16] As can be seen, however, it was a faint echo. Khrushchev now spoke of the "necessary" quantity of nuclear *bombs* but said nothing of the quantity of *rockets* available, only describing them as the world's most powerful. Moreover, he claimed only that "the aggressors," not the countries that were hostile to the Soviet camp, could be wiped from the face of the earth. Thus, the retreat in Soviet strategic claims that was evident after the U-2 incident continued and became even more pronounced in the winter of 1961. For a time Soviet leaders continued to claim that the U.S.S.R. was the strongest military power in the world, but they did not assert that they possessed what that boast necessarily implied—a large quantity of weapon-delivery vehicles capable of striking at the chief adversary. [17] Subsequently, in the fall of 1961, when American officials began to express strong confidence that the United States had a considerable margin of superiority in strategic forces over the U.S.S.R., Soviet leaders had already ceased to claim over-all military superiority.

---

[16] Khrushchev, *Stroitel'stvo kommunizma v SSSR i razvitie sel'skogo khoziaistva* ["The Building of Communism in the USSR and the Development of Agriculture"] (Moscow: Gospolitizdat, 1963), Vol. V, p. 128.

[17] An exception was Marshal Grechko's V-E Day article, which accurately quoted Khrushchev's claim of a rocket capability to wipe any hostile country from the face of the earth (*Pravda*, May 9, 1961).

EIGHT

COLLAPSE OF THE "MISSILE GAP" AFTER SEPTEMBER, 1961

In September, 1961, reports began to appear in the American press that new intelligence estimates were crediting the Soviet Union with but a fraction of the number of operational ICBM's that had previously been projected for mid-1961. Projections had reportedly been pared down annually in American estimates since 1959, which had resulted in a progressive narrowing of the "missile gap" expected in the sixties.[1] According to press reports, the new estimates altogether eliminated the gap. Joseph Alsop, who throughout the "missile gap" controversy had criticized official United States estimates as too conservative, was among the first columnists to report on the new intelligence reappraisal. He wrote on September 25, 1961:

Prior to the recent recalculation the maximum number of ICBMs that the Soviets were thought to have at this time was on the order of 200—just about enough to permit the Soviets to consider a surprise attack on the United States. The maximum has now been drastically reduced, however, to less than a quarter of the former figure—well under 50 ICBMs and, therefore, not nearly enough to allow the Soviets to consider a surprise attack on this country. The number of Soviet heavy bombers of intercontinental range meanwhile remains unchanged, at about 150.[2]

As noted previously, other press reports of that time cited similar figures, most frequently ranging from thirty-five to seventy-five Soviet ICBM's.[3] Even these figures exaggerated the size of the Soviet ICBM force: the United States Defense Department estimated several years later that the U.S.S.R. had actually deployed only "a handful" of ICBM's by 1961.[4]

About a month after these press reports first appeared, they were implicitly confirmed by high administration officials. On October 21, 1961, Deputy Defense Secretary Roswell Gilpatric delivered the first in what turned out to be a series of speeches and statements on the strategic balance by high-ranking officials of the government. Although the administration leaders did not then refer explicitly to the

---

[1] For the changing estimates, as provided to the Senate Armed Services Committee by Senator Symington, see pp. 35–36.

[2] *Washington Post*, September 25, 1961.

[3] See p. 35, n. 1.

[4] See p. 37, n. 7.

revised intelligence estimates of Soviet intercontinental capabilities, it was evident that their new appraisal of the strategic balance rested heavily upon them. What distinguished the new pronouncements from past public evaluations of the strategic balance was the unequivocal character of the claim that the United States enjoyed a wide and growing margin of strategic superiority over the U.S.S.R. and the evident confidence with which the claim was expressed.[5] Thus Secretary Gilpatric declared that even after absorbing a Soviet surprise attack the surviving United States forces would probably be greater than the forces used by the U.S.S.R. in its first strike. "In short," he said, "we have a second-strike capability which is at least as extensive as what the Soviets can deliver by striking first." [6]

The confident assertions of United States strategic superiority in Gilpatric's speech and in subsequent ones by Secretary McNamara and other high officials reflected a top-level decision by the new Kennedy administration to correct the erroneous public impression of the unfavorable strategic balance that had gained currency in the previous three or four years. According to McGeorge Bundy, special assistant to the President for national security affairs:

The new President himself had feared the missile gap and had pressed his concern in the campaign. It was with honest surprise and relief that in 1961 he found the situation much less dangerous than the best evidence available to the Senate had indicated the year before. His Administration moved at once to correct the public impression, and thereafter, throughout his term, he encouraged and supported policies of action and exposition which aimed to ensure not merely that American strategic power was sufficient—but that its sufficiency was recognized.[7]

The new appraisal of Soviet intercontinental nuclear capabilities implicitly raised a question as to the credibility of past Soviet strategic claims. Secretary Gilpatric made this explicit when he stated:

We doubt that the Soviet leadership has in fact any less realistic views, although this may not always be apparent from their extravagant claims. While the Soviets use rigid security as a military weapon their Iron Curtain is not so impenetrable as to force us to accept at face value the Kremlin's boasts.

---

[5] Secretary McNamara later expressed himself as "absolutely confident" that the myth of the missile gap was and had been a myth. Acknowledging that there was always a margin of error in such matters, he said that "the margin of error is much less than the margin of our superiority" (*Saturday Evening Post*, December 1, 1962, p. 18).

[6] *New York Times*, October 22, 1961.

[7] Bundy, "The Presidency and the Peace," *Foreign Affairs*, XLII (April, 1964), 354.

The Soviet leaders had chosen to ignore the earlier American press reports about the United States intelligence revisions, but they could ignore such a direct, high-level challenge only at the risk of permitting their silence to be taken for assent, the consequences of which might have far-reaching political implications. They quickly evaluated the series of speeches by administration leaders as a concerted effort to bring United States strategic superiority to bear politically on outstanding issues between the United States and the U.S.S.R., notably on the Berlin dispute.[8] The initial response of the Soviet leaders was prompt and angry but lacked real substance. Addressing the Twenty-second Party Congress in Moscow two days after the Gilpatric speech, Soviet Defense Minister Malinovsky declared:

On October 21 of this year—that is quite recently, Roswell Gilpatric, U.S. Deputy Secretary of Defense, apparently not without President Kennedy's knowledge, addressed a Business Council in Virginia. Brandishing the might of the United States, he threatened us with force. What can one say to this one more threat, to this petty statement? One can say just one thing: This threat does not frighten us.[9]

In the months that followed, the Soviet leaders elaborated a new policy to replace the one that had been nullified by exposure of their ICBM deception. The changes that were introduced tended to confirm the correctness of the new American appraisal of Soviet ICBM capabilities and revealed the concern that the Soviet leaders must have felt about the possible consequences of this reappraisal for Soviet foreign policy. After September, 1961, Soviet strategic pronouncements sought primarily to minimize the loss to Soviet political influence and military stature caused by the collapse of the missile gap myth. A new stage in the continuing East-West dialogue on strategic matters was thus initiated, a stage in which the Soviet leaders, for the first time in almost half a decade, found themselves on the defensive. In this chapter we shall deal with the major elements of the revised Soviet declaratory policy as it took shape after September, 1961.

Although the Soviet leaders did not allow the new United States appraisal of the strategic balance to go unchallenged, they responded

---

[8] "One's attention is drawn to the circumstance that what is under discussion on this occasion is not the speech of a single wild general or politician who has lost his equilibrium but a clearly organized campaign whose aim, judging by everything, is to intimidate the Soviet Union and exacerbate still further the international situation" (Radio Moscow Home Service commentary, November 16, 1961).
[9] *Pravda*, October 24, 1961.

publicly in such a way as to evade the crucial question of the number of Soviet ICBM's that were operational. The main objective of the Soviet response was evidently to deprive American claims of superiority of their political value by re-emphasizing that the Soviet Union had an adequate retaliatory capability, even if the Soviet intercontinental strike force was quantitatively smaller than the West had been led to believe.[10] Claims of Soviet military superiority, muted since the U-2 incident, were now virtually abandoned. There was a marked tendency to move from the military plane to the political in comparing the two sides. Khrushchev, for example, in a May 18, 1962, speech in Sofia, declared:

Our strength today is not illusory but is enormous and real. The President of the United States himself said to me that our military forces were equal. I made no objection to this although we are in fact stronger than imperialism, because our forces include not only the socialist states but all progressive and peace-loving forces on earth, all people who hold peace dear. These peace-loving forces are greater than the forces of imperialism.[11]

Similarly, in his formal report to the Twenty-second Party Congress in October, 1961, Khrushchev had stated that "now the forces of socialism, all the forces which support the struggle for peace, are more powerful than the aggressive imperialist forces." [12] These were general statements on the broad political balance of forces in the world rather than on the military balance alone; they added to the forces of the Soviet camp such non-military factors as the neutralist countries and the "peace" forces within capitalist nations. In speaking of the military balance itself, Khrushchev in a March, 1962, speech in Moscow referred to it only to remark that the United States had lost its monopoly of nuclear weapons and other types of modern arms.[13] Thus he reverted to an argument advanced half a decade earlier, when Soviet strategic nuclear capability was just emerging.

In the spring of 1962, after publication in an American magazine of an interview with President John F. Kennedy on strategic matters [14]— interpreted by the Soviet press as an effort to intimidate the U.S.S.R.

---

[10] A subsidiary theme, implying the possibility of Soviet pre-emption, is discussed below, pp. 91–93. As employed by Khrushchev, this theme also seemed designed to prevent the United States from deriving political advantages from threats to take the nuclear initiative.

[11] *Pravda*, May 19, 1962. In the live broadcast of the speech, Khrushchev actually recalled saying to the President: "It is *nice of you* to say this, but . . ." (Sofia Domestic Service, May 18, 1962; italics added).

[12] *Pravda*, October 18, 1961.

[13] *Pravda*, March 17, 1962.

[14] *Saturday Evening Post*, March 31, 1962.

by threatening a United States first strike "under certain circum-stances"—there was a temporary renewal of explicit claims of broad Soviet military superiority, although direct comparisons of Soviet and American intercontinental strike capabilities were avoided. Thus, *Pravda's* "Observer" reiterated the 1961 claim that "in military power, the Soviet Union surpasses the U.S.A." but also advanced a new formu-lation, repeated on several occasions by Soviet leaders in the early spring: "[In] its ability to deliver a massive nuclear blow the Soviet Union today surpasses the United States." [15] No specific targets were mentioned, and the claim was presumably based on Soviet strike capabilities against the European NATO countries, which United States leaders had publicly conceded were very powerful, as well as their intercontinental forces. Thus, superiority was claimed in the aggregate, but not necessarily in each of its parts, and especially not in the most crucial one—capability to deliver ICBM's in quantity to the United States.

In a major speech on military affairs in July, 1962, Khrushchev explicitly noted the changed character of American pronouncements on the strategic balance, terming the new American appraisal "groundless." However, he refuted it, not by reaffirming Soviet superiority, but by arguing that the military balance of power could be determined only during the course of war and ultimately by its outcome.[16] He recalled that Hitler had claimed an overwhelming preponderance of force but was "finally" defeated by the U.S.S.R. and its allies. Significantly, Khrushchev did not deny that Hitler's forces were superior to the U.S.S.R.'s when the war began—a point now conceded by Soviet leaders and attributed to Stalin's prewar errors and miscalculations—but recalled only that Hitler was ulti-mately defeated.[17]

A new characteristic of Soviet statements regarding the strategic balance after mid-1961 was their explicitly expressed readiness to accept strategic parity as the basic assumption from which political settlements should proceed. The theme that equal strategic forces should be translated into equal political rights was introduced by

[15] *Pravda*, March 31, 1962.
[16] *Pravda*, July 11, 1962.
[17] Marshal of the Soviet Union A. I. Yeremenko had written earlier that, although superiority in military preparedness had not proved decisive in the past, "today the center of gravity has to a large if not decisive extent shifted to the opening stage of a war." The present Soviet government, he wrote, "is doing all in its power to remove any possibility of the recurrence of the state of affairs which existed in the first stages of the Great Patriotic War" (*Mezhdunarodnaia zhizn'*, 1962, No. 1, p. 38).

Khrushchev in his speech of July 8, 1961, at a Kremlin reception for graduates of Moscow military academies, in which he stated that strategic parity was now conceded by the West. "However, the necessary conclusions are not being drawn from this fact. With equal forces, there must be equal rights and opportunities. . . ." [18]

In his radio and television speech on the Berlin crisis on August 7, 1961, Khrushchev said that President Kennedy had acknowledged during their talks in Vienna that the military forces of the two sides were equal.[19] The Soviet Premier reverted to the President's alleged concession on numerous occasions during 1961 and 1962; he referred to it, almost nostalgically, even after the President's *Saturday Evening Post* interview:

There was a time when Eisenhower, the former U.S. President, and the present President Kennedy, had a realistic attitude, stating that the military strength of the Soviet Union and of the United States was equal. President Kennedy expressed such an attitude during the meeting with me in Vienna.[20]

On another occasion when he recalled the President's statement, Khrushchev added that, although he personally believed the Soviet side to be stronger, he was prepared to act as if the forces were actually equal, since such beliefs could be verified only by war.[21] Thus, instead of playing upon the West's uncertainty regarding Soviet strategic forces, Khrushchev now began to speak of an uncertainty that was intrinsic to the strategic balance. Marshal Malinovsky adopted a similar line in January, 1962, when he replied to congressional testimony by Secretary McNamara:

Here I should like to correct Mr. McNamara. U.S. President John Kennedy once admitted that our strength is equal. *This was a more or less correct acknowledgment,* and it is high time that the American military leaders drew appropriate conclusions from it. I hold that today the socialist camp is stronger than these countries [United States and its NATO allies], *but let us even presume that the forces are equal. We are ready to agree to this* so as not to take part in stirring up a war psychosis. But since our forces are equal the American leaders should come to correct conclusions and pursue a reasonable policy.[22]

The new Soviet readiness to settle for mutual acknowledgment of parity was accompanied by a change in the character of claims

---

[18] *Pravda,* July 9, 1961.
[19] *Pravda,* August 8, 1961.
[20] *Pravda,* July 19, 1962.
[21] *Pravda,* September 9, 1961.
[22] *Pravda,* January 25, 1962 [italics added].

regarding the Soviet nuclear capability against the United States. The emphasis shifted from the *magnitude* of destruction that could be inflicted to the *certainty* that retaliation would occur. The formulation "wipe from the face of the earth," which Khrushchev had applied in 1959 and 1960 to any hostile *country* that might attack the U.S.S.R., was now applied, in regard to the United States, only to certain categories of *targets*; however, it continued to be applied to whole countries allied to the United States.

A striking expression of the Soviet retreat from the 1959–60 claim was the tacit revision of it by the then commander-in-chief of Soviet rocket troops, Marshal K. Moskalenko. Referring back to the Supreme Soviet session at which Khrushchev made the original claim, Moskalenko wrote:

A definitive characterization of the might of the rocket troops was given at the Fourth Session of the USSR Supreme Soviet—our country has means which can "literally wipe from the face of the earth *entire states*" if they should try to attack us.[23]

This claim now asserted no more than what had been claimed countless times by Soviet spokesmen for several years prior to 1960.

Country-busting claims now specified the European NATO countries. Typical of the new Soviet emphasis on the certainty of retaliation, and of Soviet failure to delineate the level of destruction that could be inflicted against the United States, was the following statement by Marshal Biriuzov:

If the U.S. imperialists who are threatening the Soviet people with thermonuclear war should dare to unleash one *they will have to pay for it.* Neither the oceans surrounding the shores of North America nor the deepest atomic shelters now so strenuously advertised by the monopolistic press *will save them from just and inevitable retribution.*[24]

Defense Secretary McNamara may have had this retreat on the part of the Soviet leadership in mind when he said on February 17, 1962: "Today not even the most boastful Russian rocket-rattler asserts that the Soviet Union has the nuclear power to destroy the United States." [25]

The Soviet rejoinder four days later avoided a direct refutation but

---

[23] *Krasnaia zvezda,* September 13, 1961 [italics added]. This was the second time that Moskalenko had amended Khrushchev's claim, each time weakening its allusion to Soviet ICBM capabilities. See p. 65 for the previous instance.

[24] *Sovetskaia Rossiia,* October 3, 1961 [italics added].

[25] News release, No. 239–62, United States Department of Defense, Office of Public Affairs, February 17, 1962.

emphasized instead Secretary McNamara's acknowledgment that the Soviet Union could inflict serious damage on Western Europe. As for the United States, the Defense Ministry newspaper warned vaguely that America would be unable "to escape at the expense of Western Europe" if it started a nuclear war.[26]

Prior to the spring of 1962, Soviet strategic pronouncements stressed the capacity of the U.S.S.R. to destroy American cities but avoided explicit references to military targets in the United States such as had appeared in Soviet statements before September, 1961. Immediately after publication of President Kennedy's interview in the *Saturday Evening Post* (March 31, 1962), however, such references began to reappear in Soviet statements.[27] In May, 1962, Defense Minister Malinovsky, replying to President Kennedy's nuclear initiative statement, gave a new formulation for targets in the United States that significantly emended his previously stated position.

JANUARY, 1962	MAY, 1962
On my part, I could state that we are capable of wiping from the face of the earth with one rocket-nuclear blow any targets, *all the industrial and administrative-political centers* of the U.S.A.[28]	No "pre-emptive" blows of any kind, no defensive measures of any kind, could enable the imperialists to avert an all-destructive retaliatory blow against *economic, transportation, military, and administrative* centers of the U.S.A.[29]

This inconsistency or change in Soviet targeting statements may have reflected uncertainty or differences among the Soviet leaders on how best to cope with the new American pronouncements on nuclear war strategy. In their public statements, Soviet leaders were concerned with two related elements in the new American position: (1) the doctrine of "controlled nuclear response" and (2) the President's allusion to a United States first strike "under certain circumstances."

Regarding the first, Soviet declaratory policy then as now stressed that a strategy of "city-sparing" was infeasible and that the U.S.S.R., if attacked, would in any event respond with all-out retaliation. Replying in February, 1962, to a speech by Secretary McNamara in which three alternative American nuclear war strategies had been set forth, *Krasnaia zvezda* warned that the United States would have

[26] *Krasnaia zvezda*, February 21, 1962.
[27] For example, in the reply of *Pravda's* "Observer" to President Kennedy, March 31, 1962.
[28] *Pravda*, January 25, 1962 [italics added].
[29] *Kommunist*, 1962, No. 7, p. 13 [italics added].

"neither the time nor the opportunity" to choose among these alternatives in the event of war.[30] A Radio Moscow military commentator asserted that if the West were to attack the Soviet Union "no appeals that blows should be directed only at military objectives could prevent the all-devastating counter-blow at the economic, transportation, military and administrative centers of the United States and its allies." [31]

Khrushchev himself attacked the United States Defense Secretary's June 16 Ann Arbor speech on "controlled response" as "a monstrous [proposal], permeated from beginning to end with hatred of people and mankind," charging that it sought "to legalize nuclear warfare and thereby the death of millions and millions of people." [32] The McNamara strategy, Khrushchev asserted, was designed to divert the main Soviet blow away from the United States and onto the territory of those countries where American overseas bases were located. He argued further that it was meant to deceive the American people as well, because bases in the United States were in or near large cities.

A nuclear-rocket war completely erases boundaries between front and rear. Moreover, it will be *first of all* the civilian population that will fall victim to the weapons of mass annihilation.

As long as they were confident that their opponents credited them with an assured massive second-strike capability, the Soviet leaders were content with a declaratory policy that threatened to destroy American cities in a second strike, even if the United States should attempt to spare Soviet cities in a first strike. But after it became evident that United States leaders had revised their estimates of Soviet strategic capabilities, the confidence of Soviet leaders may have been shaken. In particular, Moscow interpreted President Kennedy's statement on "nuclear initiative" as an effort to bring political pressure to bear on the U.S.S.R. (for example, to abandon the Berlin offensive) by threatening a first strike "under certain circumstances." Apparently recognizing that such threats implicitly questioned the capacity of the U.S.S.R. to retaliate effectively after suffering a first strike, Khrushchev responded by hinting at the possibility of Soviet pre-emption, although he was careful to express his reluctance to engage the United States in a race to strike first. In a speech in Sofia on May 18, the Soviet Premier said:

---

[30] February 21, 1962.
[31] Radio Moscow, June 29, 1962.
[32] *Pravda*, July 11, 1962 [italics added].

We cannot ignore the statement made by Mr. Kennedy because it introduces a new element in the relations between our countries. Does not this statement mean that the U.S. President wishes to urge me, as the head of the Soviet government, to compete with him in who will be the first to "push the button"? We are against any such competition. It must be clear to every clear-thinking man how dangerous, inhuman, and unwise this would be. Knowing the aggressive character of imperialism, we must keep our powder dry and be in fitting readiness.[33]

He expatiated on this theme again in July:

Certain responsible statesmen in America even declare openly their readiness to take upon themselves "the initiative in a nuclear conflict with the Soviet Union." Ponder these words. This is not only a threat of thermonuclear war, but also an imposition of a sinister competition as to who will be the first to start such a war. Since they are saying that they may be the first to unleash war, they are, as it were, prompting other countries: hurry up, they say, in order to forestall [*upredit'*] the enemy. Where can this lead? It is clear to everyone: to catastrophic consequences.[34]

Khrushchev may have been brought to respond so sharply to the President's remarks by the previously expressed concern of his military advisers. Public allusions by high-ranking Soviet military officials to the danger of an American surprise attack, first noted in the Soviet literature during the 1954–55 discussions on the revision of Stalinist military doctrine, had been revived in the fall of 1961 after a lapse of several years:

We cannot sit with folded hands and look on with indifference at the way in which the ruling circles of Western powers are pushing the world toward war. We do not want to find ourselves in the position in which we were in 1941. This time we shall not allow the imperialists to catch us unawares.—MARSHAL MALINOVSKY.[35]

We cannot and will not be in the same situation as we were at that time [June, 1941].—MARSHAL GRECHKO.[36]

We must constantly sharpen [our vigilance] in order to frustrate the plans of the imperialists for a surprise attack on our country and to prevent a repetition of the sorry lessons of the initial period of the last war.— GENERAL OF THE ARMY A. S. ZHADOV.[37]

We will not let 1941 happen again, nor let the imperialists take us unawares. —MARSHAL S. S. BIRIUZOV.[38]

---

[33] *Pravda*, May 19, 1962.
[34] *Pravda*, July 11, 1962.
[35] *Pravda*, September 14, 1961.
[36] *Krasnaia zvezda*, September 6, 1961.
[37] *Krasnaia zvezda*, September 20, 1961.
[38] *Sovetskaia Rossiia*, October 3, 1961.

Finally, Defense Minister Malinovsky, in his speech at the Party Congress in October, stated flatly that the West was preparing a "surprise nuclear attack" against the Soviet Union. Therefore, he declared,

Soviet military doctrine considers that the most important, the main and first-priority task of the armed forces is: to be in constant readiness reliably to repel an enemy surprise attack and to frustrate his criminal designs.[39]

Later, in discussing the training of the armed forces, he specified "the timely delivery of a destructive blow" on the enemy as the means to "frustrate his aggressive designs." This formulation, or variations of it, was later repeated both by Malinovsky and by Soviet writers on military doctrine.[40] They spoke of the need for a capability to deal "timely blows" as a tenet of Soviet military doctrine. Khrushchev, on the other hand, warned of the possibility that United States declaratory policy might compel him, despite his fear of the catastrophic consequences, "to engage the U.S. President in a sinister competition as to who will be the first to start a war." In expressing his concern about American efforts to derive political advantage from references to the nuclear initiative, Khrushchev once again demonstrated his extreme sensitivity to changes in the declaratory policy of the United States on strategic matters.

Although Soviet claims as to the damage that the U.S.S.R. could inflict upon the United States were tempered after the fall of 1961, analogous claims regarding Western Europe were now stated even more baldly. In September, 1961, *Izvestiia* took the unusual step of reprinting the text of the *New York Times* version of an interview granted by Khrushchev to C. L. Sulzberger, which contained the

---

[39] *Pravda*, October 24, 1961.
[40] For example, Malinovsky in *Krasnaia zvezda*, November 11, 1961, and *Kommunist*, 1962, No. 7. In his *Kommunist* article he retreated from his original position by introducing revisions that largely deprived the formulation of its pre-emptive connotations. He omitted the reference to "timely" blows and implied that frustrating "the enemy's criminal designs" was a peacetime objective. "This means that our defensive might must be such as to be able to instill in the aggressor uncertainty as to the outcome of the war planned by him, to nip in the bud his criminal designs and finally, *if war should become a fact*, decisively to destroy the aggressor" (*Kommunist*, p. 15; italics added). However, Malinovsky's original Twenty-second Party Congress formulation was repeated verbatim in articles published at the same time in the Central Committee journal for the armed forces and in the Defense Ministry newspaper (Colonel General N. Lomov, in *Kommunist Vooruzhennykh Sil*, 1962, No. 10, pp. 19–20; and Colonel I. Sidelnikov, in *Krasnaia zvezda*, May 11, 1962). Moreover, *Krasnaia zvezda* stated editorially two months later (July 7, 1962) that the foremost duty of Soviet officers "is to be in constant readiness to repel an enemy surprise attack and to frustrate his criminal designs by means of the timely delivery of a destructive blow."

following brutal reference to the Western European allies of the United States as Soviet hostages:

Khrushchev believes absolutely that when it comes to a showdown, Britain, France and Italy would refuse to join the United States in a war over Berlin for fear of their absolute destruction. Quite blandly he asserts that these countries are, figuratively speaking, hostages to the USSR and a guarantee against war.[41]

Khrushchev's remark implied that the U.S.S.R. was relying on the mortal threat against countries allied to the United States to mobilize Western European pressure on the United States to avoid policies that risked general war. On this view, the crucial question in the United States–Soviet military balance was whether the United States could prevent the Soviet Union from destroying Western Europe, not whether the United States could destroy the U.S.S.R. while preserving its own people and resources. Clearly, this strategic concept has serious military and political limitations. In the final analysis, there is a contradiction between a military strategy that relies heavily on deterring the United States by holding its allies as hostages and a political strategy that aims at detaching the allies from the United States, thus diminishing the value of the allies as hostages. But whatever its political limitations, such a strategic concept requires that the allies continue to credit the U.S.S.R. with the capability of inflicting devastation upon them, regardless of changes in their beliefs about the United States–Soviet military balance. Soviet concern to assure this minimum condition has been reflected in the disproportionate buildup of Soviet continental nuclear striking power (MRBM's, IRBM's, and medium bombers) as compared with intercontinental nuclear forces.

Insofar as NATO allies of the United States were inclined to accept the revised United States appraisal of the strategic balance, the task of the Soviet leaders, in accordance with the "hostage" strategy, was to persuade allied leaders and publics that even United States strategic superiority could not prevent the destruction of their countries in the event of war. This, indeed, had been the crux of the Soviet position before the U.S.S.R. was credited with a strategic capability against the United States, and it was now employed again.[42]

---

[41] *Izvestiia*, September 9, 1961.

[42] Khrushchev had put it bluntly to the West Germans in 1959: "[Western military men] say they have more bombers than the Soviet Union. They allege that the Soviet Union has few intercontinental rockets. They would have you believe that the United States stands to lose least from a war. Even if this were true, does this make you Germans feel any better?" (*Pravda*, May 9, 1959).

In a broadcast beamed to Japan early in 1962, for example, Radio Moscow alluded to reports circulating in Japan regarding the revised American appraisal of the strategic balance. The broadcast went on to say:

We do not know where . . . these data were obtained. However, it is certain that even if one exaggerates the military strength of a superior [sic] power that is signatory of the Security Treaty and boasts of its superiority, *the danger that the Security Treaty has brought to Japan will not decrease at all*. . . . Recall the statement of Soviet Defense Minister Malinovsky. He said that the Soviet Union with its nuclear rockets is capable of annihilating with one blow those countries which have permitted other countries to maintain military bases in areas adjacent to the Soviet Union and other socialist countries.[43]

A similar line in regard to Turkey was taken by the commander-in-chief of the Soviet navy, Admiral S. G. Gorshkov, in a *Pravda* interview on February 2, 1962. Referring to a speech by British Admiral Sir Deric Holland-Martin, in which the NATO Mediterranean fleet commander pledged that NATO forces would come immediately to Turkey's assistance in the event of a Soviet attack, Gorshkov replied:

If Turkey continues to fulfill the role to which it has been assigned in the plans of the military blocs of NATO and CENTO, then, in the event of [war], a nuclear rocket blow will, of course, be inflicted on Turkey. After this, the "assistance" which Admiral Holland-Martin so generously promises to Turkey will certainly not be asked for, because it will not be needed by anyone.

The revised United States estimates of Soviet ICBM capabilities induced a more favorable public appraisal of weapons that Soviet leaders had formerly downgraded. As already noted, Soviet leaders and particularly Khrushchev began publicly to depreciate manned bombers immediately after the U.S.S.R. launched the first Sputnik, although bombers were then the sole means available for delivering nuclear bombs against United States targets. In January, 1960, Khrushchev had announced to the Supreme Soviet that "almost the entire military air force is being replaced by missiles." He said that the Soviet Union had already sharply reduced and would probably further reduce and even discontinue production of bombers "and other obsolete equipment." [44] At that time Khrushchev was apparently willing to sacrifice credit for the U.S.S.R.'s limited heavy bomber

---

[43] Radio Moscow, January 31, 1962 [italics added].
[44] *Pravda*, January 15, 1960.

capability in order to enhance the political value of Soviet progress in developing the ICBM. But as evidence mounted that United States leaders did not credit the U.S.S.R. with the large ICBM capability that Khrushchev had claimed, "supplementary" offensive weapons systems, such as manned bombers and missile-launching submarines, again became prominent in Soviet claims. This was evident as early as the summer of 1961, when new air-to-surface missiles were displayed at the annual Soviet air show. At that time, too, Soviet leaders asserted for the first time that the Soviet Union had built nuclear submarines "in no smaller quantity" than the United States.[45]

Beginning in the fall of 1961, Soviet statements typically listed their entire arsenal of long-range delivery means, not just land-based missiles. Occasionally, land-based missiles were denied precedence, as in a statement by Marshal Biriuzov, who went so far as to rescue surface naval craft from the oblivion to which Khrushchev had consigned them years earlier:

We must mention that we also have reliable means for delivering such superpowerful warheads. We have super-long-range rocket-carrying aircraft, warships equipped with rockets of various classes, and high-speed submarines with atomic power plants and practically unlimited range. Our rocket troops have powerful intercontinental ballistic rockets and complex radio-electronic equipment to control their flight.[46]

Khrushchev himself reflected the shift away from exclusive emphasis on missiles when he said in his report to the Twenty-second Party Congress: "In equipping the armed forces with rockets and an atomic submarine fleet, we are not leaving the air force out of our reckoning; we are continuing to develop and improve it." [47]

The reintroduction of manned bombers into Soviet strategic claims, when considered in the light of the revised United States estimates of Soviet ICBM capabilities, gave the impression, not of an addition to strategic power, but rather of a means to fill the gap between large previous ICBM claims and the smaller force now credited to the U.S.S.R. Moreover, the Soviet admission of continued reliance on manned bombers effected a qualitative change in projected Soviet claims regarding the weapons balance. Previously, the Soviet leaders had sought to portray the strategic situation as essen-

---

[45] See, for example, *Izvestiia*, July 22, 1961. Previously Soviet media had contended that the United States had overrated the advantages of nuclear submarines and that conventional Soviet undersea craft could perform at least as well as American nuclear submarines.

[46] *Sovetskaia Rossiia*, October 3, 1961.

[47] *Pravda*, October 18, 1961.

tially a confrontation of a large United States bomber force, which was, however, vulnerable to Soviet air defenses, and a large Soviet ICBM force, which was invulnerable to existing means of defense. In order to depreciate the strategic value of the large United States bomber force, the Soviet leaders questioned the value of manned bombers in general, including their own much smaller force. But the new American intelligence estimates required a change in Soviet declaratory policy. If American leaders now realized that manned bombers, four years after Sputnik, still constituted the main Soviet intercontinental strategic force, it became essential to emphasize that Soviet bombers would be effective in the event of war. The Soviet leaders found a technical basis for their renewed confidence in bombers by claiming and displaying a stand-off cruise missile capability.[48] This did not, however, provide them with grounds for claiming the U.S.S.R. had acquired a unique capability, since the United States had already equipped much of its B-52 force with cruise missiles (Hound Dogs).

American press reports on the revised estimates of Soviet ICBM capabilities and the related administration statements on the strategic balance coincided roughly with the Soviet announcement that the U.S.S.R. had "worked out designs for creating a series of superpowerful nuclear bombs of 20, 30 and 50 and 100 million tons of TNT" (August 30, 1961) and with the detonation of very high-yield thermonuclear devices, including one in the 55–60 megaton range, during the Soviet test series in the fall.[49] Although the decision to develop and test these high-yield devices clearly antedated the United States intelligence reappraisal in the summer of 1961, the superbombs were to play a prominent role in the Soviet response to American claims growing out of the reappraisal. The Soviet leaders tried to compensate for the West's discovery that the U.S.S.R. still had few intercontinental delivery vehicles by making it appear that they were now able to multiply the destructive capacity of each Soviet weapon

---

[48] The argument was spelled out by *Krasnaia zvezda* on November 18, 1961, in an interview with Colonel General of the Engineering-Technical Service A. N. Ponomarev: "Rockets of the air-to-ground class . . . are weapons of bomber aircraft. Such rockets are equipped with a propulsion unit and are capable of developing great speeds independent of the speed of the aircraft which launches them. Thus the bomber not only need not enter the anti-air defense zone of the target, but need not even approach it. Its task is only to bring the rocket to a prearranged point. *It is clear that under these circumstances the vulnerability of the carrying plane will be considerably reduced*" (italics added).

[49] Atomic Energy Commission Press Release No. 352-D, December 9, 1961.

carrier by fitting it with a super-high-yield warhead. The tendency to shift the focus from the number of rocket carriers to the destructive power of their nuclear cargoes was illustrated in September, 1961, when Khrushchev remarked to Sulzberger that "*several* such super-powerful bombs at our disposal will considerably increase the defense capacity of our country. . . ." [50] A few months later, Khrushchev referred to 50 and 100 megaton Soviet bombs as "a sword of Damocles" that would "hang over the heads of the imperialists when they decide the question whether or not they should unleash war." [51]

It is noteworthy that Marshal Malinovsky, when he asserted at the Twenty-second Party Congress that American specialists had underestimated the level of damage the U.S.S.R. could inflict upon the United States, cited as the source of their alleged error the fact that they had taken as a unit for their calculations "only" a 5 megaton warhead. But "as you already know," he went on, "we have nuclear charges equivalent to several tens of thousands and up to 100 million tons of TNT, and our ballistic rockets have proved to be so splendid no one can doubt their ability to lift and deliver such charges to any point on earth." [52] Such doubts did exist, however, and the Soviet leaders failed to dissolve them.

By the end of 1961, the Soviet leaders had recognized that the old claims of strategic superiority based exclusively on the Soviet ICBM force were no longer credible. Accordingly, they muted their claims of strategic superiority, expressed readiness to accept strategic parity as the basis for East-West negotiations, scaled down claims about the level of damage that the U.S.S.R. could inflict upon the United States in the event of war, and placed new emphasis on superbombs, manned bombers, and nuclear submarines. At the same time, the Soviet leaders did not explicitly address themselves to the reported United States estimates of the number of operational Soviet ICBM's; they neither confirmed nor directly refuted them. This reticence contrasted with their readiness to refute Western assertions about other aspects of Soviet capabilities. What they said was that United States specialists underestimated both the number and power of Soviet nuclear weapons; [53] that the United States was wrong to doubt that Soviet scientists had created a rocket capable of delivering a 50

[50] *Pravda*, September 9, 1961 (italics added).
[51] *Pravda*, December 9, 1961.
[52] *Pravda*, October 24, 1961.
[53] *Pravda*, October 24, 1961.

megaton warhead;[54] and that the results of Soviet ICBM and MRBM practice launches disproved the contentions of Western observers that Soviet rockets would not perform as well in combat as they had in the Soviet space and missile test programs.[55]

Beginning in 1961 the Soviet press, in an apparent effort to provide the public with some "tangible" evidence of Soviet missile capabilities, frequently published photographs of objects identified as operational Soviet missiles. Most of the photographs were actually of surface-to-air missiles and short-range surface-to-surface missiles.[56] Photographs of what appeared to be medium- or intermediate-range missiles were also occasionally published.[57] The object in one such photograph was falsely identified as an "intercontinental" rocket.[58] Related to these photographic displays were eye-witness reports by Soviet newspaper correspondents of visits to Soviet "rocket bases" and missile-launching submarines.[59]

The key words in Soviet claims regarding the size of the ICBM force was that weapons were available in "sufficient" or "necessary" numbers.[60] This formulation was apparently adopted as far back as February, 1961, when it was introduced into Armed Forces Day propaganda by Marshals K. S. Moskalenko and I. K. Bagramian,[61] although it became widely used only after the fall of 1961. At the Twenty-second Party Congress, Marshal Malinovsky specified that the rocket troops had the "necessary quantity" of launching installa-

---

[54] *Krasnaia zvezda,* November 18, 1961.

[55] *Krasnaia zvezda,* November 15, 1961. Marshal Malinovsky said that 90 per cent of all MRBM practice launches and 100 per cent of all ICBM practice firings in 1961 were graded "excellent" or "good," but he did not reveal the absolute number of practice launches.

[56] See, for example, *Krasnaia zvezda,* November 19, 1961, January 25, 1962, and February 21, 23, 25, 1962; *Pravda,* December 21, 1961, and February 23, 1962.

[57] See, for example, *Krasnaia zvezda,* October 18, November 10, 1961, and January 25, 1962.

[58] *Krasnaia zvezda,* February 21, 1962. Not until 1964 were ICBM's publicly displayed in the U.S.S.R.

[59] See *Izvestiia,* October 10, 1961, for a correspondent's account of a trip aboard a Soviet nuclear submarine. TASS (February 20, 1962) transmitted a report on a correspondent's visit to a rocket base at which he was not shown ICBM's but their "sisters" or "little sisters."

[60] It was not until January 19, 1963, in the wake of the Cuban missile crisis, that a Soviet spokesman used specific numbers to convey the size of the Soviet strategic missile force. During a speech in East Germany, Khrushchev said in an aside that, although the Soviet Union had withdrawn its medium-range missiles from Cuba, the United States was still covered by other missiles. He mentioned "80, probably 120 missiles." From the context he presumably meant ICBM's, though shorter range submarine-launched missiles might also have been counted. (*Washington Post,* January 20, 1963.)

[61] *Sovetskaia Rossiia* and *Ekonomicheskaia gazeta,* February 23, 1961.

tions, rockets and charges of multimillion-ton power. Formulations such as this were in effect truncated versions of Khrushchev's January, 1960, claim, which asserted that the U.S.S.R. had enough rockets to "wipe from the earth all of its potential enemies." The post-1960 formulas either said nothing about the purposes for which the number of rockets was "sufficient" or "necessary" or, in some variations, asserted only that they were sufficient to "rout" an enemy or to administer a "due rebuff."

In another, weaker, variant of the formulation, only the quantity of nuclear warheads possessed by the U.S.S.R. was termed "sufficient," whereas the missile portion of the claim was expressed in strictly qualitative terms:

[The Soviet armed forces] have the necessary number of thermonuclear weapons, the most perfect means of delivery—short- and medium-range rockets and intercontinental rockets. . . .[62]

The Soviet Union has at its disposal not only sufficient stockpiles of the mightiest nuclear weapons in the world, but also the most modern means of delivering them to target.[63]

The qualitative superiority of Soviet weapons and Soviet primacy in developing new weapons became dominant themes in the Soviet leaders' statements on military affairs. Thus, Marshal Moskalenko wrote that "there are no such intercontinental or other types of rockets [elsewhere] in the world today as are now in the armament of the Soviet Army" and that Soviet weapons are "the most modern in the world." [64] Marshal Biriuzov boasted: "We have the best weapons, including rockets." [65] Marshal Malinovsky asserted in May, 1962, that the U.S.S.R. could more than hold its own in "competition for quality of armaments":

Our country possesses perfect military equipment, fully answering the tasks of ensuring defense in contemporary conditions. In the competition for quality of weapons imposed on us by the aggressive forces, we not only do not lag behind those who threaten us with war, but in many respects are even superior to them. In the future, if the arms race is not brought to an end, this superiority will grow.[66]

Publicly, Soviet leaders expressed great satisfaction with the state of the Soviet missile arsenal, without distinguishing between ICBM's,

---

[62] Khrushchev statement, *Pravda*, July 9, 1961.
[63] "Observer," *Pravda*, March 31, 1962.
[64] *Krasnaia zvezda*, September 13, 1961.
[65] *Krasnaia zvezda*, September 23, 1961.
[66] *Kommunist*, 1962, No. 7.

MRBM's, and other missile types. Khrushchev announced to the Twenty-second Party Congress that "the rearmament of the Soviet army with rocket and nuclear equipment is completely finished." "Our armed forces," he said, "now have at their disposal such powerful weapons as to enable them to crush any aggressor." [67] Malinovsky conveyed an impression of substantial numbers of weapons when he boasted that some eighteen hundred subunits of the Soviet rocket troops had been graded "excellent." [68] He did not indicate the ratio of "subunits" of rocket troops to operational missiles, and particularly ICBM's; but the number of "excellent subunits" was impressively large and was used repeatedly in Soviet propaganda during that period.

Malinovsky also told the Party Congress that the output of "rocket armaments" had increased so greatly in recent years "that not only are we completely supplied with rockets of various types and missions, but we have a large surplus." Three months later, the Soviet Defense Minister stated in a *Pravda* interview that the Soviet Union had "no particular need to increase the rocket forces or weapon stockpiles." [69] "At the present time," he said, "we no longer need to build up the quantity of weapons. Those we have are sufficient to defeat any potential enemy who attacked us or the socialist countries friendly to us." [70] In the future, Malinovsky continued, it would only be necessary to renew and improve the weapons already available.

As far as the Soviet ICBM force was concerned, these claims were blatantly false: it was only in the months after Malinovsky spoke that the Soviet Union began to acquire a substantial operational ICBM force, based on a second-generation missile. [71] But in a special sense there was some truth in the assertion that missiles able to strike the United States were already available in "sufficient" numbers. Large numbers of medium-range ballistic missiles had been produced in the Soviet Union; and there was now a socialist country from which such missiles could be aimed at the United States. While the Soviet leaders

---

[67] *Pravda*, October 18, 1961. The word "army" (*armiia*) is used in Russian to denote both the sum total of the armed forces of a state, as in the passage above, where it is employed interchangeably with "armed forces," and more narrowly to signify ground forces, as in the expression, "the Soviet Army, Navy, and Air Forces."

[68] *Pravda*, October 24, 1961.

[69] *Pravda*, January 25, 1962.

[70] The unprecedented reference to "socialist countries friendly to us," implying that there might also be unfriendly socialist countries, was presumably intended as a warning to the Albanian and Chinese Communist leaders that Soviet military support was not automatically at the disposal of all "socialist countries."

[71] See Hanson Baldwin's article in *New York Times*, July 26, 1962; and Allen Dulles, *The Craft of Intelligence* (New York: Harper & Row, 1963), p. 165.

patched together a new strategic declaratory policy designed to minimize political losses caused by the exposure of their ICBM deception, more substantial efforts were being made to redress the unfavorable military balance. Before analyzing the momentous United States–Soviet confrontation that arose out of the Soviet attempt to deploy strategic weapons in Cuba,[72] we must first review the crisis in Soviet foreign policy that led to it and the relation between Soviet foreign policy failures and the ICBM deception.

---

[72] See chapters xi and xii.

PART 3

STRATEGIC POWER
AND SOVIET FOREIGN POLICY

NINE

THE MISSILE DECEPTION IN SOVIET FOREIGN POLICY, 1957–62

FROM THE INITIATION of the Berlin crisis in 1958 until the 1962 encounter in Cuba, the attempt to deceive the West regarding Soviet missile capabilities had a central place in Soviet policy. The deception directly affected Soviet cold-war objectives and the methods used in pursuing them. To understand Soviet foreign policy in those years, therefore, it is necessary to inquire (1) why the Soviet leaders permitted the United States to widen substantially its margin of strategic superiority, even after the U.S.S.R. had acquired the technical means of reducing it, and (2) why they chose to deceive the West regarding the pace and scope of their ICBM program. In what follows, consideration of these questions will provide the basis for a reassessment of Soviet foreign policy since 1957.

First, why were the Soviet leaders willing to tolerate a widening margin of United States strategic superiority after they had acquired the technical means of reducing it? The crucial reason was their confidence in the extreme disinclination of the United States, despite its great and increasing preponderance of intercontinental power, to initiate or provoke general war.

Other considerations played a part. A decision to procure a large number of first-generation, or even second-generation, ICBM's entailed a certain risk that the force might have serious technical deficiencies and, further, might be considerably degraded within a few years by the opponent's countermeasures. New systems already under development probably promised to be superior. In view of the great demands on Soviet resources, the leaders doubtless hesitated to expend the large amounts of funds needed, especially to procure a force that was subject to early obsolescence. Whatever the limitations on Soviet resources and capacities, however, the U.S.S.R. has spent huge sums on air defense and on acquiring an "overkill" capability against Western Europe. Moreover, technical uncertainties as to how the Soviet ICBM would perform were in some degree matched by similar uncertainties about the shorter-range ballistic missiles, which were nevertheless deployed in large numbers.

None of the above-mentioned considerations, nor all of them together, would have led to a Soviet decision to procure a relatively small ICBM force at a slow pace—which left Soviet intercontinental forces highly vulnerable to United States nuclear attack—had the Soviet leaders not been virtually certain that such an attack would not come. Had there been serious doubt on this score, ordinary prudence would have required the procurement of a sizable force without much delay. Such a force would have been needed to reinforce deterrence of a United States attack and, in the event deterrence failed, to provide a more adequate capability to fight a war. Instead, because of his assurance that there would be no American attack, Khrushchev chose to procure a small force at a slow pace. In so doing, he seemingly reversed the position he had taken in 1954 and 1955, while opposing Malenkov, on the inadequacy of a minimum deterrent.

Khrushchev's subsequent assurance of Soviet security was expressed on various occasions and in various ways.[1] One of the most striking expressions of it occurred in an improvised talk he gave in mid-1962.

What kind of international situation do we have? As for our socialist countries, we consider it good. You will say: "What is good about it if such a row is taking place in the world?" Yes, we shall continue to have struggles. The struggle can assume, so to speak, the shape of high tension, or low tension, but this struggle can stop only when all the means of production are in the hands of the working people. Taking this into account, then, we have a good situation. They frighten us with war, and we frighten them back bit by bit. They threaten us with nuclear arms and we tell them: "Listen, now only fools can do this, because we have them too. . . . So why do foolish things and [try to] frighten us?" This is the situation, and this is why we consider the situation to be good.[2]

According to the Soviet leader, the situation was "good." His words did not express deep apprehension about the state of the world, about rises in the level of tension; on the contrary, he showed remarkable equanimity. Khrushchev's apparent composure, on this and other occasions contrasts strikingly with the widespread belief in the West that nuclear weapons are a principal cause of international tension.[3]

Soviet confidence that the West would not attack the U.S.S.R. unless strongly provoked was reflected in two important new doctrines. First, world war is not "fatally inevitable." "In contemporary conditions," according to Khrushchev, "the prospect is opened of achieving peaceful coexistence for the entire period in the course of

---

[1] See, for example, pp. 53–55.

[2] Remarks in Maritsa, Bulgaria, on May 15, 1962, broadcast on that date by Sofia domestic radio but not circulated in the Soviet Union.

[3] See Myron Rush, "Soviet Policy and International Tension," in *Beyond the Cold War*, ed. Robert A. Goldwin (Chicago: Rand McNally & Co., 1966).

which the social and political problems that now divide the world must be solved." [4] (As a Communist, of course, the only solution he acknowledged was the world-wide victory of communism.) Second, the victory of socialism in the U.S.S.R. is "final." At the Twenty-first Party Congress Khrushchev had originated the doctrine that there was no longer a force in the world capable of overturning it.

What were the grounds of this confidence that the U.S.S.R. was secure despite the United States preponderance of intercontinental nuclear power? In good measure it was based on experience. For many years the United States had been in a position to destroy the Soviet Union with relative impunity but had not done so. From 1945 until 1952 this had been a potential capability for the most part, but the United States showed itself in no hurry to actualize it. No serious effort was made to procure the forces needed until the Korean War demonstrated Communist willingness to engage in naked aggression. By 1953 the United States had acquired an operational capability to destroy the U.S.S.R. but clearly did not intend to employ it except in a situation of great peril. The Eisenhower administration's doctrine of "massive retaliation," although it clearly worried Khrushchev and his associates when first promulgated in 1954, was in time recognized to portend no basic change in the American strategy of containment. By the middle or late 1950's, when the Soviet leaders took the decision (or, what is more likely, the series of decisions) to program a small ICBM force, they had had time to observe that the mere existence of this massive force was no threat to Soviet security. They had learned to live with SAC. Moreover, despite Soviet propaganda against "the imperialist warmongers," they had also come to recognize that the American leadership was not bellicose. This recognition was acknowledged only in backhanded fashion by Soviet assertions that the United States leaders, prompted by sober realism, not good will, were effectively deterred from initiating nuclear war by fear of Soviet strategic power. In fact, however, the Soviet leaders were not relying on large-scale procurement of such strategic power but on the inhibitions of the American leadership, which in their eyes provided a sufficiently reliable deterrent.

Why, then, did the Soviet leaders try to deceive the United States into believing that their ICBM program was much larger than it actually was? It might be said that the deception was evidently

---

[4] Report of the Central Committee to the Twenty-second Party Congress, October 17, 1961, *XXII s"ezd Kommunisticheskoi partii Sovetskogo Soiuza* ("XXII Congress of the CPSU") (Moscow: Gospolitizdat, 1962), I, 50. See also *Pravda*, October 18, 1961.

thought necessary in order to ensure against United States nuclear attack; that is, since they had no real capability—a large operational ICBM force—they postulated one to serve as a deterrent. But in that case, the nation's survival was made to depend on a fiction, on a deception that might be found out—as, indeed, in time it was. It seems more likely that, before they undertook the missile deception, the Soviet leaders had become confident that the United States was so strongly inhibited against initiating nuclear war that even exposure of the deception would not jeopardize Soviet security.

The question why the U.S.S.R. undertook the deception of the United States therefore remains. To answer it, we must first consider, although briefly at this point, the effect that modern weapons have had on the conduct of Soviet foreign policy.

The advent of thermonuclear weapons convinced the Soviet leaders that they must avoid actions that appreciably raised the risk of nuclear war. This conviction doubtless played a part in the decision to program only a relatively small ICBM force for the early sixties. Not only were the Soviet leaders convinced that the United States would not initiate nuclear war without cause, but they had also resolved not to give cause. The decision to acquire a relatively small ICBM force, in turn, heightened the Soviet sense of the need for caution, since it meant that the U.S.S.R. would remain markedly inferior in strategic intercontinental power for years to come. As a consequence, a surprise nuclear attack on the United States, which was a major concern of many defense planners in the United States during this period, was in reality out of the question. What is more significant for Soviet foreign policy, marked inferiority in intercontinental forces also ruled out a pre-emptive attack, that is, an attack launched in the belief that the opponent has initiated a nuclear attack or is about to do so. Thus, if at any time events seemed to be moving toward a sharp confrontation with the United States, the U.S.S.R. had no alternative but to back down before the risk of general war became serious.

The Soviet leaders were aware, in view of their limited intercontinental force and the huge striking force available to the Strategic Air Command, that a nuclear war would wipe out the U.S.S.R. Therefore, Soviet deliberations on international affairs almost certainly excluded the very contingency of engaging in such a war. They found it necessary to avoid any action that appreciably raised the risk of general war or that could set off a dangerous series of events that might get out of control. Khrushchev acknowledged this situation almost in so many words:

We always seek to direct the development of events so as to ensure that, while defending the interests of the socialist camp, we do not provide the imperialist provocateurs with a chance to unleash a new world war.[5]

Of course, provocateurs who were seeking a chance to unleash world war could no doubt find it. Had he truly feared such "provocateurs," Khrushchev would surely have procured the means of fighting the war that might be unleashed at any time. The true sense of Khrushchev's remark is contained in the phrase "to direct the development of events." This need to control events extended beyond the immediate situation to the predispositions of the United States "ruling class." Khrushchev wished to avoid actions that might adversely affect American internal politics, possibly bringing to power in Washington "the madmen" who might unleash nuclear war. There is some truth, then, in the declared unwillingness of the U.S.S.R. to "accept the challenge of the imperialists to a *competition* in adventurism and aggressiveness," [6] that is, to participate in a series of moves and countermoves that could culminate in war.

Did the policy of avoiding actions that might increase the risk of nuclear war mean that Soviet foreign policy had to be passive or quiescent? The Soviet leaders did not think so. They evidently believed that if they could manage to conceal from the West their extreme unwillingness to risk war it would be possible not only to preserve an offensive posture but actually to increase substantially Soviet pressure in the cold war. To do this it was necessary to deceive the West regarding the strategic balance—in particular, regarding the Soviet ICBM program. This was feasible for two reasons: the manifest success of Soviet space activities, which made the existence of a large ICBM program appear credible; and the closed nature of Soviet society, which made it possible to preserve a large measure of secrecy about military matters. In retrospect it seems clear that the Soviet leaders decided to create a fictitious ICBM force as a means of extracting political concessions from a far more powerful opponent. The object of the missile deception, then, was to make large, possibly decisive, political gains in the cold war by creating the impression that the U.S.S.R. was superior to the United States in intercontinental nuclear forces, without incurring the expense necessary to procure such forces. A double deception was involved, since the object of the *missile deception was to deceive the West with respect to Soviet*

---

[5] *Pravda*, January 19, 1961.
[6] Open letter of the Central Committee to Party Organizations, to All Communists of the Soviet Union, *Pravda*, July 14, 1963 (italics added).

foreign policy, in particular, to make it appear that the U.S.S.R. would risk war if necessary to secure its proclaimed objectives. Thus conceived, the Soviet political strategy based on bluff and deception was born of an unwillingness to incur serious risk of war and an unwillingness to forego gains that might be had without incurring such risk.

In the Soviet view, the success of this strategy did not depend on fully persuading the United States that the U.S.S.R. possessed a powerful intercontinental capability or even that it would have one shortly. What was required was that the United States be highly uncertain regarding the intercontinental forces that might be available to the Soviet leaders in the near future. Moreover, even if, once this "future" had become present, the United States had discovered no reason to doubt its strategic superiority, Soviet strategy would not be defeated so long as the United States continued to be uncertain about the period just ahead.

In the years after 1957 the United States was in fact both uncertain and concerned about the growth of Soviet strategic capabilities. It was therefore predisposed to exaggerate the pace and scope of the Soviet program for acquiring delivery vehicles that could strike the United States. By playing upon this predisposition the Soviet leaders were able to distort the American perception of the strategic balance, and so to meet two key requirements of their strategy: they obscured the overwhelming United States superiority, thereby depriving the United States of confidence in its ability to coerce the U.S.S.R. in a crisis; they concealed the narrow limits imposed on their action by strategic deficiencies and consequently were able to raise groundless apprehensions in the West regarding actions they might take on behalf of declared objectives.

Being uncertain about the strategic nuclear balance, the West found it difficult to assess the aims of particular Soviet moves. Whereas the Soviet leaders could plan their initial moves with confidence that they ran no risk of provoking war, the United States leaders were uncertain as to the risks involved in various alternative countermoves and therefore felt constrained to respond cautiously. This caution, in turn, strengthened Soviet reliance on American restraint in the cold war and increased the U.S.S.R.'s confidence that it could control the risk of war stemming from its actions.

Uncertainty, however, has not always worked to the Soviet advantage. Although uncertainty in the United States regarding the nuclear missile balance made the Soviet strategy of deception feasible, the execution of that strategy was seriously hampered by the Soviet leaders' uncertainty concerning the further measures they could safely take if their opponents failed to make the concessions they demanded. Soviet confidence that the United States would not risk nuclear war unless its vital interests were immediately jeopardized was matched by Soviet uncertainty about the ways in which the United States would actually define its vital interests when faced by a Soviet challenge. Unlike the American uncertainty, which could be resolved —at least theoretically—by improved intelligence about the size of the operational Soviet intercontinental strike force, the Soviet uncertainty was radical and without remedy since it concerned the purely subjective question of American willingness to risk nuclear war on behalf of interests that were threatened by hostile Soviet action. The answer to this question could not be known, even to the American leaders, unless the matter were put to the test. But testing the willingness of the United States to engage in nuclear war was precisely what the Soviet leaders could not do. Since the threshold of a United States nuclear response was too dangerous a question to explore, the Soviet leaders, short of abandoning their political objectives, could cope with their uncertainty in but one way: by assuming the threshold was relatively low—not so low as to preclude sharp Soviet pressure where the West was vulnerable, but sufficiently low to preclude their use of military force. Along with the sense of security that enabled the Soviet leaders to undertake the strategy of deception, then, there was a sense of peril that limited the boldness with which they could pursue it. Moreover, and this is crucial, they evidently did not believe that the perils involved in a confrontation with the United States could be sufficiently reduced by the rapid acquisition of a large ICBM force.

Thus, the Soviet strategy of deception permitted many kinds of pressure on the West, but only within an area of action that seemed to assure the U.S.S.R. immunity from a confrontation with the West.[7] This acceptance of limits gave rise to important differences with Communist China and contributed to the split that developed during these years. The Chinese Communists, whether because they discounted the significance of the strategic weapons balance or because they did not realize the full extent of Soviet inferiority, sharply denied the need for the restraint shown by the Soviet leaders.

---

[7] There is an amplification of this discussion of the limitations imposed on Soviet foreign policy by strategic inferiority on pp. 185–87.

The disagreement of the two Communist powers on cold war strategy has stemmed in good measure from a disagreement over the amount of pressure that can be exerted by Communist initiatives and retaliatory actions without unduly increasing the risk of thermonuclear war. In this open polemic Soviet leaders have seemed to argue that the danger of general nuclear war is relatively small, or at least controllable, and that so long as Communist policy does not become more aggressive the risk will remain small. Highly provocative Communist actions, however, such as those demanded by Communist China, would seriously increase the likelihood of war.[8] Chinese Communists have disagreed on both points. First, they say that the evil nature of imperialism creates a greater risk of war than the Soviet leaders will admit.[9] Next, they argue that no appreciable increase in the likelihood of war would result from stepped-up pressure on the Western world; rather, the opposite. Any policy other than that of vigorous revolutionary struggle "will only encourage the ambitions of the imperialists and increase the danger of world war." Revolutionary wars do not create sparks that can ignite a world conflagration but strengthen "the forces which prevent the imperialists from launching a world war." In contrast to the Russian belief that deterrence of the West depends upon the avoidance of severe political and military shocks, the Chinese leaders assert that the present strategic balance is proof against shocks administered by Communists. The way to lessen the risk of world war, the Chinese Communists imply, is to accept the risk of lesser wars. Mao has been quoted in the Soviet press as having expressed the belief that international tension is good for Communists and bad for the West:

To whom is international tension advantageous? To the United States? To England? To the world proletariat? This poses a problem. I believe that none of us [that is, the Communists] need fear international tension. I personally like international tension. The United States understands that tension, which they themselves have created, is not advantageous to them, because it may force the partisans of peace and the workers of the whole

---

[8] The Chinese Communist leaders "apparently hold that the Soviet Union should reply to provocations with provocations, fall into traps set by the wild men from the imperialist camp . . ." (open letter of the Central Committee to Party Organizations, to All Communists of the Soviet Union, *Pravda*, July 14, 1963).

[9] The Central Committee of the Chinese Communist party has asked, "How can war be abolished?" and answered, on the authority of Lenin, " 'By abolishing the division of mankind into classes.' . . . However, certain persons [namely, Khrushchev] now actually hold that it is possible to bring about 'a world . . . without wars' while the system of imperialism . . . still exists. This is sheer illusion" (letter to the Central Committee of the Soviet Communist party of March 30, 1963, in *Pravda*, June 14, 1963).

world to begin to think, and will lead larger numbers of people into the Communist Party. . . . It is necessary to put an end to prejudices, including prejudices relating to international tension. . . . In some countries there exists the prejudice that international tension is unfavorable for the peoples. But in conditions of international tension, Communist parties can develop more rapidly, the tempo of their development can be more rapid.[10]

These views, which Mao allegedly expressed in March, 1959, presumably contributed to the Soviet Central Committee's

impression . . . that the leaders of the C.P.C. [Communist Party of China] regard the preservation and intensification of international tension —especially in the relations between the USSR and the U.S.—to be to their advantage.[11]

For their part, the Chinese Communists have accused the Soviet leaders of having ceased to be revolutionaries because of fear of nuclear war. The Soviet leaders acknowledge that fear of nuclear war has affected their choice of means for furthering revolution. "Prevention of nuclear war has become a precondition for carrying out the world socialist revolution in a way that would not jeopardize civilization. . . ."[12] They hold that the revolutionary process will proceed by its own momentum, assisted by prudent Soviet support, but that "provocative" support for revolution by the U.S.S.R. would risk thermonuclear war. Although remaining committed to world revolution, then, the Soviet leaders have ruled out the use of means that the Chinese Communists assert, with some reason, to be necessary.

As we have said, even short-term Soviet objectives, which are much more modest than world revolution, have been supported by disproportionate physical means for pursuing them. This disproportion lies at the heart of the Soviet strategy of deception. It could succeed only if limited pressure were sufficient to achieve the ends desired, that is, if the West did not wait for a decisive confrontation between the two sides, but hastened to make concessions as soon as the U.S.S.R. appeared to be in earnest in its demands.

The point beyond which Soviet pressure would elicit concessions from the West—what might be termed the "threshold of concession" —was for the Soviet leaders the critical unknown. Khrushchev alluded to this unknown—the West's capacity to resist Soviet pressure

---

[10] Article by a leader of the Costa Rican Communist party, E. M. Val'verde, in *Izvestiia*, June 19, 1964.
[11] Open letter of the Central Committee to Party Organizations, to All Communists of the Soviet Union, *Pravda*, July 14, 1963.
[12] B. N. Ponomaryov, "Some Problems of the Revolutionary Movement," *World Marxist Review*, December, 1962, p. 9.

—in a passage whose full meaning is masked for publication, but which is highly revealing nevertheless:

There exist instruments which measure the resistance of materials. If it were possible to invent an instrument that could measure with the same precision in politics and military affairs the resistance of both sides, the socialist camp and the imperialist states, it would show that both sides are sufficiently strong at present. Therefore, disputes today should be settled not by force, but by truth.[13]

Disputes should be settled by "truth," that is, by words. The Soviet contribution to the verbal struggle, however, took the form of untruthful claims and ambiguous threats. If these proved inadequate and if strong action were required to compel the concessions sought, the Soviet strategy was virtually doomed to defeat.[14] This would be so even in the most favorable situations in which the threshold of concession, even if moderately high, would still be far below the threshold of nuclear response, and the area of maneuver would be largest. In this case, the Soviet Union could theoretically expect to induce the West to make the desired concessions without even considering the alternative of launching a nuclear attack. The Soviet leaders, however, would be most unlikely to apply the degree of pressure needed, because of their uncertainty as to the threshold of nuclear response and their need to keep it at a great distance. Their effective area of maneuver, therefore, was much smaller than the theoretical one.

The Soviet leaders were right in supposing that the West's threshold of nuclear response was extremely high but wrong about the West's threshold of concession. They placed this second threshold too low and underestimated the West's determination to resist pressure. As low as they placed the concession threshold, the tactics they adopted were evidently designed to lower it still further. They demanded concessions that in themselves were not vital for the West and obviously not worth risking war about. Moreover, in presenting demands, the Soviet leadership employed the common bargaining tactic of minimizing their significance to the opponent—who therefore cannot reasonably offer strong resistance—while insisting upon its importance to themselves—who therefore are committed to do everything necessary to force the concession. These tactics failed,

---

[13] *Pravda*, March 5, 1959.
[14] The nature of the concession would of course determine the threshold in particular instances.

however, and throughout this period the Western leaders attached great significance to the concessions demanded of them.

From a Western standpoint, the concessions, if made, would have limited consequences only if the U.S.S.R. observed the agreements that embodied them and did not subsequently demand further concessions on the matters at issue. The Western leaders strongly doubted that the Soviet Union would rest content with an agreement even if it conceded the Soviet demands without a *quid pro quo*. Nor did they trust the U.S.S.R. to observe such an agreement should it subsequently feel that its interests were no longer served by doing so. Western leaders had not forgotten Soviet violations of agreements made with the West during and after World War II. Experience with Hitler's demands had created in the West a large body of opinion that concessions to dictators' demands did not appease them but only gave rise to new and more far-reaching demands. Moreover, it was widely recognized that unilateral concessions to the U.S.S.R. would tend to resolve the large uncertainties about the strategic balance in favor of Soviet claims. One consequence, it was thought, would be a weakening of the resolution of American allies and neutrals in future dealings with the Soviet Union. A "domino effect" would result: states in areas affected by Western concessions would opt, one after another, for accommodation with what appeared to be superior Soviet power. Since Khrushchev based his demands, in part, on the changing strategic balance, it was also thought that the satisfaction of one set of demands could only lead to new ones as the balance of power continued to shift in the Soviet favor.

For all these reasons, the Western leaders tended to magnify the importance of what was demanded and maintained a resistance to Soviet pressure that was commensurate with the high value they placed on the concessions asked. Thus the West's threshold of concession was relatively high, probably higher than the Soviet leaders had expected, and in any case too high for them to counter by the limited pressure they were prepared to mount. The Soviet error, although costly, was not foolish. A critical confrontation with the U.S.S.R. was then widely feared in the West, although such fears could yield large concessions only if a confrontation was made to appear imminent. The Soviet leaders, however, could not act sufficiently boldly to make a confrontation appear imminent, since they also lived too much in fear of it.

The clearest expression, and one decisive test, of the Soviet strategy of bluff and deception was the Soviet campaign against Berlin from 1958 to 1962. This important Soviet enterprise forms the subject of the next chapter, where it is treated, not in its full implications as a major encounter of East and West, but as an episode in the history of Soviet strategic deception.

TEN

THE POLITICAL OFFENSIVE
AGAINST BERLIN

ON NOVEMBER 10, 1958, Khrushchev suddenly declared that the Soviet Union no longer recognized obligations it had assumed under the Potsdam Agreement, specifically the provisions on Berlin. As spelled out formally later that month, this denunciation amounted to a demand that the occupation of West Berlin be ended. Thus was initiated the Berlin crisis, which remained a central issue in the cold war for roughly four years, until the end of 1962. Even more than most crises, it broke unexpectedly upon the West. There was extreme uncertainty as to the motives and calculations of the Soviet leaders, an uncertainty that continued long after the crisis was over. When we recall that, despite the West's failure to make the required concessions, the Soviet leaders never executed the measures by which they repeatedly threatened to enforce their demands, the mystery deepens. Why did the Soviet leaders undertake the Berlin offensive in the first place, and why did they fail to carry it through? Both the undertaking and the failure to consummate it are best explained by reference to the Soviet strategy of bluff and deception.

In initiating the Berlin campaign, the Soviet leaders' maximum objective, in the view of most observers, was the one they announced: to get the allies out of Berlin. A peace treaty with "the two Germanies," or with East Germany alone, was also an objective of the Soviet leaders, but, as they usually insisted, such a treaty would automatically terminate the allies' rights in Berlin. A corollary objective was probably to demonstrate the unreliability of even the most solemn Western commitments. The weakness of United States military power, or alternatively, the failure of United States will, would also be revealed to the world, and the NATO alliance would receive a shattering blow from which it might never recover. The Soviet leaders no doubt had a range of objectives and might have been content had the West made important concessions short of evacuating Berlin. Although such limited concessions would have been less shattering for the West than withdrawal from Berlin, they would have represented a good beginning toward subverting the Western alliance.

The larger the concessions sought, the heavier the pressures required. Certainly, achievement of the maximum objective required pressures exceeding anything seen before in the cold war. But the severity of the pressure that could be exerted against the allied position in West Berlin depended upon the kind and degree of risk the Soviet leaders were willing to run. The critical question was whether the risks they were prepared to assume would sustain sufficient pressures to force the Western powers from Berlin or to compel them to renegotiate access rights on disadvantageous terms. Because of West Berlin's military and political vulnerability, the U.S.S.R. could mount considerable local pressure even while keeping its risks low and controllable. The initial Soviet proposal (November 27) was designed to accomplish this and in fact did so in considerable measure. It gave the Western powers six months to negotiate an agreement liquidating their occupation of West Berlin, during which time the U.S.S.R. undertook not to interfere with access to Berlin. If this grace period were not utilized to reach an "adequate agreement," however, the Soviet Union announced that it would turn control of military traffic over to the German Democratic Republic (G.D.R.), with which the Western powers would then have to deal.

The note posed a threat to the West's position in Berlin without immediately incurring any serious risk. For six months the Soviet Union need do nothing except perhaps hold up the West's military traffic to Berlin occasionally as a reminder of its capacity to make mischief. Even after the six months, if the U.S.S.R. proceeded to transfer control of this traffic to the G.D.R., the onus of resisting the change would be on the Western powers. Nevertheless, the Soviet Union could not rule out such resistance. Serious interruption of the traffic flow as a means of forcing Western troops out of Berlin, whether caused by the U.S.S.R. or the G.D.R., could provoke the use of force. Moreover, since the concession demanded of the West threatened the viability of the NATO alliance, an effort to compel the West to make this concession inevitably involved the risk of war in Central Europe and possibly over a wider area. The Soviet leaders' willingness to assume this risk did not depend solely on the balance of local forces, in which they had a clear advantage. It must also have depended on the strategic balance of forces, particularly on the balance of intercontinental forces. How did Moscow view the strategic balance?

When the Soviet leaders initiated the Berlin crisis late in 1958, they probably knew that for several years the Soviet ICBM program would not yield even a moderately sized force. Although the Soviet nuclear capability against Western Europe would rise sharply as the Berlin crisis ran its course, the balance of intercontinental forces would become increasingly unfavorable for the U.S.S.R. It was out of the question, then, for the U.S.S.R. to provoke a military outbreak in Central Europe. The Soviet leaders could at best simulate the determination to do whatever was necessary to achieve their declared objective, for they did not possess the means to sustain a genuine determination. In order to appear willing to take risks that they knew to be imprudent, the Soviet leaders, among other actions, deliberately conveyed an exaggerated impression of the size and scope of their ICBM program.

No doubt the Soviet leaders were bound to exaggerate their ICBM capabilities even without a Berlin campaign. Indeed, such exaggeration had been going on for a year when the Berlin campaign began. After early 1959, however, the effort to deceive the West became more contrived and systematic, and it is not unlikely that this intensification resulted from initiation of the Berlin crisis some weeks earlier.

The Soviet missile deception was almost bound to have some effect on American views of the strategic balance, especially at a time when not even the best-informed Americans could be sure where the truth lay. The disparity that thus arose between what the United States believed about the Soviet ICBM program and its actual strength corresponded to a disparity between the far-reaching objectives of the U.S.S.R. in the Berlin campaign and the relatively modest risks it was prepared to take to realize them.

The bearing of the strategic balance on the outcome of the Berlin crisis was recognized in the West from the outset. The West's surprise at Soviet initiation of the campaign against Berlin stemmed from the assumption, until that moment the prevailing one, that the U.S.S.R. would not dare to embark on a course leading to a confrontation with the West on so vital an issue as West Berlin. Once the campaign had been initiated, therefore, it was widely assumed in the West that the Soviet Union anticipated a rapid shift in the balance of intercontinental forces as a result of their ICBM program. The Soviet leaders gave support to this view in the following months by menacing claims of missile superiority over the United States and by assertions that the changed balance of power made the existing arrangement intolerable. They warned that a "provocation" in Berlin could start a major war, whose flames "would inevitably spread to the continent of America, because with modern military technology, frontiers between distant and near theaters of war would disappear for all practical purposes."[1] Averell Harriman reports an interview in which Khrushchev said, menacingly though ambiguously:

"Your generals talk of maintaining your position in Berlin with force. That is bluff. If you send in tanks, they will burn and make no mistake about it. If you want war, you can have it, and remember it will be your war. Our rockets will fly automatically. . . ." And his colleagues echoed like a chorus, automatically.[2]

The Soviet leaders warned the United States that resistance to their demands by military means would mean world war. We now know that the success of Soviet missile technology did not portend a powerful capability against the American continent in the near future. From 1958 to 1961, however, the West's uncertainty about the Soviet ICBM program paralleled its uncertainty about the calculation underlying the new political offensive. These two sources of uncertainty fed upon each other, as they no doubt were meant to do. The Western governments knew that the U.S.S.R. did not want war, yet feared that the Soviet leaders, emboldened by successful development of an ICBM, might act in ways that heightened the risk of war. Only by fostering this view, by making it appear that the U.S.S.R. was really prepared to risk violence and the possibility of escalation to achieve its objectives, could the Soviet leaders expect to induce the West to withdraw from Berlin or to make other far-reaching concessions.

The fears of the Western powers inevitably inhibited their response to Soviet pressure on Berlin. These fears, however, induced caution, not paralysis. The Soviet leaders seem to have realized that a necessary condition for success in forcing the West out of Berlin was to make credible their claim to possess intercontinental forces capable of devastating the United States.[3] Mere assertions would not be enough, despite the West's uncertainty and tendency to fear the worst. To make its assertions sufficiently credible to deter an effective Western response in Berlin, the Soviet Union needed to demonstrate an operational ICBM capability. Lacking a substantial ICBM force when it initiated the Berlin offensive, and for some time afterward, the Soviet Union was unable to provide such a demonstration. As a

---

[1] Speech of Andrei Gromyko to Supreme Soviet, *Pravda*, December 26, 1958. See also Defense Minister Malinovsky on the Soviet capability to deliver "an annihilating counterblow" on the United States with powerful rockets (*Pravda*, April 11, 1959).

[2] Interview, June 23, 1959, in *Life*, July 8, 1959.

[3] A necessary condition but, as will be argued shortly, not a sufficient condition.

result, although United States leaders constantly feared that the U.S.S.R. might soon acquire a substantial ICBM force, at no time did they believe that the potential threat had become actual. Consequently, they were not willing to act on the assumption of Soviet strategic superiority but instead relied on the margin of United States superiority in intercontinental weapons (diminishing though they then believed it to be) to maintain the West's position in Berlin as long as possible and to minimize whatever concessions might finally prove necessary.

Even if the United States had come to believe that the U.S.S.R. possessed a large ICBM force, the Soviet leaders themselves knew that they did not and in the last resort could not behave as though they did. As a result, when the Western powers took measures that heightened the risk of hostilities or seemed about to do so, the U.S.S.R. had no alternative but to ease its demands and to extract what concessions it could.

No doubt the Soviet leaders had expected major gains at the West's expense from the Berlin campaign; otherwise they would hardly have initiated it. Yet they proved willing to forego such gains. When the game became too risky, they contented themselves with what the West called "eroding" its position in Berlin. Yet erosion unaccompanied by strong pressure from the U.S.S.R., although better than nothing, promised little more than compensation for the considerable costs of the Berlin offensive. Indeed, on several occasions the Soviet leaders refused to accept from the West concessions that promised to be erosive, because acceptance would have committed the U.S.S.R., at least temporarily, to the status quo in all other respects and therefore might have lessened Soviet freedom to renew pressure at will.

The Soviet incapacity to persist in the effort to force the Western powers out of Berlin was evident at several points during the campaign. The ultimatum demanding negotiations that would convert West Berlin into a free city within six months led to somewhat diffuse negotiations at the 1959 Geneva Conference of Foreign Ministers. On July 28, 1959, the West proposed what would have been in effect an interim solution of five years duration, with the object of alleviating the immediate pressure on West Berlin. This was rejected. Had agreement been reached on this basis, it might have led to demoralization of the West Berliners and to a weakening of the West's will to resist once Soviet pressure was resumed. The Soviet leaders were not enticed by this prospect, however, presumably because their basic strategy enjoined the exertion of direct pressure sufficient to compel the Western powers to make more damaging concessions and if possible sufficient to end the occupation of Berlin. Later, however, they may have had cause to regret their rejection of the West's concessions at Geneva. In the spring of 1960, when negotiations on Berlin were to be renewed, the Soviet leaders found to their annoyance and disappointment that the West had withdrawn its earlier concessions and insisted on beginning the negotiations anew.

The Geneva episode came to an end when an agreement was reached for Khrushchev to visit the United States. As a consequence of the Premier's talks with President Eisenhower at Camp David, there appeared to be a fair prospect that the tactics Khrushchev planned to employ at the Paris summit meeting in May, 1960—a combination of verbal restraint, strategic claims, and moderate local pressure—might yield substantial progress toward his goals in Berlin. Significantly, the most extreme Soviet claims of missile capabilities against the United States were made in the months preceding the summit meeting. The stiffening United States negotiatory position in the preceding weeks probably dampened his hopes, although they were not wholly dispelled until the U-2 incident.

The May 1 flight of the U-2, according to President Eisenhower, was the last of a series extending over a period of four years. "These flights have given us information of the greatest importance to the nation's security. In fact, their success has been nothing short of remarkable."[4] Khrushchev, after acknowledging that U-2's had been flying over the U.S.S.R. since 1956, indicated that the flights had occurred over areas where no ICBM's were deployed. Aware of the relatively slow pace and scope of the Soviet ICBM program, however, Khrushchev had no grounds for confidence that the United States credited this claim. Soviet uncertainty concerning what the United States believed existed even before the U-2 was shot down, of course, although it may have been aggravated by the quality of the photographs recovered from the wreckage of the U-2.[5] Moreover, by publicly revealing Soviet vulnerability to aerial espionage over an

---

[4] Speech of May 20, 1960, U.S. State Department Bulletin, June 6, 1960.
[5] According to Raymond Bissell, Jr., the CIA official in charge of the U-2 program, "the detail [of the photographs] was so sharp that one could almost read the tail-markings" on bombers photographed from an altitude of around 14 miles (quoted by Charles J. V. Murphy, in "Khrushchev's Paper Bear," Fortune, December, 1964, p. 227).

extended period of years, the incident tended to lessen the effectiveness of Soviet strategic threats, since it was ultimately through such threats, combined with limited local pressures, that the U.S.S.R. hoped to achieve its objectives in Berlin. In these circumstances, the prospects for gain at the Paris summit meeting were so sharply diminished that Khrushchev chose to disrupt the conference.

He did not proceed to implement the measures he had threatened against Berlin, as was then feared. On the contrary, he hastened to call off for the time being the campaign against Berlin. He was to act similarly two years later at the time of the Cuban missile crisis and for the same reason: unwillingness to risk strong pressure against the Western position in Berlin at times when international tension, through other causes, had become acute.

Khrushchev made it clear, however, that he was only postponing the campaign against the allies in Berlin, not ending it. He promised to resume pressure on them the following year. With the ending of the U-2 flights, he may have hoped that in a year, regardless of the Soviet ICBM deployment program, the credibility of missile threats against the United States would have improved.

For almost a year, except for light probes by the East German regime acting as the Soviet proxy, the campaign against Berlin was in abeyance. In mid-1961, however, the offensive was resumed with new intensity. On May 4, Premier Khrushchev finally accepted President Kennedy's invitation of February 22 to meet with him for a discussion of outstanding world problems. During the interval of more than two months, the new and untested administration had suffered a debacle at the Bay of Pigs.[6] On the second and last day of the meeting in Vienna (June 4), Premier Khrushchev presented the President with an *aide-mémoire* defining the Soviet position on Germany and Berlin. In it, the Soviet government renewed its previous demands for a peace treaty with Germany and for the conversion of West Berlin into a free city. Several days later, the document's text was released by the official Soviet news agency, TASS, which marked open resumption of the offensive against the allied position in Berlin.[7] In a televised speech several days later Khrushchev announced a new deadline for

---

[6] In view of the importance of the subjective element in Khrushchev's campaign on Berlin, that is, his assessment of the opponent, it is arguable that Khrushchev might not have renewed the offensive in 1961 had it not been for the United States failure in Cuba in April.

[7] June 10. According to the *New York Times*, Dean Rusk had privately made nondisclosure of the text a test of Soviet seriousness in negotiation with the West (June 12, 1961).

the acceptance of his proposals: "A peaceful settlement in Europe must be attained this year." [8]

Subsequently, on July 6, Khrushchev announced a decision to increase defense spending "in the current year" by almost one-third. Since such an increase could not be spent on a rational program within that year, a major purpose of the announcement must have been to demonstrate the seriousness of Soviet intentions in regard to Berlin. Later in the month, however, on July 26, President Kennedy countered Khrushchev by requesting from Congress a supplementary military appropriation of over $3 billion. Thus the immediate effect of Khrushchev's renewed effort to exert pressure on the West was to accelerate the arms race, a consequence that the U.S.S.R. could ill afford.

In addition, the United States moved to strengthen its capacity to engage in military operations in Central Europe. Well over half the supplementary appropriation was intended to improve American conventional capabilities. Reserve and Air National Guard units were to be expanded, and draft calls and civil defense expenditures sharply increased. The scheduled retirement of B-47 bombers was postponed. Troops numbering forty-one thousand and matériel began to move to Germany. The display of resolution implicit in the strengthening of United States military capabilities in Europe must have made a painful impression on Khrushchev, particularly in view of his reduction of personnel in the Soviet armed forces during 1960 and the continuing Soviet incapacity to engage in general war.

In the midst of the renewal of the crisis over Berlin, and at a time of serious political deterioration in East Germany, the G.D.R. suddenly, on August 13, closed the sector border between East and West Berlin to prevent further defection of the East German population. The measure was of course authorized by the Soviet regime, presumably as a defensive maneuver that was unlikely to provoke a strong response. Once taken, the measure was almost welcomed by many in the West, since it seemed to resolve an acute problem for Soviet security in Central Europe and thereby to stabilize the situation. [9]

The wall dividing Berlin did not immediately bring the hoped-for

---

[8] June 15, 1961. Khrushchev reaffirmed the deadline in a speech on June 21.

[9] It has sometimes been suggested that the Soviet offensive against Berlin was largely a cover operation designed to make the West accept the wall. This explanation seems defective, however, since the political and economic costs to the U.S.S.R. of the Berlin offensive were great, whereas its contribution to the West's acceptance of the wall was probably not significant.

lessening of Soviet pressure on the West's position in Berlin. Its unopposed construction damaged confidence in the West's resolve and seriously damaged the morale of West Berlin's population. These effects may have encouraged Soviet hopes for important gains. But the United States continued to respond sharply to Soviet pressures, insofar as pressures could be distinguished from merely defensive measures. There was a sixteen-hour confrontation of United States and Soviet tanks at a Berlin checkpoint on October 27, an experience that was probably as sobering for Moscow as it was for Washington.

About this time, responsible United States leaders began to deny publicly the credibility of Soviet missile claims and to speak with new confidence of a large margin of American superiority in strategic forces. In their public assessments of the strategic balance, the Soviet leaders were now very much on the defensive. A moderation of Soviet claims to strategic superiority had become apparent as early as the end of 1960, when the Soviet leaders, in order to justify their failure to take the aggressive and risky actions demanded by Communist China, had begun to emphasize the mutual destructiveness of thermonuclear war instead of its dire consequences for the capitalist world. A year later, when the United States confidently asserted its strategic superiority, the Soviet leaders were quick to dispute the claim but cautious in asserting their own superiority. As a result, the effectiveness of Soviet threats against the West was seriously impaired.

Shortly before, in his speech to the Communist Party Congress on October 17, Khrushchev lifted the deadline he had placed on the signing of a peace treaty with Germany. "The question of a time limit for the signing of a German peace treaty will not be so important if the Western powers show a readiness to settle the German problem; we shall not in that case absolutely insist on signing the peace treaty before December 31, 1961." [10] He still insisted, however, that such a peace treaty would be signed "with or without the Western powers" and would end their rights of occupation in Berlin. Subsequently, deprived of a deadline and of bold strategic threats, the Berlin campaign lost its momentum. Despite some renewed Soviet pressure on the Berlin air corridors,[11] the offensive had ground to a halt by mid-1962 in desultory and inconclusive negotiations.

---

[10] *Pravda*, October 18, 1961.
[11] In February and March, 1962, Soviet planes began to buzz commercial airliners in the air corridors and to drop metal chaff that interfered with their radars.

ELEVEN

SEARCH FOR A WAY OUT:
FROM BERLIN TO CUBA

THE FIRST PHASE of the Berlin offensive ended in 1960, the second and last phase in 1962. Failure in both cases stemmed from the adverse strategic balance. The Soviet Union's effort to deceive the West regarding its ICBM capabilities had only a limited success. Probably more important, the constraints imposed upon the Soviet leaders by their own understanding of the strategic balance limited their willingness to apply the pressure needed to realize their objectives. The mere threat of measures to impair the West's position in Berlin proved inadequate. This was crucial, and it was something the U.S.S.R. could not know in advance. Nor did it become apparent at once. The U.S.S.R. could discover the West's will to resist only by testing it. During the course of the Berlin campaign and probably by the end of 1961, the Soviet leaders became sufficiently convinced of the quality of the West's will to resist.

Even if the Soviet Union had cut off traffic with Berlin, transferred control of access routes to the East Germans, or signed a peace treaty with East Germany, there was still no assurance that these measures would have led directly to their objective. And after 1958, it appeared more likely that these measures would be resisted and that any attempt at effective counteraction by the U.S.S.R. would further heighten the risk of war. Since war was wholly unacceptable, not even the first step on the road that might lead to it could be taken.

The Western powers were unwilling to make the concessions demanded by the U.S.S.R. merely in response to threats of forceful measures; at the same time, they could not discount possible Soviet readiness to accept the increased risk of war that these measures implied. Realizing this, Khrushchev, even after twice retreating from his commitments to act against Western interests if his demands were not met, retained the freedom to resume the offensive almost at will. By 1962, however, Western leaders were persuaded that the U.S.S.R. was unwilling to accept the risks involved in taking the necessary measures to end the occupation of Berlin. By then, Khrushchev's opponents no longer saw his failure to act as a pause before a new storm but as a retreat before their power and their firm resolution to use that power if necessary. Now many in the West were beginning to regard the problem of Berlin less as a threat posed to allied interests than as a source of great discomfiture to Khrushchev and a threat to his position of leadership in the Communist bloc.

Since the adverse strategic balance had twice led to failure in the Soviet offensive against Berlin, it was clearly folly to attempt it a third time without first altering the strategic balance. Evidently some time in the first half of 1962, Khrushchev decided to seek some quick and dramatic means for achieving a breakthrough that would strengthen the U.S.S.R.'s position—militarily, diplomatically, and psycho-logically—on a whole range of outstanding issues and particularly on Berlin. His search led to the decision to deploy strategic missiles in Cuba.

The Cuban missile episode was a bold effort to alter the unfavorable strategic environment in which the U.S.S.R. found itself in 1962 as the result of the United States intercontinental arms buildup and the collapse of the "missile gap" myth.[1] Other hypotheses regarding Soviet objectives treat the Soviet missiles and bombers deployed in Cuba essentially as bargaining counters emplaced on the island only so that they could be withdrawn in exchange for desired local political or military concessions by the United States. Although, according to these hypotheses, broader consequences might have followed from Soviet success in extracting American concessions under these cir-cumstances, the Cuban missile venture was not intended primarily to alter the over-all strategic balance; in particular, Berlin was not a major target of the Cuban deployment. Since the Cuban missile crisis plays such a central role in this study of Soviet efforts to manipulate and capitalize on world beliefs about the strategic balance, it is necessary to deal with these alternative hypotheses before presenting our own.

Some observers have imputed to the Soviet Union certain limited aims, which, they believe, Khrushchev in fact achieved. Among such aims was the securing of political concessions from the United States, such as a public pledge by the President not to invade Cuba. In the end, these observers argue, Khrushchev was able to make some general political gains. In some quarters, for example, he was given credit, which he claimed, for having saved the peace.

From our point of view, even if these objectives had been fully achieved, they would have been manifestly disproportionate to the

[1] See Arnold L. Horelick, "The Cuban Missile Crisis: An Analysis of Soviet Calculations and Behavior," in World Politics, April, 1964. The discussion of Cuba in this and the following chapter is largely taken from that article.

costs and risks incurred by the Soviet Union in undertaking to place missiles in Cuba. At least forty-two IL-28 bombers and an equal number of strategic missiles were brought into Cuba by Soviet ships. Nine missile sites were established, six with four launchers each for the MRBM's, and three fixed sites, to include four launching positions each, for the IRBM's.[2] Yet a token force of a few conspicuously deployed MRBM's would doubtless have sufficed to provoke a United States demand that the Soviet Union remove them from Cuba.

The magnitude and character of the Soviet strategic weapon deployment in Cuba also throws doubt on another hypothesis that has been advanced—namely, that the Soviet Union merely sought to compel the United States to withdraw its missiles from Turkey in exchange for the withdrawal of Soviet missiles from Cuba. Since the United States had only one squadron (fifteen missiles) of Jupiters deployed in Turkey,[3] no more than one-third the number of MRBM's with a 1,100-mile range known to have been shipped to Cuba would have been necessary to make such a trade seem quantitatively plausible. The costly and essentially unsalvageable fixed sites that were being prepared to receive IRBM's with a 2,200-mile range were altogether superfluous to any intended Cuba-Turkey missile base exchange since the United States had no equivalent missiles in Turkey or anywhere else, for that matter.

Of course, a mutual withdrawal of missiles from Cuba and Turkey was explicitly proposed by Khrushchev in his October 27 letter to President Kennedy. But the mere fact that Khrushchev proposed such an exchange at one point during the crisis, after the United States had demanded the withdrawal of Soviet strategic weapons, does not prove that this was his objective from the start any more than his subsequent withdrawal of the missiles without such a *quid pro quo* proves that his ultimate objective was simply to get President Kennedy to promise not to invade Cuba. It is true that the withdrawal of United States strategic weapons from Turkey, under apparent Soviet duress, would have given Khrushchev a more tangible return for his trouble than a conditional verbal pledge by the United

---

[2] Briefing by John Hughes, of the Defense Intelligence Agency, *Department of Defense Appropriations for 1964*, Hearings before a Subcommittee of the House of Representatives Committee on Appropriations, 88th Cong., 1st sess., 1963, Part 1, p. 7 (hereinafter cited as *Hearings on Department of Defense Appropriations for 1964*).

[3] *Missiles and Rockets*, January 7, 1963, p. 26.

States not to invade Cuba.[4] It was one thing for the United States and an allied host country to decide jointly to substitute other means of defense for some bases, such as Polaris submarines in adjacent waters; it would have been quite another for the United States, under Soviet duress, to withdraw from its bases, regardless of the wishes of its allies.

It seems questionable, however, that the Soviets would accept the costs and risks of deploying missiles in Cuba merely to have them available to exchange for the withdrawal of United States missiles from Turkey. The phasing out of United States missiles deployed overseas, without a Soviet *quid pro quo,* was already known to have been under consideration long before the October 1962 crisis,[5] though the Soviet leaders may not have been certain regarding American intentions. Moreover, for reasons of geography and because the United States already possessed a large advantage in intercontinental nuclear delivery capabilities, a strategic missile base in Cuba would have been a far more valuable military asset to the Soviet Union than a comparable base in Turkey was to the United States. Finally, as pointed out earlier, if the Soviet leaders intended no more than to lay the groundwork for an agreement on the mutual withdrawal of strategic missiles, they need not have deployed more than a token force of MRBM's and need not have constructed installations for IRBM's at all. It is more likely that the base-exchange proposal was an improvised, or perhaps even a prepared fallback, position to cover unfavorable contingencies than that it was the culmination of Soviet hopes for the Cuban venture.[6]

Khrushchev's official explanation of Soviet policy was that Soviet strategic weapons were deployed in Cuba solely to defend the island

---

[4] Had the United States accepted the Soviet base-exchange proposal of October 27, Khrushchev would have received such a pledge in any case, since a reciprocal exchange of no-invasion pledges was part of the proposed bargain.

[5] Secretary McNamara has testified that the long-standing program to replace the obsolete Thor and Jupiter missiles dated from early 1961 (*Hearings on Department of Defense Appropriations for 1964,* p. 57).

[6] If the base-exchange proposal was a prepared fallback position, the Soviet leaders failed to prepare their propagandists for it. On the same day (October 28, 1962) that Khrushchev's letter to the President proposing an exchange of bases was made public on the front page of *Izvestiia,* a commentary on an inside page stated: "There are those in the U.S.A. who speculate that in exchange for denying Cuba the ability to repel American aggression, one might 'give up' some American base close to Soviet territory. . . . Such 'proposals,' if you can call them that, merely serve to betray the unclean conscience of the authors." The editor of *Izvestiia* was then Alexei Adzhubei, Khrushchev's son-in-law.

against attack by the United States and that once the threat of such an attack was removed (by the President's conditional undertaking not to launch one) the Soviet weapons, having served their purpose, were withdrawn and peace was preserved. But the credibility of this assertion was seriously impaired when Khrushchev, presumably to demonstrate that his decision to withdraw the missiles was not a needless concession, acknowledged that he took that decisive step only when urgent word reached him that an American attack on Cuba appeared imminent.

Far from paralyzing the "imperialists" by giving them, in Khrushchev's words, "a more realistic idea of the danger of thermonuclear war," the discovery of Soviet strategic missiles in Cuba provoked a United States naval quarantine, a rapid buildup of army and tactical air forces in the southeastern part of the country, and a world-wide alert of the Strategic Air Command. Thus it would seem that the deployment of Soviet strategic weapons in Cuba did not succeed, as Khrushchev said he had expected, "in bringing the aggressors to their senses." In his words:

In the morning of October 27 we received information from our Cuban comrades *and from other sources* which directly stated that this [U.S.] attack would be carried out within the next two or three days. We regarded the telegrams received as a signal of *utmost alarm*, and this alarm was justified. Immediate action was required in order to prevent an attack against Cuba and preserve peace.[7]

The action, of course, was Khrushchev's proposal to the President to withdraw from Cuba all the weapons "which you regard as offensive" in exchange for cessation of the quarantine and a pledge by the President not to invade Cuba. It must have appeared to Khrushchev, then, that the United States had been prepared to attack Cuba, not only despite the presence of Soviet weapons, but precisely because of it, since evidently only by agreeing to withdraw the weapons did Khrushchev believe he could secure from the President assurances that the United States would not attack.

The strange logic of Khrushchev's face-saving explanation of Soviet motives and behavior does not in itself disprove his contention that Soviet missiles were deployed in Cuba solely to deter an attack by

---

[7] *Pravda,* December 13, 1962 (italics added). The "other sources" presumably included "Mr. X," the head of Soviet intelligence in the United States, who acted as Khrushchev's private and unofficial agent for communicating (through John Scali, ABC correspondent) with high United States officials during the crisis (Roger Hilsman, "The Cuban Crisis: How Close We Were to War," *Look,* August 25, 1964, pp. 17–21).

the United States; if deterrence of an attack on Cuba was the sole Soviet objective, however, the plan backfired: the Soviet weapons provoked rather than deterred strong American action.

Khrushchev's account of Soviet objectives is vulnerable on another ground—the appropriateness of the weapons deployed in Cuba for the ostensible purpose of deterring an American attack on that country. Surely, a threat to destroy several southeastern cities of the United States, or Miami alone, *if credible*, would have been adequate to deter such an attack. For this, tactical missiles with a range of several hundred miles would have sufficed. It could have been claimed that such weapons were designed to strike at airfields and marshaling and embarkation points in the Florida area from which a United States invasion might be mounted. Perhaps by employing a high-lofting technique, the MRBM's that were deployed and the IRBM's that were being prepared could have been used to strike close-in targets, but such long-range missiles are not designed for that purpose. Whatever the deployment of missiles with ranges in excess of several hundred miles may have added to deterrence of an attack was more than outweighed by the additional provocation they offered.

Had the Soviet missiles remained in Cuba, declarations regarding the control arrangements established for them would have been important indicators of the Soviet Union's objectives. To maximize the effectiveness of Soviet missiles deployed in Cuba as a deterrent against an American attack on Cuba and to reduce the risk that their employment, in the event of an attack, would bring down United States nuclear retaliation upon the U.S.S.R., it might have been desirable for Khrushchev to have the American government believe that the Soviet missiles were at Castro's disposal and under his control. In the United States Castro had gained a reputation for impulsive, irresponsible behavior. Whether authentic or not, the post-crisis remarks attributed to Ernesto Guevara, that the Cubans were prepared, in the event of an American attack, to strike "the very heart of the United States, including New York," [8] conformed to the image of the Cuban leadership that was widely held in the United States. Once an operational missile capability was established in Cuba, such beliefs on the part of Americans might have lent substantial deterrent value to the missiles deployed there.

---

[8] According to Theodore Draper, these remarks were reportedly made by Guevara in an interview with a London *Daily Worker* correspondent but did not appear in the version published on December 4, 1962 ("Castro and Communism," *Reporter*, January 17, 1963, p. 44).

On the other hand, to bring Cuba-based missiles to bear in support of Soviet interests in confrontations with the United States (for example, in Berlin), the Americans would have to believe that the missiles were at the disposal of the Soviet leaders. Until such time as the Soviet Union might wish to bring the missiles to bear for this purpose, however, its leaders would probably prefer to keep the question of control in an ambiguous state.

Thus, it seems obvious that a premature explicit announcement on control would have obliged Khrushchev to accept certain political liabilities. Whether he proclaimed Soviet or Cuban control over the missiles, Khrushchev would have had to acknowledge that the Soviet Union was engaging in a military practice that he had repeatedly denounced. A claim to Soviet control implied a strategic Soviet base on foreign territory; an announcement of Cuban control implied proliferation of nuclear strategic weapons.

On October 22, 1962, President Kennedy impaled Khrushchev on one of the horns of this dilemma by unilaterally resolving the ambiguity: "It shall be the policy of this nation to regard any nuclear missile launched from Cuba against any nation in the Western Hemisphere as an attack by the Soviet Union on the United States requiring a full retaliatory response upon the Soviet Union." [9] Initially, the Soviet Union attempted to evade the issue by refusing to acknowledge that it had emplaced strategic weapons in Cuba, though it affirmed in its first official statement on the crisis (October 23) that Cuba alone had the right to decide what kinds of weapons were appropriate for the defense of Cuba.[10] The Soviet denial that the military equipment provided to Cuba included strategic weapons reflected concern that the United States government might feel impelled to strike quickly to prevent operational missiles from falling into Castro's hands. Moscow therefore offered the following oblique reassurance: "Nuclear weapons, which have been created by the Soviet people and which are in the hands of the people, will never be used for the purpose of aggression." [11]

On the same day, Khrushchev made this reassurance explicit during

---

[9] *New York Times,* October 23, 1962. The phrase "full retaliatory response upon the Soviet Union" may have implied to the Soviet leaders not only that the United States would not treat the Soviet Union as a sanctuary area if the Cuba-based missiles were fired but that it did not intend to restrict itself to a limited strategic response ("tit for tat" retaliation).

[10] *Pravda,* October 24, 1962.

[11] *Ibid.*

a three-hour private conversation in Moscow with the vice-president of Westinghouse Electric, William E. Knox, through whom he presumably wished to communicate informally with the United States government. According to Knox, Khrushchev acknowledged that Soviet ballistic missiles had been furnished to Cuba but insisted they were completely controlled by Soviet officers. ". . . The Cubans were very volatile people, Mr. Khrushchev said, and all of the sophisticated hardware furnished for their defense was entirely under the control of Soviet officers; it would be used only in the event that Cuba was attacked, and it would never be fired except on his orders as Commander in Chief of all of the Soviet Union." [12]

Finally, in his October 27 letter to President Kennedy, the first Khrushchev letter published during the crisis, the Soviet Premier informed the President that "the weapons in Cuba that you have mentioned and which you say alarm you are in the hands of Soviet officers. . . . Therefore, any accidental use of them whatsoever to the detriment of the United States is excluded." [13]

Despite the advantages to be gained from ambiguity regarding control of the missiles in Cuba, Khrushchev evidently felt compelled to reassure the President explicitly that Castro could not order the missiles to be fired and that there was therefore no need for the United States to make an immediate attack before the missiles became operational in order to forestall a possible irrational act by the "volatile" Cubans.[14] Whatever value the Soviet weapons may have been intended to have as a deterrent of a local United States attack on Cuba was seriously diminished by this reassurance.

It is questionable, however, whether deterrence of a local United States attack on Cuba was ever regarded by the Soviet leaders as more than a subsidiary and derivative effect of a venture intended primarily to serve other ends. Certainly, the size and character of the intended deployment indicate that it was meant to achieve some broader purpose. As we have said, the American cities within the range of the MRBM's (including the capital) would have been a sufficient hostage to deter an attack on Cuba by the United States. The

---

[12] *New York Times*, November 18, 1962.

[13] *Pravda*, October 28, 1962. The implication is that, if the weapons had been under Cuban control, the possibility that they might be "accidentally used" could not be excluded.

[14] This did not occur for all MRBM systems until October 28; the IRBM's never achieved operational status, nor, apparently, did the IL-28 bombers (*Hearings on Department of Defense Appropriations for 1964*, pp. 12, 16).

introduction of IRBM's can therefore most reasonably be explained as providing a capability against strategic-bomber and missile-base targets, which could not be reached by the MRBM's.

Some circumstantial evidence from the Cuban side tends to support this interpretation. Castro has been quoted by a friendly source, the correspondent for *Le Monde*, Claude Julien, as having said that the Cuban leaders had considered among themselves the possibility of requesting that the U.S.S.R. furnish Cuba with missiles, but had not come to any decision when Moscow proposed to emplace them:

They explained to us that in accepting them we would be reinforcing the socialist camp the world over, and because we had received important aid from the socialist camp we estimated that we could not decline. That is why we accepted them. It was not in order to assure our own defense, but first of all to reinforce socialism on the international scale. Such is the truth even if other explanations are furnished elsewhere.[15]

Subsequently, Castro gave conflicting accounts of the origin of the proposal to emplace strategic missiles in Cuba, but the above account has the ring of truth.[16] Moreover, in March, 1965, after the ouster of Khrushchev, he reverted to the original position he had taken in the Julien interview:

We speak in the name of the people who, for the sake of strengthening the revolutionary movement, for the sake of strengthening the socialist camp . . . without hesitation accepted the risk of thermonuclear war, the

---

[15] *Le Monde*, March 22, 1963.

[16] *Prensa Latina* (Havana), March 22, 1963. Castro questioned published reports of the interview, denying, for example, that "I expressed myself in an unfriendly way at any time about Soviet Prime Minister Nikita Khrushchev." Castro's general refutation pointedly referred only to the UPI version of *Le Monde*'s article: "I do not believe that Julien, whom we consider a friend of Cuba, can be guilty of untruths like *some* of the statements the UPI attributes to him" (italics added). The March 22 TASS version of Castro's denial omitted both of the statements quoted above.

Castro was subsequently questioned by two other journalists regarding the origin of the plan to deploy Soviet missiles in Cuba. According to Herbert L. Matthews (*Return to Cuba* ["Hispanic American Report Series"; Stanford, Calif.: Stanford University, 1964], p. 16), Castro stated flatly on October 23, 1963, that "the idea of installing the nuclear weapons was his, not the Russians'." However, three weeks later, according to Jean Daniel's account of his interview with the Cuban Premier, Castro appeared to confirm the account given earlier in the Julien interview: "We thought of a proclamation, an alliance, conventional military aid. . . . They [the Russians] reasoned that if conventional military assistance was the extent of their assistance, the United States might not hesitate to instigate an invasion, in which case Russia would retaliate and this would inevitably touch off a world war. . . . Under these circumstances, how could we Cubans refuse to share the risks taken to save us?" (Jean Daniel, "Unofficial Envoy: An Historic Report from Two Capitals," *New Republic*, December 14, 1963, pp. 18–19). Matthews writes that he telephoned Castro after Daniel's account was published and was again told: "We were the ones who put forward the idea of the missiles" (Matthews, *loc. cit.*).

risk of a nuclear attack upon us, when, exercising our full right, which we did not decline, and in complete accord with law, we ·agreed to the emplacement of strategic nuclear rockets in our country . . . and we never had any regrets (*applause*). We not only agreed to the emplacement of these rockets but we also did not agree to their removal (*applause*). And I think this is no secret to anyone.[17]

Of course, the deployment of Soviet missiles in Cuba, to the extent that it strengthened the Soviet position in its "world-wide" confrontation with the United States, would also have added credibility to Soviet strategic threats, including the threat to defend Cuba against United States attack. In fact, the implication of the official Soviet rationale for deploying strategic weapons in Cuba—namely, that the threat posed to the United States by Soviet weapons *based in the U.S.S.R.* lacked sufficient credibility to deter an American attack on "socialist" Cuba—later embarrassed Khrushchev when he was obliged to defend his erratic behavior in the missile crisis.[18]

Before the crisis, Khrushchev's expressions of strategic support for Cuba were framed in notably cautious and equivocal terms: the U.S.S.R.'s capability to defend Cuba with Soviet-based missiles was affirmed, but a commitment to do so was carefully avoided.[19] Cuban leaders, however, consistently interpreted Khrushchev's words as if they represented a firm, though tacit, commitment. For example, as far back as January, 1961, according to Guevara, it was "well known that the Soviet Union and all the socialist states *are ready to go to war* to defend our sovereignty and that *a tacit agreement* has been reached between our peoples." [20]

---

[17] *Pravda*, March 18, 1965.
[18] Khrushchev handled this question gingerly in defending his Cuban policy against Chinese and Albanian criticism in his speech at the Congress of the East German Communist Party in Berlin on January 16, 1963: "One may object that, under the influence of the most unrestrained incitement, the U.S. imperialists will not keep their promise and will again turn their arms against Cuba. But the forces which protected Cuba now exist and are *growing in strength every day*. It does not matter where the rockets are located, in Cuba, or elsewhere. They can be used with equal success against any particular aggression" (*Pravda*, January 17, 1963; italics added). The implicit question is: If so, why were Soviet missiles deployed in Cuba in the first place? And the implicit answer: Soviet-based strategic power was not then great enough to deter a United States attack, but it was "growing in strength every day" and soon would be (or would appear to be).
[19] In July, 1960, Khrushchev said that "figuratively speaking, in case of need, Soviet artillerymen can support the Cuban people with their rocket fire . . ." (*Pravda*, July 9, 1960). The conditional form of this threat ("can," not "will," support was retained in the Soviet government's statement on Cuba on September 11, 1962, which asserted that the U.S.S.R. "has the capability from its own territory to render assistance to any peace-loving state" (*Pravda*, September 11, 1962).
[20] *Obra revolucionaria*, January 25, 1961, quoted by Draper, *op. cit.*, p. 39 (italics added).

It may be assumed that the Cuban leaders had pressed Khrushchev for an explicit and unequivocal commitment to defend Cuba with Soviet-based weapons in the event of an attack by the United States. It was presumably to secure such a commitment, which the Soviet Union was evidently reluctant to give, that Castro in effect volunteered Cuba for membership in the "socialist camp" in 1961. Given a choice between an explicit and unequivocal Soviet guarantee, on the one hand, and the stationing of Soviet strategic weapons on Cuban soil, on the other, Castro might well have preferred the former, under certain circumstances. To the extent that Castro (1) could have had confidence that the Soviet Union would honor such a commitment, or (2) believed that it would be credited to some serious extent in the United States, or (3) believed that a United States attack was unlikely in any case, he might not have thought it necessary to request the Soviet Union to establish strategic missile bases in Cuba and might have been wary of the political consequences of such a move throughout Latin America and in the United States.

The reasons for not requesting Soviet missiles in Cuba did not prevent Castro from accepting the missiles when the Soviet Union proposed to deploy them there. Castro probably believed the likelihood of an American attack was not negligible. He may have agreed to the Soviet proposal not only because of his general dependence on the Soviet Union, but also because the apparent desperation of the Soviet leaders to reinforce their world-wide position vis-à-vis the United States had led him to regard the already equivocal Soviet pledges to defend Cuba with Soviet-based weapons as seriously compromised.[21] In brief, he may have felt compelled to accept Soviet missiles under Soviet control as the only means available to deter a United States attack on Cuba.

How could the emplacement of strategic weapons in Cuba reinforce the world-wide position of the Soviet Union? The deployment of strategic weapons in Cuba may have recommended itself to the Soviet leaders as a "quick fix" measure to achieve a substantial improvement in Soviet strike capabilities against the United States. A large increase in the programmed Soviet-based ICBM forces or

---

[21] In the immediate aftermath of the crisis, the positions prior to the crisis of the Soviet Union and Cuba on the firmness of Soviet pledges to defend Cuba were sharply reversed. Whereas the Soviet leaders, presumably to placate Castro, offered increasingly strong pledges to defend Cuba, Cuban leaders ignored them and vowed to resist any United States attack with their own resources. Later, however, as Soviet-Cuban relations recovered from the estrangement of the fall of 1962, Cuban leaders began to welcome Soviet pledges with great public enthusiasm.

missile-launching nuclear submarines would have provided the Soviet leaders with a military capability far more effective for second-strike purposes than the emplacement of highly vulnerable MRBM's, IRBM's, and light bombers in Cuba; but such an expansion of intercontinental delivery means could be achieved only gradually and at far greater cost. The Cuban deployment may have been undertaken not as a substitute for such a buildup but as a stopgap measure pending its completion.

Certainly, the deployment of limited numbers of MRBM's and IRBM's in Cuba would not have solved the Soviet Union's strategic problem. The evident deficiencies of such a force have led some observers to conclude that military considerations were of little importance in the Soviet decision. It is true that the missile sites were soft, very close to the United States, and after detection, under close and constant surveillance. Presumably, they would have been highly vulnerable to a United States first strike, even with conventional bombs. As a Soviet first-strike force, the missiles, deployed or being readied in Cuba in October, 1962, were in themselves too small a force to destroy the United States strategic nuclear strike force. Even together with the larger long-range strategic force based in the U.S.S.R., they would have been inadequate for this purpose in the fall of 1962. Moreover, there would have been a problem, though perhaps not an insurmountable one, of co-ordinating salvos from close-in and distant bases so as to avoid a ragged attack.

On the other hand, the installation of Soviet strategic missiles in Cuba would have complicated a United States first strike; and it would have substantially improved Soviet capabilities to launch a pre-emptive attack. It will be recalled that Defense Minister Malinovsky had stated at the Twenty-second Congress of the CPSU in October, 1961, and several times thereafter that "the most important, the main, and the first-priority task" of the Soviet armed forces was to be prepared to deal a "timely blow" in order to "frustrate the aggressive designs" of a would-be attacker.[22] Politically, an improved Soviet capability to pre-empt might have reduced the credibility of American threats to respond with strategic weapons to local Soviet aggression, even in Europe. As to the first-strike potential of Cuba-based Soviet missiles, they could have brought a substantial portion of United States nuclear striking power under attack, essentially without warning. Moreover, there is no assurance that the buildup would have

---

[22] See p. 93.

stopped with the sites already completed or under construction when the Soviets were compelled to abandon the operation.

Whatever their strategic shortcomings, the additional capabilities provided the Soviet leaders by Cuba-based missiles were not insignificant. It is difficult to conceive of any other measure that promised to produce so large an improvement in the Soviet strategic position as quickly or as cheaply. That the Cuban missile deployment would not in itself have provided the Soviet Union with a retaliation-proof first-strike capability against the United States is hardly a reason for dismissing it as of limited strategic importance, as some observers have attempted to do. As the President subsequently said, the Soviet leaders tried materially to change the balance of power. Certainly, the deployment of Soviet missiles in Cuba, in his words, "would have *politically* changed the balance of power; it would have appeared to [change it] and appearances contribute to reality." [23] The world-wide position of the Soviet Union that needed to be reinforced in the fall of 1962 was not only its strategic position vis-à-vis the United States but also its bargaining position on a range of political issues whose outcomes would be importantly affected by the strategic imbalance in favor of the United States.

It had become evident at least as early as the second half of 1961 that the forward momentum of the Soviet Union in international affairs had largely exhausted itself without yielding the gains that the Soviet leaders had expected and the West had feared since the mid-1950's. The West's fears had been fed by mounting evidence of the growing military, scientific, technological, and economic power of the Soviet Union. Some of this evidence was real enough, but much of it, particularly in the realm of strategic power, was illusory. Yet this very realm was central in the conduct of the cold war. The effects of the striking Soviet achievements in space exploration were amplified, sometimes out of all proportion to their intrinsic political and military worth, by their presumed bearing on the strategic balance. With the discovery in 1961 that the missile gap had all along favored the West rather than the Soviet Union, there was a perceptible change in the world political climate. Western self-confidence was restored, and Soviet anxieties were evidently intensified.

Moreover, confident Soviet expectations of dividends from military and economic aid to the underdeveloped countries had failed to materialize. Western European prosperity had reached a new peak,

---

[23] *Washington Post*, December 18, 1962 (italics added).

and despite De Gaulle's intransigence the prospects for growing European economic and political unity must have looked distressingly good to Moscow. At the same time, the unity of the Communist camp was being shattered by the escalating conflict between its two most powerful members. Indeed, the Chinese Communist attack on Khrushchev centered precisely on the unfavorable trend in the cold war, which the Chinese attributed to Khrushchev's faulty and erratic leadership.

Finally, there was the long-smoldering, still unresolved problem of Berlin. That the Cuban missile deployment and Khrushchev's Berlin strategy were linked in some way was borne out to some extent by the Soviet government's statement of September 11, 1962, in which the U.S.S.R. acknowledged that it was providing military assistance—though of a strictly defensive type—to Cuba, warned that a United States attack on Cuba might unleash a thermonuclear war, but at the same time declared a moratorium on new moves in Berlin until after the United States congressional elections.[24] Khrushchev may have hoped to discourage any new American action against Cuba until after the elections (that is, until after the MRBM's, at least, became operational) by offering in return to desist from fomenting a new crisis in Berlin. After establishing a strategic base in Cuba, he may have hoped to use this new leverage to press for a favorable settlement in Berlin.

Success in the Cuban venture would have contributed greatly to a future political offensive against Berlin. The presence of a large operational missile force in Cuba was sure to become known, thus satisfying the need to demonstrate a strategic capability against the United States that would not, by the very act of disclosure, be deprived of military significance. Popular opinion in the United States would be considerably more impressed, and perhaps in some measure intimidated, by an acknowledged missile capability against American cities based in Cuba than by the previous hypothetical capability based thousands of miles away in the U.S.S.R. If Soviet deployment of missiles in Cuba was preliminary to a renewed offensive against Berlin, by frustrating the first, the United States prevented the second.

The link between Berlin and Cuba is clearly direct and undeniable; yet there are crucial differences between the two crises. The Berlin offensive inevitably hinged on a confrontation with the Western

---

[24] *Pravda*, September 11, 1962.

powers; the Cuban offensive required that every effort be made to avoid a confrontation with the United States. The objective in the Berlin offensive was to inflict a crushing defeat on the West, a defeat that could be decisive in the cold war; the objective of the Cuban offensive, although also far-reaching, was largely to set the stage for future engagements. Finally, the success of the Berlin offensive depended on making false strategic claims that would be credible to the West; the Cuban offensive was based on actual capabilities and was designed to change the strategic balance in reality. Such Soviet deception as was practiced in the Cuban offensive took the opposite form than previously—a denial that the U.S.S.R. was in the act of acquiring a new strategic capability.

The true relation of the Berlin problem to the Cuban crisis was obscured for many at the time of the crisis and afterward. There were widespread fears as the confrontation over the Soviet missiles in Cuba developed that the U.S.S.R. might counter United States pressure for their removal by renewed pressure to force the Western powers out of Berlin. American strategic superiority, however, made it too risky for the Soviet Union to use or even threaten to use Berlin as a trump card. The Soviet leaders apparently feared that a threatening Soviet move against that city, particularly in the midst of a crisis in the Caribbean, would be dangerously provocative. Emphasizing that the Cuban crisis "had brought the world one step, perhaps only half a step, from an abyss," Foreign Minister Gromyko told the Supreme Soviet in December, 1962: "This [Cuban] crisis . . . made many people think how the whole matter might have developed if yet another crisis in Central Europe had been added to the critical events around Cuba." [25] Indeed, Soviet quiescence in Berlin during and immediately after the Cuban missile crisis demonstrated the severe limitations of even overwhelming local military superiority in the hands of a strategically inferior power when the issue at stake is of central, not peripheral, importance to the opponent. [26]

---

[25] *Pravda*, December 14, 1962.

[26] For an illuminating discussion of this point and its relevance for decisions regarding the extent to which NATO should rely on conventional weapons for the tactical defense of Europe, see Bernard Brodie, "What Price Conventional Capabilities in Europe?" *Reporter*, May 23, 1963, pp. 25–33.

TWELVE

THE CUBAN MISSILE CRISIS
AND ITS AFTERMATH

THE SOVIET EFFORT to deploy strategic missiles in Cuba was an application of the strategy of bluff and deception under new conditions, not an abandonment of that strategy. As already noted, it was designed to compensate for the increasing failure of the missile deception in which the U.S.S.R. had been engaged since 1957. Now in 1962, along with the hypothetical and concealed ICBM capability in the U.S.S.R., a visible IRBM and MRBM capability was to be created in Cuba. As in previous political offensives, the Soviet leaders sought to make large gains but were prepared to forego them whenever persistence seemed to increase the danger of war significantly.

Soviet calculations throughout the Cuban missile crisis can be reconstructed with some degree of confidence, because the confrontation with the United States was so open. For this reason, and because the crisis over Cuba, together with that over Berlin, provided a major test of these calculations, it will be useful to examine them in considerable detail and to show how they stood the test of battle in a political encounter almost without parallel in history.

It may seem to some that the risk assumed by the U.S.S.R. in attempting to deploy missiles in Cuba is incompatible with our contention that the Soviet leaders were unwilling to take actions that significantly increased the risk of nuclear war. Certainly, this contention would be hard to support if Khrushchev had consciously and deliberately accepted the possibility that his action in Cuba might directly provoke a thermonuclear attack on the Soviet Union. But although the Soviet leaders evidently accepted unusually high military and political risks in embarking on the Cuban venture, they almost certainly did not believe that an immediate United States thermonuclear response against the Soviet Union was one of them. In view of the adverse strategic balance, which the rockets in Cuba were to help rectify, the Soviet leaders would hardly have undertaken their venture unless they had been virtually certain that the United States would not respond by attacking the U.S.S.R. Whatever errors they made in anticipating the character and intensity of the response of the United States, they were doubtless correct in excluding nuclear attack. A very crucial upper limit on the risks they did accept was thus established. No doubt, as the crisis unfolded, the Soviet leaders became concerned that a real danger of nuclear war might arise. In fact, the sudden withdrawal of their missiles apparently resulted from a decision to end the crisis quickly before it became necessary to face a serious risk of nuclear war in order to avoid even greater losses. Nevertheless, the Soviet leaders did run greater risks in the Cuban venture than in Berlin.

In Berlin, the Soviet leaders were unwilling to press ahead because the United States was insufficiently intimidated. In Cuba, they hoped to acquire additional means of intimidation and thereby lessen the likelihood of a dangerous United States response to measures the U.S.S.R. might take against Berlin. Although the risks involved in the Cuban venture were greater than those previously assumed, they were substantially smaller than the risks of directly implementing the measures that had been threatened against Berlin from 1958 to 1962. That is to say, the risks of the Cuban venture were intermediate between those assumed by the U.S.S.R. in its cautious offensive against Berlin from 1958 to 1962 and those it would have assumed had it acted boldly against Berlin thereafter. If the Cuban venture had succeeded, the risk of taking action against Berlin would have been lessened, although such action would probably still have exceeded the risk of deploying missiles in Cuba.

Confidence that it would not directly provoke nuclear war was a prerequisite for the Cuban missile venture, but it could not be a sufficient condition for success. Aside from their belief that the United States would not respond by striking the Soviet Union, what were the calculations that led the Soviet leaders to believe their venture could succeed? Undoubtedly, their understanding of the Cuban policy of the United States was a major factor in their decision. The ill-fated Bay of Pigs invasion of April, 1961, demonstrated American hostility toward Castro, but it may also have convinced Soviet leaders that American reluctance to engage its own forces directly in military action against Cuba was so great that even the emplacement of Soviet strategic weapons on the island would be opposed by means that fell short of the use of armed force.[1] The

---

[1] At the same time, the fact that the United States had attempted, even though ineffectually, to overthrow Castro by using Cuban exile proxies both increased Castro's desire for Soviet military assistance and made such assistance seem legitimate to many third countries.

United States government's apparent acceptance of increasingly open Soviet involvement in Cuban affairs after the Bay of Pigs incident, including the shipment of arms and military technicians, may have further encouraged a belief among the Soviet leaders that the United States would intervene militarily only in response to the actual use of Cuba-based weapons against a state in the Western Hemisphere.

The Soviet arms buildup in Cuba was conducted in phases: first, basic conventional weapons, second, sophisticated weapon systems of a tactical type, and finally, advanced SA-2 surface-to-air missiles, which had been at least partially deployed before strategic missiles were introduced into the island in September, 1962. The American reaction to the arrival of each new type of weapon doubtless was observed closely in Moscow. The problem of interpretation became increasingly difficult, however, because as the character of the weapons shipped to Cuba grew more complex their delivery and deployment became increasingly covert. There was probably uncertainty as to whether the United States government was tacitly accepting the presence of new Soviet weapons or had not yet learned of their arrival. If there was uncertainty, the Soviet leaders evidently resolved it by assuming American forbearance.

By the spring of 1962 the Soviet Union had supplied the Cuban army with what Secretary McNamara has described as "great quantities" of conventional weapons and supplies, from pistols and rifles to heavy artillery and medium tanks. In addition, MIG-15, -17, and -19 aircraft and helicopters had been provided to the Cuban air force, and motor torpedo boats and coastal patrol vessels of the Kronstadt class had been delivered to the Cuban navy.[2] Arrival of these weapons was known to the United States government and was a matter of public record. The President and other administration spokesmen spoke of these weapons as "defensive" and indicated that they posed no threat to the security of the United States or of other Western Hemisphere countries.

In late July and early August, an unusual number of Soviet ships brought cargo and passengers to Cuban ports. There were reports that Soviet personnel who accompanied the equipment had unloaded it and that Cubans had been denied access to the dock area. By mid-

---

[2] *Department of Defense Appropriations for 1964*, Hearings before a Subcommittee of the House of Representatives Committee on Appropriations, 88th Cong., 1st sess., 1963, Part I, p. 2 (hereinafter cited as *Hearings on Department of Defense Appropriations for 1964*).

August, Secretary McNamara has testified, analysis of these reports strongly suggested the possibility that the Soviet Union was introducing surface-to-air missile systems in Cuba. A high altitude reconnaissance mission flown on August 29 positively identified two SA-2 surface-to-air missile sites and tentatively identified six others. Later a short-range, coastal-defense, cruise-missile installation was also identified.[3] Interpretation of these photographs was not yet available when the President, at his August 29 press conference, dealt with Senator Capehart's call for a United States invasion of Cuba. The President stated that he opposed an invasion of Cuba "at this time" and that it could "lead to very serious consequences for many people." He went on to say there was as yet no evidence of surface-to-air missiles or Soviet troops in Cuba, although Soviet military technicians might be there.[4]

On September 3, Moscow and Havana released the text of a joint communiqué signed in Moscow at the conclusion of the visit of Ernesto Guevara and Emilio Aragones. In it the U.S.S.R. acknowledged that, at the request of the Cuban government, it was sending "armaments" and technical specialists to train Cuban servicemen.[5]

On the following day, the White House issued a special presidential statement on Cuba: Information reaching the government in the previous four days had established the presence in Cuba of a number of anti-aircraft defensive missiles with a slant range of twenty-five miles, several Soviet-made motor torpedo boats equipped with fifteen-mile-range guided missiles, and approximately thirty-five hundred Soviet military technicians, some still en route. As the President stated, however, there was no evidence of any organized combat force in Cuba from any Soviet bloc country; of military bases provided to the U.S.S.R.; "of the presence of offensive ground-to-ground missiles; or of other significant offensive capability either in Cuban hands or under Soviet direction and guidance." The President warned: "Were it to be otherwise, the gravest issues would arise."[6]

On September 7, the President requested from Congress power to call up one hundred fifty thousand reservists without having to declare a national emergency, in order "to permit prompt and effective responses, as necessary, to challenges which may be pre-

---

[3] *Ibid.*, p. 3.
[4] *New York Times*, August 30, 1962.
[5] *Pravda*, September 3, 1962.
[6] *New York Times*, September 5, 1962.

sented in any part of the free world."[7] Four days later, ostensibly in response to this presidential request, the Soviet government authorized TASS to issue a statement on Soviet-Cuban policy in which the United States was warned that an attack on Cuba would be "the start of the unleashing of war." Since the statement alluded to "reactionary" pressure in the United States for "an attack on Soviet ships carrying necessary goods and foodstuffs to the Cuban people," it may have been intended to deter American interference with this shipping. Strategic missiles and their associated equipment were probably still in transit on the high seas on September 11, since it is now estimated that this equipment first began arriving in Cuba about September 8.[8] The Soviet government acknowledged that armaments and military equipment were among the goods being shipped to Cuba by the U.S.S.R. and asserted that this was "a purely internal affair of the states sending these cargoes and those which buy and receive them." But the statement went on to offer an ambiguous assurance:

The arms and military equipment sent to Cuba are intended solely for defensive purposes. The President of the U.S.A. and the American military, like the military of any country, know what means of defense are. How can these menace the United States of America?[9]

This assurance was amplified in a manner clearly meant to suggest that the Soviet Union did not intend to deploy strategic nuclear weapons on Cuban soil:

The Government of the Soviet Union has also authorized TASS to state that there is no need for the Soviet Union to set up in any other country—Cuba, for instance—the weapons it has for repelling aggression, for a retaliatory blow. The explosive power of our nuclear weapons is so great and the Soviet Union has such powerful missiles for delivering these nuclear warheads that there is no need to seek sites for them somewhere beyond the boundaries of the Soviet Union. We have said and we repeat that if war is unleashed, if the aggressor attacks one or another state and this state asks for help, the Soviet Union has the capability to extend help from its own territory to any peace-loving state, and not only to Cuba.

At his September 13 press conference the President repeated that the Soviet shipments to Cuba did not constitute a serious threat to

---

[7] *New York Times*, September 8, 1962. There was no reference to Cuba or to any other trouble spot in the presidential message accompanying the proposed measures. The reference to "challenges . . . in any part of the free world" might have been taken to suggest West Berlin rather than Cuba.

[8] *Hearings on Department of Defense Appropriations for 1964*, p. 3.

[9] *Izvestiia*, September 12, 1962.

any part of the Western Hemisphere and that unilateral United States military intervention could not "currently either be required or justified." [10] But he also reiterated his previous warning that "if the Communist build-up in Cuba were to endanger or interfere with our security in any way," or "if Cuba should become an offensive military base of significant capacity for the Soviet Union, then this country will do whatever must be done to protect its own security and that of its allies." Further, the President now specifically stated that United States action would not have to await an overt act but would occur "if Cuba should possess a capacity to carry out offensive actions against the United States."

In his statements of September 4 and 13, then, the President had drawn a clear line between weapons of the type that had already been announced as present in Cuba, which the United States was presumably willing to tolerate, and weapons with an offensive capacity, specifically ground-to-ground missiles, whose presence in Cuba he declared was unacceptable to the United States government. Whatever the Soviet leaders may have thought of the general statements previously made by American leaders about "offensive" and "defensive" weapons in Cuba, the President's early and middle September statements left them no margin of doubt, for he explicitly placed ground-to-ground missiles in the "offensive," and hence unacceptable, category.

The President's first explicit statement on ground-to-ground missiles appeared several days before the earliest estimated date—around September 8—that the first Soviet missiles and associated equipment, clandestinely transported in the holds of large-hatch Soviet ships, could have reached Cuban ports.[11] His second statement, which warned that the mere presence of such weapons, even without any overt act, would require the United States government to act, was made before the earliest estimated date—between September 15 and 20—for the initiation of site construction and deployment activity.[12] Thus, shortly before the plan to emplace strategic missiles in Cuba entered its final and decisive phases, the Soviet leaders had two opportunities to reconsider their action in the light of the commitment of the United States to oppose it. The President's warnings may have raised anxiety in Moscow, but they clearly did not deter the Soviet leaders.

---

[10] *New York Times,* September 14, 1962.
[11] *Hearings on Department of Defense Appropriations for 1964,* p. 25.
[12] *Ibid.*

Although the Soviet leaders no doubt regarded the President's statements as a commitment by the United States government to oppose the emplacement of Soviet strategic weapons in Cuba, they may have believed that, at least initially, the United States would restrict itself to diplomatic means. They may further have relied on their ability to make the missiles operational quickly enough to ensure the venture's success. The deployment was carried out with a rapidity that the United States intelligence community found "remarkable." [13] Had the Soviets succeeded in attaining an operational capability clandestinely and then confronting the United States with a *fait accompli*, as they evidently meant to do, we may wonder what the outcome might have been.[14] Speaking of the week-long deliberations that preceded the President's crucial decision in October, Theodore C. Sorensen, special counsel to the President, has said that the pressure of time was felt keenly:

For all of us knew that, once the missile sites under construction became operational and capable of responding to any apparent threat with a nuclear volley, the President's options would be drastically changed.[15]

The Soviet leaders may not have relied entirely on avoiding detection until they had completed the missile deployment. Given their difficulties in maintaining complete secrecy and their apparent willingness to do without feasible measures of concealment in order to achieve greater speed, they could hardly have excluded the possibility that some evidence of the deployment would be available to the United States government before it was completed. Allegations that Soviet strategic missiles were present in Cuba, sometimes attributed to Cuban refugees, sometimes even to unnamed members of the intelligence community, had been publicized in the United States even before the first shipment of these weapons is believed to have arrived in Cuba. As it turned out, the airing of these charges may have assisted the Soviet operation, since the administration felt obliged to deny the allegations publicly and to insist repeatedly that the Soviet

---

[13] *Hearings on Department of Defense Appropriations for 1964*, p. 6.

[14] Actually, if the United States would have adopted the same policy for dealing with the situation, the outcome need not have been different even if the Soviet missiles had been operational at the time of their detection. The missile sites would still have been highly vulnerable to attack, and Soviet reluctance to initiate a United States–Soviet nuclear exchange would presumably still have been sufficiently great to make the threat of an attack on Cuban bases highly credible. However, sufficient doubt might have arisen on the United States side to cause the adoption of a different policy in dealing with the crisis.

[15] Sorensen, *Decision-making in the White House: The Olive Branch or the Arrows* (New York: Columbia University Press, 1963), p. 31.

arms buildup in Cuba posed no threat to American security. The Soviet leaders may have calculated, reasonably, that the President and his advisers would subsequently hesitate to withdraw their denials as long as the available evidence remained ambiguous. Moreover, the Soviet leaders may have believed that the administration, on the eve of national elections, would be reluctant to expose what the Soviet Union had done, since unfavorable domestic political repercussions might be expected if strategic missiles were known to be in Cuba and no Soviet commitment to withdraw them had been demanded.[16]

The Soviet leaders obviously believed that speed was essential and that deception and diplomacy must be employed in order to minimize the time between the discovery and the completion of the missile bases. They could hardly expect to maintain their deception indefinitely; and in fact, the very objectives they pursued required that the new Soviet military capabilities be revealed at some point after the missiles became operational. In the event of premature detection, the Soviet leaders may have planned to rely on diplomacy to substitute for concealment. They probably thought the likelihood of a strong United States reaction would be reduced as the Soviet strategic missiles became operational and the American people and their government grew accustomed to their presence in Cuba.

Because of their past experiences and their understanding of the American decision-making process, the Soviet leaders may have concluded that the United States government would be unable to assess the situation and devise a policy for dealing with it in the short time available. They may also have supposed that the United States government, before acting, would consult its NATO allies, who could be expected to view the situation with much less urgency than the United States. They may have expected significant opposition from the Organization of American States to any United States proposals for immediate joint action requiring the use of military force. In short, the Soviet leaders had reasons for supposing that there was little likelihood of prompt unilateral action by the United States. They may have expected to reduce the likelihood further by presenting the United States with a *fait accompli*, so that prompt unilateral action to reverse it would appear to require the initiation of violence.

---

[16] By the same token, however, the fact that the elections were but two weeks away when the President bluntly demanded that the Soviet leaders withdraw their strategic weapons from Cuba may have helped persuade Moscow, from that moment, of the President's determination to act quickly and to use whatever means were necessary to compel Soviet compliance.

The President's earlier decisions on Cuba, according to Sorensen in his discussion of decision-making in the White House, limited his choice of an appropriate response to the Soviet strategic deployment:

To refer once again to this nation's response to the presence of Soviet missiles in Cuba, this decision was not wholly developed during the seven days preceding its announcement. President Kennedy, on the morning of the first of those seven days, sent for copies of all his earlier statements on Cuba—on the presence of offensive, as distinguished from defensive, weapons—on threats to our vital interests—and on our armed intervention in that island. These earlier decisions made it *unlikely that he would respond to the October crisis by doing nothing and unlikely that his first step would be an invasion.*

Here, too, the nation's basic commitment to tradition and principle was involved. *An air strike on military installations in Cuba, without any advance warning, was rejected* as a "Pearl Harbor in reverse"—and no one could devise a form of advance warning (other than the quarantine itself, which was a type of warning) that would not leave this nation *vulnerable to either endless discussion and delay* (while work on the missiles went forward) *or to a harsh indictment in the opinion and history of the world.*[17]

The Soviet leaders presumably did not expect the United States government to solve this apparent dilemma quickly enough to prevent them from securing their new positions.

If these were among the calculations of the Soviet leaders, events proved them wrong at almost every point. The collapse of confidence that caused Khrushchev to send President Kennedy a private communication on October 26 in which he reportedly indicated his readiness to yield may have been the culmination of a series of disappointed expectations.[18] Although these expectations were not realized, they were not necessarily unreasonable. Many observers in the West were also surprised—though pleasantly—at the speed and efficiency of the American reaction to the receipt of reliable evidence of Soviet strategic weapons in Cuba.

As we noted previously, the United States had little reason to fear that the Soviet venture in Cuba would be accompanied by an aggressive move against Berlin. Yet such fears did arise, and the Soviet

---

[17] Sorensen, *op. cit.*, pp. 34–35 (italics added).
[18] Apparent inconsistencies and contradictions in communications received in Washington from Moscow and in Soviet press treatment of the crisis (see, for example, n. 6, p. 129.) suggest that Soviet decisions were being made in an environment of considerable uncertainty and perhaps even sharp controversy among political and military elite groups. See Roman Kolkowicz, *Conflicts in Soviet Party-Military Relations: 1962–1963* (RM-3760-PR; Santa Monica, Calif.: The RAND Corporation, 1963).

government may have relied on their deterrent value. If, contrary to Soviet expectations, the United States government was inclined to take military action against Cuba in spite of the missiles installed there, the Soviet leaders may still have hoped that fear of possible Soviet retaliation against Berlin would paralyze American action. In his first letter to President Kennedy eighteen months earlier, during the landings at the Bay of Pigs, Khrushchev obliquely invoked the threat of Soviet retaliation in another part of the world if the United States intervened in Cuba:

We are sincerely interested in a relaxation of international tension, but if others choose to aggravate it, we shall reply in full measure. And in general, it is hardly possible to handle matters in such a way as to settle the situation and put the fire out in one area while kindling a new conflagration in another area.[19]

Abundant evidence was available to the Soviet leaders that United States policy on Cuba might be critically influenced by concern over West Berlin. President Kennedy, for example, in his press conference of August 29, 1962, had directly linked the need for American restraint toward Cuba with American obligations in West Berlin:

The U.S. has obligations all around the world, including West Berlin . . . and therefore I think that in considering what appropriate action we should take we have to consider the totality of our obligations and also the responsibilities we bear in so many different parts of the world.[20]

And on October 22, the President made a special point of warning the Soviet leaders against threatening diversions in Berlin:

This latest Soviet threat or any other threat which is made either independently or in response to our actions this week must and will be met with determination.

Any hostile move anywhere in the world against the safety and freedom of peoples to whom we are committed, including in particular the brave people of West Berlin, will be met by whatever action is needed.[21]

Although, as it turned out, United States fears for Berlin did not inhibit the United States reaction to the deployment of strategic weapons in Cuba, Soviet expectations of American paralysis had not been unreasonable.

Why did Khrushchev change course so precipitately and withdraw his strategic missiles and bombers from Cuba? Some reasons have been adduced implicitly in the preceding discussion of Soviet calcula-

[19] *Pravda*, April 19, 1961. The reference at that time was presumably to Laos.
[20] *New York Times*, August 30, 1962.
[21] *New York Times*, October 23, 1962.

tions prior to the crisis. It remains to make these points explicit and to amplify them.

1. The Soviet leaders had evidently hoped to present the United States with a *fait accompli* in Cuba (like the hastily erected Berlin wall in August, 1961). As it turned out, however, the Soviet deployment was not complete when the President instituted the quarantine and demanded the withdrawal of Soviet strategic weapons.

2. By effectively preserving the secrecy of its initial deliberations in the crisis, the United States government itself was able on October 22 to present the Soviet Union with its own *fait accompli*: the quarantine.[22]

3. The United States response, as set forth by the President on October 22, apparently confounded the Soviet leaders. By imposing a quarantine on strategic arms shipments to Cuba as the first in a series of measures designed not only to prevent a further buildup but to secure the removal of weapons already on the island—the other measures remained deliberately unspecified—the United States shifted to the Soviet Union the immediate burden of deciding whether or not to resort to violence. The quarantine was something less than the direct application of violence but far more than a mere protest or verbal threat. The United States Navy placed itself physically between Cuba and the Soviet ships bound for Cuban ports. Technically, had Khrushchev chosen to defy the quarantine, it might still have been necessary for the United States to fire the first shot, though other means of preventing Soviet penetration might have been employed. But once the quarantine was effectively established—and this was done quickly—the decision whether to risk a military confrontation was up to Khrushchev.

In dealing with the quarantine, the Soviet leaders had essentially three choices, all of them unpleasant and one quite dangerous: (1) they could submit to the quarantine by permitting their vessels to be stopped, searched, and, if contraband was aboard, seized; (2) they could avoid a showdown by keeping their ships out of the quarantine area, which (except for an oil tanker clearly identifiable as such) is what they actually did;[23] or (3) they could precipitate the use of

---

[22] Speaking of the deliberations that led up to the President's October 22 speech, Sorensen has said: "All of us knew that once the Soviets learned of our information and planning, our prospects for surprise and initiative would be greatly lessened" (*op. cit.*, p. 31).

[23] Sixteen out of eighteen dry-cargo Soviet ships en route to Cuba, presumably those containing contraband items, reversed course and returned to the Soviet Union (*Hearings on Department of Defense Appropriations for 1964*, p. 13).

force by violating the quarantine, perhaps with the aid of submarines. The prospects for success of the last alternative were very poor; more important, the Soviet Union had nothing to gain by raising the conflict to higher levels of local violence.

4. United States success in securing prompt and unanimous support for the quarantine from the Organization of American States, and the active participation of naval elements from some Latin American countries, must have dampened Soviet hopes of success in bringing diplomatic pressure to bear for a lifting of the quarantine.[24] At the same time, United States military preparations made a "waiting strategy" increasingly risky.

5. The President's decision to confront the Soviet Union directly while ignoring Castro also compelled the Soviet leaders to determine their course of action quickly. It removed the basis for any Soviet effort to involve the United States in negotiations with the Cuban government, as the Soviet leaders subsequently attempted unsuccessfully to do in connection with the IL-28 bombers. Diplomatically and morally, the United States decision to confront the Soviet Union directly kept the issue of the menacing Soviet weapon deployment in Cuba separate from the broader and more controversial issue of United States–Cuban relations.

6. Finally, among the factors that must have influenced Khrushchev was the speed and evident resolution with which the United States government acted. The prompt and successful implementation of the quarantine, the rapid securance of OAS co-operation and NATO support, the speed of the American conventional military buildup in the southeastern states, and the alert measures taken by American strategic forces around the world must all in varying degrees have impressed the Soviet leaders. There is no doubt that these preparations were carefully noted by Moscow. We can probably take at face value Khrushchev's statement of December 12, 1962, that he had decided to withdraw Soviet missiles from Cuba upon receiving urgent word that a United States attack was imminent. American preparation doubtless had persuaded him that he had to act quickly in order to limit his losses. He was evidently unwilling to gamble further on the possibility that the United States government would ultimately stop short of

---

[24] Sorensen has suggested that if the OAS had failed to provide the vote necessary to authorize a Cuban quarantine, "the Soviets and possibly others might have been emboldened to challenge the legality of our actions, creating confusion and irresolution in the Western camp and giving rise to all kinds of cargo insurance and admiralty questions that this nation would not enjoy untangling" (*op. cit.*, pp. 24–25).

direct military action, for losing such a gamble would have meant accepting far greater local losses than immediate withdrawal entailed and perhaps even risking general war.[25]

It is useless to debate whether conventional military superiority in the Caribbean area or over-all strategic nuclear superiority won the day for the United States. The United States possessed superiority in both types of military force and brought both to bear in the crisis; each reinforced the effectiveness of the other. The immediate military threat confronting the Soviet leaders, of course, was that posed locally to Soviet forces in Cuba and to the Castro regime. But this threat was amplified by American strategic superiority, which made credible the announced determination of the United States government to employ force locally if other measures, such as the quarantine, proved inadequate and to retaliate against the Soviet Union if Cuba-based weapons were launched against targets anywhere in the Western Hemisphere. Extraordinary alert measures taken by the Strategic Air Command, including such conspicuous ones as the dispersal of B-47's to auxiliary civilian airfields, underscored this determination.

Manifest strategic superiority made it impossible for the Soviet strategic forces to deter an American attack on Cuba, so that withdrawal was the only path consistent with the firm policy of avoiding any appreciable rise in the likelihood of general war. The attempt to rectify the strategic balance, so that it would form a basis for future political offensives, had failed.

The Cuban missile crisis of October, 1962, dramatized and sharpened even more the main military-political problem that has confronted the Soviet leaders in acute form since at least the fall of 1961: how to achieve, in the face of manifest United States strategic superiority, a military posture adequate to support Soviet foreign

---

[25] Alluding to the role played by the danger of general war in Khrushchev's decision to withdraw Soviet strategic weapons from Cuba, Secretary McNamara testified before a subcommittee of the House Committee on Appropriations in February, 1963: "We had a force of several hundred thousand men ready to invade Cuba. . . . Had we invaded Cuba, we would have been confronted with the Soviets. . . . Had we been confronted with the Soviets we would have killed thousands of them. . . . Had we killed thousands of them the Soviets would probably have had to respond. . . . They might have had nuclear delivery weapons there [that] might have been operational and they might have been launched. . . . In any event, Khrushchev knew without any question whatever that he faced the full military power of the United States, including its nuclear weapons. . . . We faced that night the possibility of launching nuclear weapons and Khrushchev knew it, and that is the reason, and the only reason, why he withdrew those weapons" (*Hearings on Department of Defense Appropriations for 1964*, p. 31).

policy objectives? As we have argued, the introduction of strategic missiles into Cuba was motivated chiefly by the Soviet leaders' desire to overcome, or at least to narrow, quickly and at comparatively small cost, the existing large margin of United States strategic superiority. The attempt failed precisely because American strategic power, together with overwhelming local military superiority, was quickly and effectively brought to bear in a manner that the Soviet leaders had not expected. Not only did they fail to improve their strategic and related political positions, but their failure revealed more starkly than before the limitations upon Soviet policy imposed by strategic inferiority.

The prospect now facing Khrushchev was bleak. The United States had regained confidence in its strategic superiority and had wrested the initiative from the Soviet Union. Khrushchev found it necessary to cease using strategic threats for offensive purposes, and he scaled down accordingly the objectives of Soviet foreign policy. He pursued a policy of *détente* toward the United States with a single-mindedness of which he had been incapable while he was tempted by the prospects of large gains. In the summer of 1963 he finally accepted the partial nuclear test-ban treaty that the United States and Great Britain had offered him several times previously. This action was facilitated by the acute worsening of Sino-Soviet relations and was in fact intended by the U.S.S.R. to discomfit the CPR leadership. Several lesser agreements also furthered the American-Soviet *détente*, including the establishment of a "hot line," or emergency communication link, between Washington and Moscow and a subsequent agreement that weapons of mass destruction were not to be placed in orbit. The latter accord was embodied in a United Nations resolution approved by acclamation in the General Assembly on October 17.

Soviet policy on Berlin remained quiescent, though occasional incidents on the *Autobahn* served to remind the West that the U.S.S.R. retained the option to renew pressure. Soviet policy toward Western Europe centered on preventing the creation of a NATO multilateral nuclear force, and it was on this issue, above all, that Khrushchev uttered his strongest warning during these years. Even so, his threat was only the possible deployment of Soviet nuclear weapons in the Warsaw Pact countries.

When President Kennedy was assassinated on November 22, 1963, the Soviet leaders seemed genuinely shocked and dismayed. They hastened to impress upon the new President their desire to maintain the *détente*. Khrushchev announced on December 13 that the U.S.S.R. intended to reduce its military budget for the coming year and was considering the resumption of the troop reductions that had been interrupted during the 1961 Berlin crisis. Subsequently, the Soviet military budget was cut by 600 million rubles, around 5 per cent, a reduction that paralleled a $500 million cut in the United States defense budget announced later by President Johnson. Khrushchev hinted that progress in disarmament might be achieved by a process of "mutual example," in which each side reciprocated the arms reduction measures undertaken by the other, presumably without formal agreement and without inspection.

Meanwhile, the strategic forces of the two sides grew in accordance with programs established some years earlier. In 1962 the Soviet Union finally began to deploy significant numbers of operational ICBM's (until then only "a handful" had been emplaced),[26] but by then United States strategic missile programs were operating in high gear: in fiscal 1963 alone the long-range missile forces almost tripled, according to Secretary McNamara, and they were programmed to double again the following year.[27] The Soviet ICBM force grew far less rapidly in those years, so that by April, 1964, the American force was more than four times as large as the Soviet.[28] There is no evidence that Khrushchev decided during these years to make a serious bid to overcome the lead of the United States in strategic forces. On the contrary, he apparently either decided that such an effort was too costly and unpromising or simply postponed making the relevant decisions, perhaps hoping that future technological changes would facilitate a solution. One such decision that Khrushchev evidently postponed was whether to undertake substantial deployment of an anti-ballistic-missile defense system.[29]

Opposition to Khrushchev's decisions affecting the future Soviet strategic force conceivably played some part in his sudden ouster in October, 1964. Shortly before his removal, he issued a sharp challenge

---

[26] See p. 37.

[27] *New York Times*, January 28, 1964.

[28] See "Department of Defense Statement on U.S. Military Strength," April 14, 1964, quoted below, p. 163 (*New York Times*, April 15, 1964).

[29] Defense Minister Malinovsky had announced the successful testing of an ABM as early as October, 1961, and Khrushchev himself had boasted in July, 1962, of an antimissile missile that "can hit a fly in outer space" (*New York Times*, July 17, 1962). In the November 8, 1963, military parade in Red Square a new type of surface-to-air missile had been displayed and identified in Soviet commentary as an anti-missile missile (Radio Moscow, November 12, 1963; *Krasnaia zvezda*, November 16, 1963).

to military dissidents and their political supporters in a speech that set the guidelines for the U.S.S.R.'s long-range economic plan, gave highest priority to consumer-goods production, and expressed satisfaction that the defenses of the country were "at the proper level." [30] No doubt Khrushchev's record in his half-dozen years as head of the party and the government made him vulnerable on several scores. During these years agriculture had stagnated, and industrial growth had slowed down. Soviet leadership of the international communist movement had been openly challenged, and the movement itself seemed on the verge of an historic split. Perhaps equally important, as we have seen, his strategy of bluff and missile deception directed against the West had met with evident failure. For these reasons, and no doubt others that the future will reveal, on October 14, 1964, Khrushchev's reign came to a sudden end. The problems he had failed to solve, in agriculture and industry, in foreign and military policy, now faced his successors.

[30] *Pravda,* October 2, 1964.

PART 4

SOVIET STRATEGIC CHOICES AND THEIR POLITICAL IMPLICATIONS

INTRODUCTION

THE SOVIET LEADERS who succeeded Khrushchev were no strangers to the strategic problems that confronted the U.S.S.R. Although Khrushchev had evidently reserved for himself the initiative in vital military-political matters, his lieutenants certainly had ample opportunity to ponder them, to take part in deliberations, and perhaps to propose alternative measures. As we have seen, Khrushchev, in the final years of his rule, had evidently taken no strikingly new strategic decisions. The problems that had faced him, therefore, devolved upon his successors, along with the alternative solutions among which they now had to choose.

Chapters xiii–xv, which constitute Part Four of this book, deal primarily with the political considerations that may influence future Soviet strategic choices and with the political implications of alternative Soviet strategic postures. Of course, the choices made by the Soviet leaders will be significantly influenced by other, non-political considerations, costs and constraints. The alternatives that we shall discuss do not simply comprise a menu of postures from which Soviet leaders may freely choose solely on the basis of expected political advantage. If this were so, the choice could be narrowed considerably, say, to something between a manifest strategic superiority conferred by a militarily effective first-strike capability and a far-reaching disarmament agreement on Soviet terms. Not only do different strategic postures have distinctive advantages and limitations as political instruments; they also vary greatly in terms of their economic cost and technical feasibility.

The spectrum of Soviet strategic postures we have elected to analyze ranges from continued acceptance of strategic inferiority, through strategic parity, to postures that might confer some ambiguous forms of strategic superiority. An analogous spectrum of politically plausible United States strategic postures would probably not be as broad. This is so because the Soviet leaders have accepted and under certain circumstances might continue to accept a prolonged state of strategic inferiority, whereas it is almost certain that no American government would willingly accept such a state for itself.

Of course, this broad spectrum of Soviet postures does not exhaust the theoretical possibilities. A decisive strategic superiority, such as would be conferred by a manifestly effective first-strike capability,[1] is one such possibility, but it has been excluded from present consideration on the ground that, even if it were technically feasible for the Soviets, it would be prohibitively costly for them in the foreseeable future.

As the Soviet economy grows, the Soviet leaders will be in a position to increase military expenditures without increasing the percentage of the gross national product devoted to military purposes. But even so, resources available for military programs are not and will not be unlimited. Moreover, competition from high-priority non-military programs may increase despite over-all economic growth. As Secretary McNamara expressed it a few years ago,

The Soviets could, over the next few years, build a large force of hardened second generation ICBM's; they could develop and deploy an ICBM delivery system for the large yield nuclear warheads they have been testing since 1961; they could expand and improve their MRBM/IRBM systems; they could continue to maintain and improve their active defenses against manned bomber attack; they could maintain a large and modernly-equipped army; they could develop and deploy some sort of system of active defense against ballistic missile attack; they could modernize and improve their large fleet of submarines including ballistic missile-firing types; they could continue the space race; they could expand both military and economic aid to the non-aligned nations; they could make the great investment needed to create an efficient agricultural economy; they could continue to push the development of heavy industry; or they could increase the standard of living of the Soviet people—but they cannot do them all at the same time.[2]

The pressures upon available resources exerted by the competing demands of non-military programs evidently have not been eased since the ouster of Khrushchev. Although the new leaders soon cut back Khrushchev's ambitious investment planning targets for the Soviet chemical industry,[3] the savings that may thus have been achieved were swallowed up by the massive obligations for new agricultural investment—71 billion rubles in the 1966–70 period—assumed by the Leonid I. Brezhnev–A. N. Kosygin regime.[4] In the

---

[1] The distinction between such a capability and more ambiguous types of first-strike capabilities that might have varying degrees of political effectiveness is discussed below, pp. 200–202.

[2] United States, House of Representatives, *Hearings before the Committee on Armed Services on Military Posture and H.R. 2440, To Authorize Appropriations during Fiscal Year 1964 for Procurement, Research, Development, Test, and Evaluation of Aircraft, Missiles, and Naval Vessels for the Armed Forces, and for Other Purposes,* 88th Cong., 1st sess., pp. 302–3.

[3] *Pravda,* December 10, 1965.

[4] *Pravda,* March 27, 1965.

first post-Khrushchev Soviet budget, outlays for defense were reduced by 500 million rubles, which represented almost 4 per cent of Khrushchev's last defense budget.[5]

Limited resources continue to place serious constraints on Soviet military policy, although, if necessary, vast resources could be diverted from other sectors to that of strategic arms. Another constraint—one that the Soviet leaders cannot control so readily themselves—is that imposed by the strategic choices of the United States. The Soviet Union's difficulty in achieving strategic parity, not to speak of some form of superiority, depends in no small degree on the magnitude and success of countervailing efforts of the United States. Unless the programmed United States strategic forces are sharply cut back, the Soviet leaders will be obliged in the years immediately ahead to continue investing heavily in strategic weapon systems simply to maintain their present relatively unfavorable strategic position. Substantial increases in the pace and scope of the United States buildup of strategic weapons would probably render infeasible some of the more ambitious Soviet postures that we shall consider here and might also preclude the attainment of strategic parity, even of a kind that did not require matching numbers of weapons.

In addition to the pace and scope of United States strategic weapons programs, developing technology will also determine how great an effort the Soviet Union must make in the future to maintain or improve its present strategic position vis-à-vis the United States. In general, the trend has been for technological advances to boost the cost of successive generations of strategic weapons and hence to magnify economic constraints on Soviet strategic buildups. Nevertheless, the possibility cannot be ruled out that the U.S.S.R. might make a series of breakthroughs that would enable it to leap-frog the opponent and, at comparatively low cost, overcome the effects of Western superiority in weapon systems acquired over the years at great cost—weapon systems that for one reason or another had become obsolescent.

---

[5] *Pravda*, December 10, 1964. According to Kosygin, projected military expenditures for 1965 were 12.8 billion rubles, as compared with 13.3 billion for 1964. It should be noted that the single published line-item for defense expenditure in the annual Soviet budget has not been a reliable guide in the past to actual allocation of resources for military purposes. See Thomas W. Wolfe, *Problems of Soviet Defense Policy under the New Regime* (P-3098; Santa Monica, Calif.: The RAND Corporation, 1965), pp. 3–5.

THIRTEEN

ACCEPTANCE OF STRATEGIC INFERIORITY

ONE CHOICE THAT IS obviously open to the Soviet leaders is to continue to accept strategic inferiority in one form or another. This is the condition under which the Soviet leaders have thus far conducted the cold war, sometimes suffering large failures, but other times achieving considerable successes, and meanwhile averting disaster. The degree of strategic inferiority with which the Soviet leaders have lived has varied over time. The difficult years when the United States had a monopoly in nuclear weapons and long-range delivery means are behind them. Yet, as the October, 1962, Cuban confrontation demonstrated, United States strategic superiority, even when it is no longer monopolistic, can still be a potent force in international relations.

Clearly, strategic inferiority compels the Soviet leaders to observe certain limitations in the conduct of their foreign policies that otherwise they might not have to. On what grounds, then, might they choose to forego the effort that would be required to overcome their strategic inferiority and the political limitations it entails?

Much would depend, of course, on how great an effort the Soviet leaders believed would be required to overcome American strategic superiority. If they estimated the costs and risks to be very great and the prospects for success uncertain, they might be disinclined to make the effort even if they believed strategic parity or superiority might yield substantial political benefits. Conversely, if the costs were estimated to be low, the risks negligible, and the probability of success high, the Soviet leaders might make the effort even if they expected only modest political benefits to ensue from an improved strategic posture. It is necessary, therefore, to say something about the magnitude of the disparity, inherited by the new Soviet leaders, between American and Soviet strategic capabilities, so that the distance the Soviet Union must cover to overtake the United States can be more accurately gauged. In the spring of 1964, a half-year before the ouster of Khrushchev, the United States Department of Defense, responding to questions raised by critics of the administration regarding the magnitude of American strategic superiority, summarized the United States–Soviet balance of intercontinental strategic forces then obtaining:

Today the United States Air Force has 540 strategic bombers maintained constantly on alert which could take off and fly to their targets in the face of a surprise missile attack. In contrast, it is estimated the Soviets could place over this country, on two-way missions, no more than approximately 120 heavy bombers plus perhaps an additional 150 medium bombers, the targets for which would be limited to Alaska and the northwest areas of the United States. Our Air Force has today on launchers approximately 750 intercontinental ballistic missiles; the Soviets have less than one-fourth of that number in operation. We have 192 Polaris missiles deployed; the Soviets have substantially fewer submarine-launched ballistic missiles in operation. Each of our Polaris missiles is carried in a nuclear powered submarine—only a small percentage of the Soviet missile carrying submarines are nuclear powered. Each of our Polaris missiles can be launched from below the surface—none of the Soviet missiles have that capability. Each of our missiles has a range of 1500 miles or more—the range of the Soviet missiles is less than one-third as much.[1]

This was the strategic balance that Khrushchev, chief architect of the Soviet Union's intercontinental nuclear force, bequeathed to his heirs. In June, 1965, eight months after the new Soviet leaders assumed power, the strategic balance was still evolving along the lines established by Khrushchev and by the Kennedy and Johnson administrations. According to an April, 1965, statement by Defense Secretary McNamara, by June 30 the United States would have a total of 1,270 long-range missiles (including 800 Minuteman ICBM's in hardened and dispersed silos underground and 416 Polaris missiles in submarines) and 935 intercontinental bombers (630 B-52's, 80 B-58's, and 225 B-47's, some 50 per cent of the bombers being maintained on fifteen-minute strip alert to reduce their vulnerability). According to the Secretary, these forces would give the United States a quantitative superiority "of approximately 3 or 4 to 1" and a qualitative superiority far exceeding that.[2]

Despite this impressive margin of American superiority—which is expected to grow in the next few years, at least until the completion of the programmed Minuteman ICBM and Polaris missile programs [3]

---

[1] "Department of Defense Statement on U.S. Military Strength," April 14, 1964 (*New York Times*, April 15, 1964).

[2] Interview with Robert S. McNamara, *U.S. News & World Report*, April 12, 1965, pp. 52, 56.

[3] By 1967, according to Secretary McNamara, 1,000 Minuteman missiles will have been deployed. The last 200 will be Minuteman II ICBM's, which are expected to have a kill capability four to eight times that of the earlier model because of increased ac-

—the advent of a state of strategic parity is widely predicted as imminent. Of course, the disappearance of United States strategic superiority has been heralded many times in the past, both by Soviet leaders who knew their statements to be premature or false, and by Western observers who did not. Current predictions regarding the early advent of a state of strategic parity, however, are not so closely linked as in the past to estimates of the future size of the Soviet strategic force; instead, they are based on the relative invulnerability of the weapons now entering the Soviet force. It is argued that the new strategic weapons assure that the U.S.S.R. will nullify United States strategic superiority by the end of the present decade, if not sooner, even without a substantial acceleration of the Soviet strategic buildup. In this view, strategic stalemate is the inevitable consequence of the U.S.S.R.'s acquisition of hardened ICBM's and nuclear-powered, ballistic-missile-launching submarines. Once the Soviet Union acquires a sizable force of such relatively invulnerable weapons, some believe, even very large increases in the opposing American strategic force would not suffice to give the United States a significant margin of strategic superiority; there would then be parity of a non-quantitative type.

The assumptions underlying the prediction of an imminent improvement in the Soviet strategic position relative to the United States appear to be (1) that the Soviet Union will acquire in the near future a sizable force of relatively invulnerable strategic weapons and (2) that the relative invulnerability of these weapons will not be seriously degraded by technological advances that might improve the capabilities of opposing offensive or active defensive forces. Although both of these assumptions seem plausible, the realization of neither is inevitable. Soviet leaders have more than once chosen not to procure large numbers of new offensive strategic weapons even when the U.S.S.R. appeared to have the capacity to do so. As Khrushchev's military policies demonstrated to the very end, the temptation to wait for the next, more advanced generation of weapons—and by so doing to postpone new heavy military expenditures—is strong. As a result, even after Khrushchev's fall from power, Soviet procurement of

---

curacy, payload, and range; eventually, all of the Minuteman I missiles will be replaced by retrofitted Minuteman II's. The Polaris force is scheduled to grow to 656 missiles by 1967. The older model missile-launching submarines are to be retrofitted with improved versions of the Polaris missile with a range of 2,200 to 2,400 nautical miles, as opposed to the range of 1,500 nautical miles of the early model. The 1967 intercontinental bomber force of the United States is expected to consist of 600 B-52's and 80 B-58's (*ibid.*, p. 56).

intercontinental weapons continued to lag behind American expectations.[4]

Actually, there is another, more basic difficulty in the view that the Soviet Union will shortly achieve strategic parity. This arises in part from the looseness with which the term "strategic parity" is often used, despite its being a very complicated military-political concept. Parity, according to *Webster's New International Dictionary*, is "the quality or condition of being equal or equivalent." It is this distinction between "equal" and "equivalent" that is central to the concept of strategic parity in the nuclear age. Those who predict parity believe that the strategic forces of the U.S.S.R., although inferior to those of the United States, can nevertheless provide the Soviet Union with capabilities equivalent to those of the United States. This "equivalence" will be achieved when the U.S.S.R. possesses a certain minimum number of relatively invulnerable intercontinental weapons. But how does one determine that minimum number? The criterion of sufficiency is (or rather, should be, since the term is often used without a definite connotation) the following: the Soviet strategic force must be sufficient to deprive the superior United States strategic force of any political advantage in peacetime or, if the two forces are used in combat, of any military advantage. It would be well to distinguish between the military parity and the political parity of strategic forces. Military parity implies that in the event of all-out war neither side would gain a significant military advantage over the other, advantage being defined according to such objective criteria as residual military and economic capabilities and comparative population losses. In principle, the number of strategic weapons of given types required by one side to deprive the other of any significant military advantage can be calculated with some degree of precision. But the number of weapons required to deprive a superior strategic force of any substantial *political* advantage may be considerably smaller, since political advantage is determined essentially by subjective factors that are influenced only in part by objective military capabilities.

Moreover, the minimum number of hardened ICBM's and ballistic missiles launched from nuclear submarines that would be needed by the Soviet Union to achieve military parity of strategic forces cannot

---

[4] Secretary McNamara, referring to the expected growth of Soviet strategic capabilities against the United States, stated in April, 1965: "Our estimates of the Soviet threat have changed since last year. We now estimate that the Soviet program will lag compared with what we previously estimated . . ." (*ibid.*).

be fixed in advance. The number would depend not merely on the degree of hardness of the Soviet ICBM's or on the extent of other vulnerability-reducing characteristics of the Soviet force but also upon such factors as the quality of the target intelligence available to the opposing side; the accuracy, penetration capacity, and warhead size of its weapons; and the number of weapons that it could direct at each Soviet target. Finally, though it may now seem unlikely, highly effective antimissile defense systems or new means for attacking hardened ICBM sites and missile-launching submarines might eventually become available. Such breakthroughs could radically alter current notions about the feasibility of achieving invulnerability with strategic forces that are greatly inferior numerically to those of a potential attacker.

Granted, such breakthroughs may fail to occur, or they may occur on both sides and more or less cancel each other out. The Soviet Union may be acquiring a sizable force of hardened ICBM's and undersea mobile missiles, although, as Secretary McNamara said in April, 1965, the Soviet "rate of expansion today is not such as to allow them even to equal, much less exceed, our own 1970 force." [5] The effort required to narrow substantially the quantitative gap—not to speak of closing or reversing it—will probably continue to be very great for years to come.

It has been argued that, once the Soviet Union acquires a force of relatively invulnerable strategic weapons such that United States leaders can no longer preclude "major damage" to the United States from Soviet retaliation, American quantitative preponderance in strategic weapons will have lost its political value, particularly in deterring attacks on third areas. The confidence of United States leaders, however, should not be the sole criterion; the possible effects of marginal kinds of American strategic superiority upon the calculations and behavior of Soviet leaders in various contingencies continue to be highly relevant.

The Soviet leaders have for many years heard expressions of doubt by responsible American officials regarding the ability of the United States strategic force, despite its superiority to the opposing Soviet force, to prevent "major damage" to the United States in the event of war; but in spite of these comments, American strategic preponderance has not been deprived of its political value. As early as December, 1953, President Eisenhower foresaw "civilization destroyed" in the

---

[5] *Ibid.*, p. 52.

event of a new world war,[6] but United States commitments to defend allies, if necessary by launching nuclear weapons against the U.S.S.R., remained in force and were not challenged. In his famous Cuban crisis speech of October 22, 1962, President Kennedy acknowledged that the fruits of victory in a thermonuclear war would be "ashes in our mouth,"[7] but this prognosis did not prevent him from successfully bringing United States strategic superiority to bear in support of his demand that the Soviet Union remove its strategic weapons from Cuba.

It is one thing for American leaders, while the guns are silent, to express lack of confidence that their superior strategic force could destroy a sufficiently large proportion of the opposing Soviet force to preclude "major damage" to the United States. Such lack of confidence reinforces their already strong general aversion, fed by many sources, to engage in thermonuclear war with the Soviet Union and, specifically, their concern, as President Kennedy put it in the same speech, not to risk the costs of general nuclear war "prematurely or unnecessarily." It may be quite another thing, however, for Soviet leaders, facing a strategic force that is manifestly stronger than their own, to decide to risk a grave provocation of the United States on the strength of doubts expressed by American leaders before the crisis. Even if such doubts were perceived to be very strong, the possibility that they might not remain stable under the strain of acute crisis would also have to be considered by the Soviet leaders. The Soviet leaders would have to be confident of the following: that their United States opponents would not, even when facing a grave threat to their security or in actual military adversity, (a) revise downward their precrisis estimate of the upper limit of damage that the Soviet Union could inflict on the United States in retaliation (or their estimate of the probability that this upper limit, rather than some lower level of damage, would be reached)[8] or (b) revise their notions, formed in precrisis conditions, of the limits of damage that would be "acceptable" to the United States in the given contingency. The Soviet leaders would have to be confident that, under such circumstances, United States leaders would not decide that the costs and risks, as now reassessed, of striking first with their undamaged and numerically

[6] New York Times, December 9, 1953.

[7] New York Times, October 23, 1962.

[8] For example, on the basis of new information (accurate or otherwise) acquired during the crisis or, possibly, as the result of a sudden crisis-connected degradation of certain aspects of Soviet strategic capabilities (or what is mistakenly believed to be such a degradation).

superior strategic force were preferable to the costs and risks of not striking.

There is no way to predict precisely how and under what conditions marginal forms of United States strategic superiority might success-fully be brought to bear to deter the Soviet leaders from undertaking or persisting in courses of action hostile to the United States. We shall return later, in a different context, to a more detailed considera-tion of the potential political uses and limitations of marginal or ambiguous types of strategic superiority. In this chapter we have confined ourselves to establishing the following points:

1. The Soviet leaders could not be indifferent to the existence of an American strategic force that enjoyed great quantitative preponder-ance over their own, even if it were evident to them that their opponents lacked confidence in peacetime in the premium on a first strike that could be derived from such preponderance. The extent to which Soviet behavior might be inhibited by the existence of such a force would depend upon a great number of factors, but among them would certainly be the extent of the preponderance enjoyed by the United States strategic force.

2. The numerical disparity between United States and Soviet intercontinental strategic forces in the mid-sixties is so great that for the Soviet leaders to reduce it in this decade to the point where it could cease to be a matter of special concern to them would require a substantial increase in the modest growth rate they have thus far assigned to their intercontinental strike force.[9]

Before considering some of the factors that might bear on a decision by the Soviet leaders either to continue for the time being to accept a large degree of United States strategic superiority or to undertake a large-scale weapons buildup in an effort to overcome or substantially reduce it, mention should be made of two conceivable developments that might permit the U.S.S.R. to achieve strategic parity without engaging in an extraordinary arms effort. Theoretically, a decision by the United States to adopt some form of a minimum-deterrence strategy and to adjust its strategic posture accordingly could result in parity. Such a decision might be implemented by the cancellation or sharp reduction of additions to the strategic force already programmed, the phasing out of some of the more vulnerable elements of the present strategic force, and the institution of a freeze

---

[9] The matter of special concern referred to here is the disparity between the forces, not the existence of the United States strategic force as such, which would under any circumstance continue to be a matter of great concern to the Soviet leaders.

on the strength level of the remaining force. Although conceivable, this development is not likely, however, since a United States policy of severe unilateral arms restraint would probably not long survive knowledge that the Soviet leaders were failing to curtail their own arms programs.

A second way in which a state of strategic parity might arise is from a formal United States–Soviet arms reduction accord. Given the present strategic imbalance between the United States and the U.S.S.R., the achievement of "instant parity" by means of a far-reaching disarmament agreement that would eliminate at a single stroke all intercontinental nuclear weapons, save for small "nuclear umbrella" forces of equal size on both sides, might appear to the Soviet leaders an attractive alternative to (1) acceptance of a prolonged period of strategic inferiority or (2) a costly, perhaps risky, arms buildup that might fail in the end to improve the Soviet position at all and might even worsen it. Moreover, if relations between the United States and the Soviet Union were to deteriorate after such an advanced phase of disarmament had been implemented, or if for other reasons the Soviet leaders decided to rearm, the U.S.S.R. would find itself starting out in any such renewed strategic armaments race from a far more advantageous position relative to the United States than it has yet enjoyed or than it could otherwise attain, if at all, without great cost.

It is for these very reasons, however, among many others, that the Western powers have rejected Soviet proposals to begin the process of general and complete disarmament with the kind of unbalanced radical arms slashes that would be required to achieve instant parity in strategic weapons. The Western allies have insisted instead upon phased and balanced reductions in strategic weapons that would maintain a progressively diminishing margin of United States superiority in strategic weapons, until the very end of the process.

If the Soviet leaders should conclude that neither substantial, disproportionate cuts in American strategic forces nor American agreement to a Soviet-type "instant parity" disarmament proposal are likely in the near future, they could try to deal unilaterally with United States strategic superiority by engaging in an intensified buildup of their intercontinental nuclear force. A decision to adopt such a course would not be taken lightly by Moscow, for it would entail great costs, drawing resources away from other high-priority programs that offer alternative means of achieving the regime's political objectives. Certain serious risks would also have to be faced, not the least of which is the risk that any large-scale Soviet strategic weapon buildup is likely to be conspicuous and hence known to the outside world.[10] The Soviet leaders might fear that evidence of a Soviet buildup would provoke the United States, with its superior production capabilities, to step up its own strategic weapons programs and thus initiate a new phase of the arms race that could well end with the U.S.S.R. lagging even farther behind the United States than before. Given past American responses to evidence—fictitious as well as real—of Soviet strategic arms buildups, the Soviet leaders would have to reckon seriously with this danger.

Under the circumstances, it is not a foregone conclusion that the Soviet Union would make such an effort even if other means of eliminating United States strategic superiority were unavailing. Here we return to the questions raised at the beginning of this chapter: Under what conditions might the Soviet leaders choose continued strategic inferiority rather than the major attempt needed to overcome it? And what kinds of changes might tend to make strategic inferiority less tolerable to them than it has evidently been until now?

That the Soviet leaders have for many years conducted the cold war from a position of strategic inferiority does not mean that they have been unaware of the advantages of strategic parity or superiority. They have made every effort to avoid the appearance of inferiority—every effort, that is, short of actually procuring the necessary strategic forces. Moreover, they have sought, systematically and with considerable success, to overcome deficiencies in their strategic nuclear technologies. Thus, the Soviet Union ended the atomic bomb monopoly of the United States several years earlier than most Western experts had expected; thermonuclear weapons were developed in the two countries almost simultaneously; and the U.S.S.R. was the first successfully to flight-test an intercontinental ballistic missile. The Soviet drive for parity or superiority in military technology is already vigorous, has powerful momentum, and can be expected to continue in the years ahead. In regard to the procurement and deployment of intercontinental delivery vehicles, however, the Soviet Union has lagged behind the United States; and Soviet leaders do not seem to have been strongly motivated in the past to close the gap as quickly as they might have. According to Secretary McNamara (in the spring of 1965), the Soviet leaders "have decided that they have lost the quan-

---

[10] The U.S.S.R. has shown (1959–61) that it can "conceal" missiles that do not exist; it would be much more difficult to conceal missiles that were there.

titative race, and they are not seeking to engage us in that contest. . . . There is no indication that the Soviets are seeking to develop a strategic nuclear force as large as ours." [11]

In the previous chapters we have analyzed the conditions that have tended thus far to make a state of strategic inferiority acceptable to the Soviet leaders, in the sense that they were unwilling to bear the costs of a radical improvement in the Soviet strategic position. No doubt the Soviet leaders have found it possible to live with strategic inferiority because they felt United States strategic superiority did not directly threaten the security of the Soviet Union and the Communist bloc.[12] Maintenance of this situation, however, has depended on the acceptance by the Soviet leaders of certain important limitations on their prosecution of the cold war against the West. The Soviet leaders have given strong evidence of their willingness to accept these limitations: implicitly, by seeking to avoid dangerous confrontations with the United States and by quickly disengaging from them on the infrequent occasions when they have occurred; explicitly, by rejecting the alternative cold war strategy and tactics advocated by the Chinese Communists, who have argued that Soviet acceptance of limitations is incompatible with the goal of communist transformation of the world.

Strategic inferiority might not be so readily tolerated by the Soviet leaders (1) if it appeared to them that American forbearance could no longer be secured merely by their continued acceptance of the limitations they have so far observed or (2) if the limitations themselves ceased to be acceptable to the Soviet Union. The first contingency might arise, for example, if the Soviet leaders perceived a change in the character of the American government of such magnitude as to raise doubts about what has been the bedrock assumption of Soviet defense policy: the extreme disinclination of the United States to engage in general war. It is impossible to know how likely the Soviets estimate such a change to be, but they probably do not altogether exclude it. In the Soviet view, American governments have within them conflicting groups of "sober realists" and "madmen." Both are regarded as "imperialist" and deeply hostile to the Soviet Union and communism, but the "sober realists," who are said to tend toward moderation and reasonableness, display a healthy awareness of the dangers of thermonuclear war and of the "real correlation of forces" in the world, whereas the "madmen," who overrate their own

---

[11] *U.S. News & World Report*, April 12, 1965, p. 52.
[12] But see below, pp. 173–74.

capabilities, incline toward an "adventurism" that is marked particularly by a predisposition to use or threaten the use of force to turn back the wheel of history.[13] Significantly, since Stalin's death, the American President has always been placed, explicitly or implicitly, in the camp of the "sober realists," not among the "madmen." Responsibility for actions by the American government that have been termed "adventurist" (the U-2 and Bay of Pigs incidents, as well as the Cuban quarantine *before* the Soviet capitulation took place) has been attributed to the temporarily dominant influence of "madmen" in government and military circles rather than to the President personally.[14]

The Soviet leaders probably feel that a major political change, such as would be entailed by the advent to power of an American administration dominated by "madmen" and bent on "rollback" or preventive war, would cast long shadows before it. Accordingly, there would still be time to undertake a large-scale strategic buildup, if it were deemed necessary, provided the U.S.S.R. had remained technologically abreast of the United States.

A related but less radical change—in United States strategy and tactics for conducting the cold war rather than in the basic political character of the government—might make strategic inferiority seem more onerous to the Soviet leaders than it does at present. Throughout the cold war the United States has exploited its strategic superiority only to achieve limited defensive objectives. During the 1962 Cuban missile crisis, for example, the United States limited itself to preventing the establishment of a Soviet missile base in Cuba. Although this was certainly a serious defeat for the Soviet leaders, in the larger sense such defeats may not be intolerable to the Soviet Union so long as they result in nothing worse than the *status quo ante*. Had the United States employed its strategic superiority not only to secure the withdrawal of Soviet strategic weapons from Cuba but also to cover the military liquidation of the Castro regime, Soviet incentives to nullify American strategic superiority, even at very great cost, would almost certainly have risen significantly.

---

[13] In many respects the Soviet image of the conflict between "sober realists" and "madmen" for control of American policy mirrors Moscow's version of the Sino-Soviet dispute.

[14] President Johnson's standing in Moscow as a "sober realist" apparently even survived his order to initiate a bombing campaign against targets in North Vietnam in February, 1965. As the bombings continued, however, signs began to appear that the evaluation of the President might be changing, at least publicly. On May 23, *Izvestiia* charged President Johnson with "embarking on the path of the raving Fuehrer."

In short, so long as American strategic superiority is used only to resist Soviet encroachments and not to penalize the Soviet Union for attempting them, the Soviet leaders are unlikely to find strategic inferiority intolerable. However, neither are they likely to be easily dissuaded from further attempts to change the status quo in the non-Communist world through the use of moderate pressures. Although the prospects for large Soviet gains in the near future might be poor, the possibility of long-term success through the gradual erosion of Western positions might hold out great promise to the Soviet leaders. Western hopes for an end to the cold war rest largely on the assumption that repeated frustrations and failures will diminish the offensive ardor of the Soviet leaders and lead them to seek a general accommodation with the West. But if it costs little or nothing to chip away at Western positions, the Soviets might not tire of it at all, even if they enjoyed only occasional success. They might be satisfied to continue, intermittently, to exert only moderate kinds of pressure at opportune moments and to devote the greater part of their resources to internal development, foreign aid, and so on.

On the other hand, if the Soviet leaders believed that the United States would use its strategic superiority to penalize them for attempted encroachments (for example, by forcing changes in the status quo to the disadvantage of the Communists)—although they might be deterred from new offensive undertakings so long as they remained strategically inferior—they would probably be strongly motivated to correct their strategic deficiencies. If the price exacted by the United States were high, there would be a considerable likelihood of a spiraling arms race and of greatly increased tension.

Soviet incentives to overcome United States strategic superiority in the future may also depend on the actions of parties not wholly subject to the control of either the Soviet Union or the United States. The increasing autonomy of allies and clients and their growing capacity to involve the two superpowers in crises and even military conflicts against their inclinations may complicate the international scene in ways that cannot now be foreseen. Since February, 1965, for example, the Soviet Union has had to seek means to fulfil its commitment to defend a small Communist state, North Vietnam, which has provoked American bombing attacks upon itself by directing and supporting a war in South Vietnam in pursuit of objectives to which Moscow itself assigns a relatively low priority.

The American air attacks upon North Vietnam constitute the most severe challenge yet made to the long-standing Soviet pledge to defend Communist states against attacks from hostile quarters. That pledge is at the very heart of the U.S.S.R.'s claim to leadership of the Communist world, for the Soviet leaders have asserted time and time again that only the U.S.S.R. among the Communist states has sufficient power to deter the United States. A direct test of the Soviet claim was barely averted at the time of the Cuban missile crisis. In Vietnam, the claim has been directly challenged for the first time, as the result of actions on the Communist side that were not even carried out at the behest of the Soviet leaders or, apparently, with their consent. At present, this is a novel situation; but since the process that has brought about the fragmentation of authority inside the Communist world movement seems destined to continue, the Soviet leaders may have to face such situations again, perhaps in even more severe form. How they propose to deal with chestnuts thrust into the fire by independent-minded allies will certainly influence the decisions they make about the future Soviet strategic force.

Just as adverse changes in the political environment, like those described above, might increase Soviet incentives to match or surpass the United States in strategic power, so too might unexpectedly favorable technological developments. The Soviet leaders might come to believe that they had previously overestimated the difficulty of overcoming their strategic inferiority. New or improved technologies for radically reducing the vulnerability of Soviet strategic forces (or rendering United States forces highly vulnerable) might reduce the costs of such programs, perhaps enough to make them economically feasible. The size and character of the opposing American strategic force, however, would still be crucial. If it were to grow obsolescent, or if the margin of American quantitative superiority were to decline sharply, even without a significant acceleration in the current pace of Soviet strategic weapon programs, the Soviet leaders might find irresistibly attractive the prospect of achieving parity or superiority cheaply.

Extensive research and development programs, such as the Soviets have evidently been conducting, would place them in a position to move quickly to capitalize on new technological opportunities that might arise, particularly if American efforts slackened. These programs would also enable them to take appropriate measures should political changes in the United States cause the danger posed by American strategic superiority to grow. A fast technological arms race is hardly a low-cost venture, but it is far cheaper than a race to procure and deploy on a large scale generation after generation of new intercontinental weapons.

The changes noted above that might make strategic inferiority less tolerable to the Soviet leaders than in the past are changes in the political character or strategy and tactics of the United States, or of Communist allies that are largely autonomous, or in the technological environment. Assuming that such changes do not occur, still another condition must be satisfied if the Soviet Union is to continue to find inferiority acceptable: the Soviet leaders must not themselves change in their willingness to accept the political limitations imposed upon them by American strategic superiority. Should continued acceptance of these limitations lead to a stabilization of international politics in which Communist advances are halted, the Soviet leaders would have to choose between (1) accepting this situation and modifying their objectives accordingly and (2) making new efforts, including strategic ones, to overcome the hampering limitations. The fate of the world may well depend on the choice made by the Soviet leaders. Khrushchev asserted that the advance of communism would not be hampered by acceptance of the ground rules of "peaceful coexistence." His erstwhile Chinese comrades denied this contention. How will Khrushchev's successors respond if evidence accumulates that the Chinese Communists are correct?

A major theme of this book has been the limitations imposed on Soviet foreign policy in the past by deficiencies in Soviet strategic capabilities. In the next chapters we shall consider how such limitations might be overcome by improvements in the Soviet Union's strategic posture, supposing that such improvements might actually be achieved or otherwise made credible to the West.

FOURTEEN

ACHIEVEMENT OF PARITY

THE TERM "STRATEGIC PARITY" means many things to many men. In the West, some observers believe it has existed for years, whereas others believe it will come into existence shortly.[1] Some believe its coming is inevitable; others that it is probable; still others that it is unlikely. The complexity of the concept and disagreement about its meaning have contributed to these differences of view, although they are grounded on real differences in estimates of the future state of the world.

Here we shall take "strategic parity" to mean the *political* parity of strategic forces:[2] it is a condition in which the Soviet strategic forces are sufficient to deprive even a more powerful American strategic force of its political usefulness. How large a disparity between the forces of the two sides could be consistent with a state of strategic parity and how stable any state of parity based on disparate forces might prove to be cannot be predicted with precision. The clearest form of strategic parity, and the one that provides the point of departure for this chapter, is that in which either side could virtually destroy the other as a viable state *after* suffering an all-out nuclear attack.[3] This is the most stable form of parity, the one best able to withstand political and military shocks; it provides the limiting case for Soviet exploitation of a state of parity. Yet what is true of this most unambiguous form of parity is also true in varying degrees of less stable forms.

The Soviet leaders, although they themselves do not actually use the term "parity" [*paritet*], have talked for years as if strategic parity had already become a well-established fact of international life. Since late 1960, when Khrushchev began to retreat from his explicit claims of strategic superiority, Soviet spokesmen have repeatedly emphasized the catastrophic destruction that thermonuclear war would entail, without distinguishing between the consequences for the two sides.

---

[1] Those who contend that a state of strategic parity has already existed for some years appear to define parity simply as any strategic state in which one side does not possess a highly effective and confidently assessed first-strike capability (that is, one that is virtually retaliation-proof).

[2] See p. 165 for a more complete definition.

[3] The late Leo Szilard termed this strategic state "saturation parity." He wrote in March, 1964, that the Soviet Union had not yet achieved such parity, but that it would do so in time, perhaps "within a very few years" ("'Minimal Deterrent' vs. Saturation Parity," *Bulletin of the Atomic Scientists*, March, 1964, pp. 8–9).

Of course, Soviet comments on modern war have always been strongly conditioned by rhetorical considerations. The statements of the early sixties, especially, seem to have been designed to serve Soviet purposes in the mounting conflict with the Chinese Communists, who disputed the Soviet view on the magnitude and implications of the thermonuclear war danger. When it was the West that most needed persuasion regarding the U.S.S.R.'s determination to pursue courses of action that threatened Western interests, the Soviet leaders stressed not the general consequences of nuclear war but the consequences for the West, even claiming strategic advantages for the U.S.S.R. in the event of war. Since the exposure of the missile gap myth in late 1961 and the Cuban missile episode a year later, however, claims of Soviet superiority have had a hollow ring. Manifestly lacking credibility, they have been replaced almost entirely by assertions that nuclear war would annihilate both sides without distinction. In the aftermath of the Cuban missile crisis, Khrushchev painted this grim picture:

According to the calculations of scientists the very first blow [in a thermonuclear war] would destroy between 700 and 800 million people. All large cities, not only in the United States and the Soviet Union, the two leading nuclear powers, but also in France, Britain, Germany, Italy, China, Japan, and many other countries would be razed to the ground and destroyed. The consequences of atomic-hydrogen bomb war would persist during the lives of many generations and would result in disease, death, and would cripple the human race.[4]

"The atomic bomb," stated the Soviet Party Central Committee in its open letter of July 14, 1963, to the Communist Party of China, "does not adhere to the class principle: it destroys everybody within range of its devastating force." [5]

In addressing the West, the Soviet leaders have repeatedly insisted that it must acknowledge the loss of strategic superiority by making appropriate concessions designed to bring political relations between the two sides into line with the new global distribution of strategic power. In fact, the alleged existence of a strategic stalemate has been the principal theme of Soviet declaratory policy on the strategic balance since 1960. Soviet statements have repeatedly noted the discrepancy between the kind of American behavior that would be consistent with the Soviet-preferred image of the strategic balance (shared at one time, it may have seemed to Moscow, by United States

---

[4] *Pravda*, January 17, 1963.
[5] *Pravda*, July 14, 1963.

leaders) and actual American behavior. In one of his Cuban crisis communications to Kennedy, for example, Khrushchev complained that the United States was demanding the removal of Soviet missiles from Cuba at the same time that it surrounded the Soviet Union with American missiles deployed on allied territory: "How then does the admission of our equal military capabilities tally with such unequal relations between our great states? This cannot be made to tally in any way." [6]

So far the Soviet leaders have enjoyed but limited success in their efforts to extract political gains from what they have represented as a strategic standoff. But this can by no means be taken as evidence that a real state of strategic parity could not provide the U.S.S.R. with a secure platform from which to conduct intensified political warfare or even limited military aggression. Despite Soviet claims, the U.S.S.R. has in fact remained strategically inferior to the United States, and the essential condition for successful Soviet exploitation of parity—acknowledgment of such a strategic state by the opponent—has not yet been realized, or only in part and for brief periods. The West's confidence in its ability to resist Soviet threats and offensive probes has been acquired in an environment of United States strategic superiority. Moreover, the Soviet leaders have known this to be the true balance, and their knowledge has strongly inhibited their conduct of the cold war.

The concern expressed a few years ago by some students of thermonuclear strategy that the Soviet Union would derive large political gains from its emergent capacity to wage nuclear war against the United States has so far proved exaggerated. In part, this is because Soviet strategic capabilities have not grown as quickly as had been expected. In part, too, it may be because these observers underestimated both the strategic capabilities that would be required to support bold new Soviet political strategies and the means available to the Western powers to cope with these strategies. Only if the Soviet initiatives were based on some credible form of strategic superiority, or at least on acknowledged parity, would this kind of concern be fully justifiable.

Nevertheless, this concern reflected recognition of certain fundamental asymmetries in the circumstances of the two major powers engaged in the cold war. These asymmetries (desire to maintain the status quo versus activist revolutionary aims, a relatively open demo-

---

[6] *Pravda*, October 28, 1962.

cratic society versus a secretive totalitarian one, and so on) make it easier for the Soviet Union than for the United States to extract political gains from military strength. American strategic superiority has tended to balance the Soviet advantages. In this sense it has been an equalizing factor and has contributed to the stability of international politics.

The stabilizing and politically equalizing effects of United States strategic superiority are often overlooked by those who contend that strategic parity is a precondition for reaching a stable understanding with the Soviet Union and ending the cold war. The assumption underlying this position is that the Soviet leaders want to reach a stable understanding with the United States, but are prevented from seeking it by their strategic inferiority. But historical experience strongly indicates that the Soviet leaders do not want a lasting understanding with the United States for its own sake, but only as an accompaniment of American acquiescence in the global expansion of Soviet power, influence, and control. The Soviet Union's strategic inferiority lessens the prospects for securing such acquiescence and makes a policy of *détente* seem more attractive, at least for the time being. Khrushchev, replying to Chinese Communist charges that the Soviet Union was abandoning the cause of world revolution, expressed the distinction between desire and capability in characteristically pungent language:

Well, you know, if it depended only on our desire to make revolution, comrades, I guarantee you that the Central Committee (*voice rising to a shout*) would have done everything to see that the bourgeois world was no more and that the red flag flew over the whole world (*applause*). But, comrades, let us not indulge in fantasies about this, but act like people able to think realistically. The desire by itself is little . . . even the party's desire is little. . . .[7]

It is well to remember that the *détente* which began in 1963, and gave rise to renewed speculation that the Soviet leaders might at last be prepared to consider long-term settlements with the West, was born in an environment of strategic imbalance, not parity. It is true that the Soviet leaders initiated the *détente* by signing the partial nuclear test-ban treaty, but the test-ban had been proposed several years earlier by the United States and Great Britain. The U.S.S.R. agreed to it only after its efforts to circumvent United States strategic superiority by bluff and by short-cut methods had been thwarted. The

---

[7] Live Radio Moscow broadcast of speech by Khrushchev at Soviet-Polish Friendship Rally in Moscow, April 15, 1964.

American intelligence re-evaluation of Soviet strategic capabilities in the autumn of 1961 had destroyed the myth that the strategic balance in the early sixties would be dominated by a "missile gap" in favor of the Soviet Union. Soviet failure to budge the Western allies in Berlin had underlined the limitations imposed on Soviet policy by strategic inferiority; and the failure of the Cuban missile deployment a year later showed that the Soviet strategic force was also too weak to bolster provocative short-cut efforts to augment it. The Cuban missile crisis also demonstrated to the Soviet leaders more strongly than any other experience the high risks they faced in attempting to conduct offensive policies against interests deemed vital by the United States government so long as Soviet strategic power remained manifestly inferior.

The *détente* was in a sense the natural outgrowth of these failures. Whether it will prove to be merely a pause before new storms, or a phase of a prolonged period of relaxed tensions leading to a general settlement of outstanding differences, cannot be foreseen. There is no reason to suppose, however, that an atmosphere of *détente* can be prolonged and deepened only if Soviet strategic inferiority—which is the condition that brought it about—is replaced by a state of parity.

This is not to say that the advent of strategic parity would necessarily lead the Soviet Union to abandon policies of *détente*. Many other factors, including non-military ones, would bear on such a decision. But the Soviet leaders would find the alternative courses of action open to them different in several important respects from what they have been. If the leaders of the two superpowers believed, and especially if they publicly acknowledged, that the outcome of general nuclear war could only be mutual genocide, threats by either to initiate nuclear war against the other (for example, in defense of allied third countries) would probably lose their credibility. Forms of conflict that had become muted during the emergence of the nuclear stalemate might then be liberated. Highly provocative measures, including strategic threats, or conceivably even military action, against allies of the United States might be adopted with sustantially reduced fear of triggering an all-out war.[8]

A Soviet belief that both sides possessed genocidal retaliatory capa-

---

[8] However, fears that a given course of action hostile to the interests of the opponent might eventuate in general nuclear war (inadvertently, by escalation or otherwise) might arise regardless of the credibility attached to the opponent's threat. On this point, see below, p. 185.

bilities might lead to the adoption of one of several highly divergent military policies: (1) acceptance of this strategic state and adoption of measures designed to perpetuate it; (2) an intensified technological arms race to break the strategic stalemate; or (3) a race in non-strategic arms (compatible with either of the first two possibilities).

As regards political strategy, the chief alternatives might be (1) strongly hostile actions against the United States, strong political or military pressures on American allies to become neutral, and active assistance to Communist or other anti-Western insurgent forces in countries where political conditions were ripe, or (2) serious efforts to reach a general accommodation with the West, possibly including far-reaching disarmament measures.

Less extreme, intermediate courses of action of a more familiar type might also be seriously considered and perhaps adopted. The actual choice between these alternative military and political strategies, of course, would depend on the political circumstances in which the decisions were made. But in the changed strategic environment postulated here, Soviet leaders might believe, perhaps for the first time, that more aggressive military and political strategies had become live options. Presumably, certain military strategies would be inconsistent with some political strategies. For example, a Soviet decision to intensify the technological arms race in order to gain a military advantage would probably be incompatible with a serious effort to reach a general settlement with the United States. Interim *détente* tactics might be used to inhibit American military progress, however, and ultimately, the improvement in the Soviet posture might be used to exact more favorable terms from the United States.

On the other hand, many diverse political strategies would be compatible with Soviet adoption of a military policy grounded in acceptance of a continuing nuclear stalemate. Their common point of departure would be a strategic balance more favorable to the Soviet Union than any that has yet existed, for the advent of a mutually acknowledged state of strategic parity would signify to the Soviet leaders a major improvement in the relative strategic position of the U.S.S.R. and a deterioration in that of the United States.

As indicated above, Soviet cold war policy toward the West, during both moderate "rightist" and offensive "leftist" phases, has been based consistently and often explicitly on the assumption that political relationships between the powers must conform to the world "correlation of forces"; the balance of strategic power is acknowledged to be a central aspect of the "correlation of world forces," particularly in the present era. During periods of moderation in Soviet foreign policy, the effects of the still unfavorable balance of power have tended to dominate Soviet calculations and to inhibit Soviet behavior. Offensive periods have been characterized by attempts to capitalize on real or fictitious shifts in the balance favoring the Soviet side. Soviet leaders have traditionally fluctuated between conciliatory or defensive policies toward the West, grounded on sober, "realistic" appraisals of the world balance of power (viewed statically at a particular point in time) and, at the other extreme, hostile or offensive policies based on optimistic estimates of the dynamics of future change in the world correlation of forces. In a state of parity, choices would still have to be made between offensive and moderate, "left" and "right," policies, and fluctuations between the two would doubtless continue to occur as in the past. But the specific content of the policies pursued during offensive or moderate phases might be significantly altered. In particular, offensive policies might be conducted with greater directness and boldness than in the past.

At the same time, if there were a conjunction of favorable political conditions, a mutually acknowledged state of strategic parity could conceivably provide a surer basis for a *rapprochement* between the United States and the U.S.S.R. What might first be required to bring this about is some modification of the totalitarian character of the Soviet regime and of its commitment to world revolution. A Soviet regime that had been modified in this way might be especially inclined to seek agreements that would end or curtail the arms race, once it was confident that the U.S.S.R. possessed a capability for genocidal retaliation and that the United States so credited it. For such a modified regime, the hazard to Soviet security arising from the proliferation of modern weapons might conceivably appear to exceed that arising from the existence of United States strategic forces. The prospect of eliminating that threat by a single-minded hostility to the United States as the main enemy might then seem less attractive than the promise of stabilizing the world political system in concert with the United States.

But the emergence of a state of strategic parity would not of itself cause the Soviet leaders to abandon or basically modify their long-term international objectives. The Soviet leaders freely acknowledge that it is their awareness of the unprecedented destructiveness of thermonuclear war that has caused them to revise old Leninist and Stalinist dogmas about the inevitability of war and the universal necessity for violent revolution. However, their fear of the destructive consequences of thermonuclear war does not arise from some hypothetical future state of strategic parity in which both the U.S.S.R. and the United States would possess genocidal retaliatory capabilities but from the actual possession of such capabilities by the United States now and for many years past. The acquisition by the U.S.S.R. of intercontinental capabilities comparable to those possessed by the United States would do nothing to enhance Soviet awareness of the potentially destructive consequences of thermonuclear war for the U.S.S.R. or to intensify Soviet concern to avoid actions that might bring such destruction to the Soviet Union. On the contrary, acquisition of a comparable capability by the U.S.S.R. would reduce even further the Soviet leaders' estimates of the likelihood of general war, even if it did not reduce significantly their estimates of the damage that the U.S.S.R. would probably suffer in such a war.

If the Soviet leaders do not abandon or fundamentally modify their objectives while they are strategically inferior, it is not easy to see why the achievement of parity should lead them to do so. Yet there are special circumstances in which this might occur, although they could probably be realized only after the Soviet leaders had made an attempt to pursue their long-standing goals under the new and improved strategic conditions. If the facts of life in the thermonuclear age have not yet led the Soviet leaders to seek a fundamental accommodation with the West (that is, acceptance of the present international system, if not of the status quo in every detail), it may be because they believe that their strategic inferiority, and not merely American possession of large quantities of thermonuclear weapons, has impeded their progress. If so, and if the Soviet leaders, having achieved strategic parity, were to find that a renewed aggressive pursuit of their objectives still raised unacceptable risks of catastrophic consequences, they might finally conclude that the time had come to liquidate the cold war and to make a long-term political settlement with the West, including perhaps far-reaching disarmament agreements. In conditions of strategic parity, the Soviet leaders might be more optimistic about the bargain they could strike with their adversaries, hence more positively motivated to enter real rather than sham negotiations on such basic questions as Germany, European security, and disarmament. But to repeat, what would probably first be required would be a demonstration that strategic parity in fact did not offer a substantially more satisfactory basis than the old inferiority for pursuing traditional Soviet global objectives in the thermonuclear era. And the period of demonstration might be a dangerous one for mankind.

Although a basic modification of Soviet objectives cannot be ruled out, therefore, it is less likely to be brought about in the near future by the emergence of the Soviet Union from strategic inferiority than by the prolongation of that inferiority. In the short term, following acquisition of a strategic force that could deprive the United States of the political advantages of strategic superiority, the Soviet leaders might decide to resume the offensive abandoned in 1962, this time prepared to exert greater pressures than before against exposed Western positions like Berlin. If they were confident that Western European and United States leaders shared their estimate of the strategic balance—this would be a critical requirement—the Soviet leaders might conclude that even extremely hostile actions, including perhaps limited military operations against NATO forces, could now be contemplated, credibly threatened, and if necessary executed with far less risk of general war than before.

Thus, because of its comparatively high stability, a strategic balance wherein both sides were credited with genocidal retaliatory capabilities might appear capable of supporting highly provocative Soviet foreign policies. Expectations regarding the outcome of general war would no longer depend in any substantial measure on which side initiated hostilities since both the attacker and the attacked would expect to be annihilated (that is, the United States would no longer possess or be credited with possessing a politically or militarily meaningful "damage-limiting" capability). Neither side, then, would be inclined to initiate general hostilities in order to secure the advantages of striking first; nor would either side believe that its opponent was so inclined. A marked decline in the likelihood of preemption by either side would virtually eliminate fears of deliberate surprise attack. To sum up, if each side credited the other with an assured second-strike capability to destroy the opponent's state, and if each believed the other so credited it, there could be high confidence on both sides in the ability of the strategic equilibrium to withstand severe political as well as military shocks. If there were no uncertainty about this on either side—a condition that is probably unrealizable—mutual deterrence would be absolute and there would be absolute strategic parity.

Under these circumstances, as we have said, threats by one side deliberately to launch a central attack on the other, except in retaliation for an attack upon itself, would probably be deprived of credibility. Even though each side might proclaim that its closest allies were to be regarded as virtually physical extensions of itself, it is not likely that such declaratory guarantees would be persuasive, particularly if current alliance-loosening trends on both sides continued. In a state of strategic parity based on mutual genocidal capabilities, the credibility of a power's pledge to defend allies against attacks of various kinds would depend less on its over-all military power and the extent of its verbal commitment than on the specific and demonstrable military dispositions it made for such defense in peacetime.

This does not mean that the Soviet leaders would feel free to commit any hostile act of which they were capable other than launching a strategic attack against the United States. Having made their country for the first time in its history the equal in strategic military capabilities of the most powerful Western capitalist state, the Soviet leaders would have reason to feel exhilaration, but it is most unlikely that they would suddenly begin to behave like the irresponsible adventurers they allege the Chinese Communists to be. As long as there existed in American hands a secure strategic force capable of destroying Soviet society, Soviet awareness of its existence and of its destructive potential would necessarily exercise a restraining influence on all major Soviet foreign policy calculations and behavior. This would be so even if threats by American leaders deliberately to set in motion the machine of mutual destruction were not believed, because the possibility that general war might nevertheless occur through accident, irrational action, or miscalculation or as the uncontrolled culmination of a process of escalation from lower to higher levels of violence would leave a residual fear of war that would tend to rise and fall with rises and falls in tension between the United States and the U.S.S.R. How powerful a restraining, deterrent effect such a residual fear of war might have on Soviet policy cannot be predicted; it would vary according to circumstances. The inhibiting effect upon Soviet foreign policy, however, would necessarily be weaker than the effect produced by fear that war might arise from deliberate action by the opponent.

Fear that a United States nuclear attack on the U.S.S.R. might be imminent has almost certainly never been a consideration influencing Soviet foreign policy decisions, despite continuing United States strategic superiority. Experience taught the Soviet leaders to discount the danger of an unprovoked American attack; prudence instilled in them a firm resolve not to provoke one themselves. As we have shown, a central Soviet concern in the cold war has been to avoid courses of action that might create the extreme circumstances in which American leaders might seriously contemplate the military employment of strategic forces. In order to observe the political effects of American strategic superiority, it is necessary to distinguish between two classes of action that the Soviet leaders have so far been induced to avoid: (1) acts so intrinsically violent or so manifestly and immediately threatening to the most vital Western interests that their commission might conceivably draw an immediate nuclear response from the United States directly against the Soviet Union, and (2) much less violent or threatening acts to which an immediate nuclear response from the United States would be wholly inappropriate and would therefore be ruled out by the Soviet leaders but which might be sufficiently grave to provoke some lesser American military response that could initiate a chain of events (escalation) culminating in general war.

Two different thresholds are associated with these two classes of action: one dividing actions in the second category from those in the first; and the other dividing actions in the second category from all others. So long as the Soviet leaders are resolved to avoid actions in both catagories, the second, or lower, threshold will be the crucial one in their deliberations, and the higher threshold will be considered only in so far as crossing it might add to the peril of inadvertently crossing the lower one. This has been the basic situation throughout the cold war. Probably seldom if ever have Soviet leaders deliberated seriously about whether a contemplated action might inadvertently bring them over the higher threshold and spark a general war— although the decision to deploy missiles in Cuba may have been one instance of this.[9] Rather, they have been mainly preoccupied with the avoidance of acts that would lead to military conflict of any kind with American forces. Short of such acts, the Soviet leaders have employed threats, pressures, and various other expedients in order to make political gains. Since this limitation on the means that the U.S.S.R. was prepared to employ was not always apparent to the West (indeed, it could be known only in retrospect), and since the United States, too, has wished to avoid direct military confrontations with the U.S.S.R., there has been an area in which the Soviet leaders could maneuver with very high assurance of immunity to military response, though not always with great confidence in political success. Even

---

[9] But only in the sense that they may have deliberated about the danger of touching off a general war before concluding that the risk was negligible; see pp. 141–42.

within this restricted area of maneuver, success could create new difficulties for the Soviet leaders: if the U.S.S.R. registered some unexpected gain, or one that was perceived (rightly or wrongly) by American leaders to be potentially very harmful to broader Western interests, the United States government might be led to enlarge the area of interests it was willing to defend by force, thus further constricting the "safe" area of cold war maneuver for the U.S.S.R. Under the circumstances, it is small wonder that moderate, carefully applied, and graduated pressure has been the preferred Soviet mode of political offensive in the cold war.

The advent of some form of strategic parity might lessen the virtually absolute Soviet aversion to engaging in actions that might precipitate military conflict with the United States even at low levels of violence. If parity were achieved, the upper threshold might become important for policy. In some circumstances, the Soviet leaders might then be willing to cross the lower threshold—that is, risk provoking a limited Western military response—but only if they were confident that their action would not spark a United States nuclear attack on the U.S.S.R.—that is, inadvertently lead them across the upper threshold. Whether the location of the upper threshold did gain appreciably in significance, however, would depend on the stability of the strategic balance. If the form of strategic parity postulated were what we have termed "mutual genocidal retaliatory capabilities," the strategic balance would be highly stable and the dangers of inadvertently sparking general war would probably not be a matter of serious concern.[10] The Soviet leaders, doubtless, would not begin by exploring the upper limits of the lower threshold, but they might test American tendencies to escalate hostilities by taking actions in the less dangerous part of the spectrum. It is toward such actions that Soviet attitudes might be soonest and most substantially modified by the termination of United States strategic superiority. Let us consider why this is so.

The present great reluctance of the Soviet leaders to risk testing the threshold of American forbearance, even at the lowest levels of violence, does not stem fundamentally from fear that the United States might prevail in limited military actions against Soviet forces. Since the initiative in undertaking offensive moves rests in Soviet hands, the Soviet leaders can choose where and when to offer violent

---

[10] This is not to say that the likelihood of general war would be non-existent, since the willingness of both sides to cross the lower threshold might conceivably heighten the danger of hostilities escalating to general war.

challenges to United States interests or to engage in actions that could be resisted only by violence. Even in situations where the U.S.S.R. has enjoyed substantial local military superiority, the Soviet leaders have feared to employ their superiority militarily when threats have been insufficient to compel their Western opponents to make the desired political concessions. Evidently, the Soviet leaders have feared that, in actual military conflict, the United States, possessing superiority at higher, strategic levels, would be, or would become, progressively more unwilling to accept as final any defeats inflicted by the U.S.S.R. at lower, tactical levels. At each successively higher level of violence, therefore, the risks associated with military "success" would be less acceptable to the Soviet Union. The higher the level of conflict, the closer it would edge toward the decisive area of United States superiority.

The Soviet leaders may be quite confident that American leaders are unwilling even to contemplate general war except as a last and desperate resort and that they wish to avoid, if possible, direct military conflict of any kind with the U.S.S.R. Yet so long as America enjoys strategic superiority, the Soviet leaders must fear that the United States, if engaged in the armed defense of a Western interest and threatened by the opponent's superiority in local military force, might threaten to extend the war, and might actually do so, in order to meet the Soviet Union on terms of equality or superiority. The U.S.S.R. must therefore seek to achieve its objectives without provoking armed resistance by the United States. And if military conflict should appear imminent or actually break out, prompt disengagement or withdrawal is enjoined, in order to avoid the risks of escalation.[11]

In conditions of mutually acknowledged strategic parity, this crucially important difference in willingness to escalate might no longer be characteristic. As before, the Soviet leaders would strongly prefer to make political gains without military conflict, particularly against the United States. But actions that risked the outbreak of small-scale violence involving American forces might no longer be precluded. In the event Soviet and American military forces actually became engaged in conflict, the Soviet leaders might be prepared to cope with American threats to escalate and to match such escalation, if

---

[11] Only to the extent that the U.S.S.R. remains a relatively free agent in its relations with allies and clients can it act in accordance with its own inclinations. As the other Communist states become more autonomous, the Soviet Union finds itself increasingly drawn into dangerous situations that it would prefer to avoid. See the discussion of the 1965 Vietnam crisis on pp. 173–74.

necessary. This would be true particularly if the United States could not match Soviet military capabilities except at very high levels of violence and could no longer surpass them even at the highest level. The effect of such a change in the predispositions of Soviet leaders might be to encourage more aggressive and tenacious conduct of political offensives.

In embarking on a new offensive against Western interests and positions, however, the Soviet leaders, even in conditions of strategic parity, would still strongly prefer to achieve success by threatening to employ force rather than by actually employing force. A major problem for the Soviet leaders, then, would be to convince their opponents of their preference for avoiding military conflict, if possible, but of their willingness to engage in it if necessary to secure their objectives. The Soviet leaders might actually be prepared for the first time to engage in limited military actions. Moreover, they might suppose that once their opponents recognized the willingness of the U.S.S.R. to fight they would prefer small concessions to wars.

Yet the Soviet Union might find it very difficult to persuade its adversaries that under conditions of strategic parity the West should give more credibility to Soviet threats. To demonstrate that the Soviet Union's improved strategic position vis-à-vis the United States had brought new resolve to its leaders, it would not suffice to resume issuing the now familiar "empty threats," that is, threats accompanying demands that a Western power abstain from doing what it had no intention of doing in any case, perhaps for reasons quite apart from the Soviet deterrent threat.[12] The renewal of such threats might signal to the West that Soviet foreign policy was entering a new hostile phase but not necessarily that Soviet behavior would be different from what it had been or that Moscow might find it necessary to carry out its threats if the demands associated with them were not satisfied.

The Berlin question would probably still be the key issue on which to apply pressure. It would have all the advantages as a lever against the Western powers that it has had since the end of World War II: (1) the objective, West Berlin, remains a highly exposed, locally

---

[12] Such contrived threats are not without political value: they can impress potential blackmail victims, who may not realize how unlikely is the act "forestalled" by the Soviet threat. In addition, some third countries may be encouraged by the ostensible success of such threats to seek Soviet support in future conflicts with the United States or with countries allied to the United States. The Soviet leaders have often employed ambiguous strategic threats covering highly unlikely contingencies as a cheap means of establishing Soviet interest in far-flung corners of the world where the U.S.S.R. previously played no significant political role.

indefensible Western salient; (2) the initial threats could be non-violent (that is, the U.S.S.R. could threaten to sign a peace treaty with the German Democratic Republic and to turn over to the East Germans control of the access routes to West Berlin); and (3) the only threats of force would be those of retaliation against a Western violation of G.D.R. "sovereignty."

The Soviet leaders might adopt a Berlin strategy designed to confront the Western allies with a series of non-violent but progressively more provocative moves, inviting them at each stage, individually as well as jointly, to avoid further escalation by agreeing to negotiate on Communist terms. For example, the Soviet leaders might provoke a new crisis over Berlin by reviving "for the last time" their demand for a conference of all members of the former anti-Nazi coalition to sign a peace treaty with both German governments that would involve Western recognition of the G.D.R. The Soviet leaders would threaten once more to sign a separate peace treaty with the East Germans if the Western powers did not agree to a peace conference. Presumably, the allies, having called the Soviet bluff on this issue in the past, would refuse. This time, however, Western refusal might actually be answered by the often postponed signing of a Soviet-G.D.R. peace treaty. In accordance with the provisions of such a treaty, the Soviet Union might turn over to the East Germans formal control over West Berlin access routes and invite the Western powers to deal with the East German authorities on questions of access. If the Western powers chose to avoid a showdown by treating the East Germans as mere agents of the Soviet Union, which they would continue to hold responsible, the Russians (and East Germans) might permit traffic to continue to move in normal fashion for some time. At some point a series of measures might be implemented by the East Germans to hinder communications between West Germany and West Berlin. The Western powers would be invited to iron out any misunderstandings with the East German government. Pending agreement, allied convoys would be detained at checkpoints. The Soviet Union might proceed in this manner on the assumption (1) that the Western allies would be unable to agree among themselves to resort to violence rather than negotiate with the East Germans; (2) that even if agreement were reached, or if the United States decided to act alone, the Soviet and East German forces could cope with any limited Western military action; and (3) that the Western powers, facing the prospect of defeat at every local level of conflict and now no less fearful than the Communists of escalation toward unlimited war, could be quickly compelled to open negotiations with the G.D.R. regarding access to West Berlin. By such tactics, if the West failed to adjust its military posture and strategy rapidly to meet the new threat, the U.S.S.R. might hope to destroy the NATO alliance without employing its strategic force militarily. That force would be used principally to deter United States threats of, or resort to, unlimited war.

The employment of such tactics would still be risky, however, even if the Soviet assumption proved correct that important political concessions could be extracted from the Western allies once they were convinced of Soviet willingness to engage in limited military conflict. Risks would result from the increased danger that the West might miscalculate, through a failure to recognize the new Soviet resolve to persist in pursuing offensives once begun.

Whether the Soviet leaders would decide to exploit the emergence of strategic parity by such tactics and how successful they might be would depend in some measure on the manner in which awareness was brought home to the West and its leaders that the United States no longer enjoyed an effective margin of strategic superiority over the Soviet Union. If awareness came suddenly, perhaps as a consequence of some dramatic new Soviet military demonstration or in conjunction with a sharp diplomatic confrontation after a prolonged period of Western unconcern over the likelihood of nuclear war, it might greatly inhibit Western reactions and might lead to virtual paralysis in some quarters. An estimate of such an effect in the West appears to have been one of the calculations underlying Soviet "Sputnik diplomacy" between 1957 and 1962, most notably in regard to Berlin.[13] If, as seems more likely, Western reliance on strategic weapons for the defense of key areas declined slowly and deliberately, the emergence of a mutually acknowledged state of strategic parity might appear

---

[13] In the new circumstances postulated here, the Soviets might again time a demonstration of some new strategic weapon (for example, a new antimissile missile) to coincide with a diplomatic confrontation with the West. The actual military value of the new weapon might be negligible, and even recognized as such by most Western leaders and their advisers; yet public opinion in Western countries might be influenced by such a demonstration, at least temporarily, during the acute phase of the diplomatic crisis. On the basis of the demonstration, Soviet leaders might even claim that they had achieved some margin of strategic superiority over the United States (for example, that the Soviet Union had some damage-limiting capability, whereas the Western powers did not). If the Soviet claim was not believed or was later discredited, little harm might result, since Western beliefs that the Soviet Union had achieved strategic parity would not depend on the credibility of the new Soviet strategic claims, as they did during the years of the missile gap. See below, pp. 205–6.

somewhat less promising to the Soviet leaders as the basis for a renewed political offensive, although, as we shall show in what follows, such an offensive might still be adopted.

Since 1961 United States defense policy, in addition to strengthening and improving the strategic retaliatory force, has sought to strengthen and improve major non-strategic components of the American and allied military posture so as to reduce gradually the burden that the American long-range nuclear strike force has carried in defense of third countries. Presumably, these recent efforts, together with optimistic expectations regarding the extent to which United States and allied general-purpose forces can be further strengthened in the years ahead, are among the considerations that have led some Western observers to discount the new political and military dangers that might arise if the United States lost its strategic superiority. Of course, if the U.S.S.R. should overcome its strategic inferiority and achieve parity, it would be particularly desirable for the NATO powers to correct the present conventional military imbalance in Europe.[14] Strategic parity, however, will not automatically bring about parity in conventional arms.

The difficulties encountered by the United States in attempting to persuade the Western European allies to make substantial peacetime increases in their conventional forces are well known and need not be reviewed here. It is often overlooked, however, that if substantial cuts in Soviet conventional forces since 1955 have made the goal of conventional parity seem more feasible than before, substantial increases in these forces, even back to the 1955 level (5,763,000), are also a possibility under certain circumstances. Whereas American

---

[14] This does not mean that elimination of United States strategic superiority would necessarily destabilize the present over-all military balance in Europe or that stability could be maintained only if the present conventional military imbalance were corrected. American tactical nuclear power might serve to maintain the equilibrium, provided the necessary forces were made available and the Western allies could agree on appropriate strategies and tactics for bringing them to bear politically and militarily. Analysis of this complex and controversial question, however, lies beyond the scope of this book. For some Western discussions of conventional versus tactical nuclear defense of Western Europe, see Henry A. Kissinger, *The Necessity for Choice* (New York: Harper & Row, 1961), pp. 57–98; Bernard Brodie, "What Price Conventional Capabilities in Europe?" *Reporter*, May 23, 1963, pp. 25–33; Malcolm Hoag, "What Interdependence for NATO?" *World Politics*, April, 1960; W. Kintner and S. Possony, "NATO's Nuclear Crisis," *Orbis*, Summer, 1962. Given present Soviet superiority in immediately available and rapidly mobilizable conventional forces in Europe, Soviet policy on tactical nuclear warfare is more likely to be reactive to Western policy and posture than to grow out of Soviet preferences. The standard contention of publicly expressed Soviet military doctrine is that the use of nuclear weapons in any form in a United States–Soviet conflict would inevitably mean escalation to general nuclear war.

governments have had their hands full for years trying (with but partial success) to persuade reluctant allies to raise larger armies, Khrushchev was kept busy trying to force troop cuts down the throats of his marshals and generals.[15] Should strategic parity come about at relatively small cost to the U.S.S.R., because the United States decided that the effort to maintain strategic superiority was futile, Soviet as well as American resources might be freed for use by non-strategic forces. And if, under the conditions of a thermonuclear standoff, it appeared to the Soviet leaders that the Western powers were relying on a balance of conventional military forces to preserve world political stability, the Soviet Union's incentives to restore its conventional establishment to something like its former dimensions would probably grow. (By concentrating on large ground forces, the Soviet leaders would then be doing what comes naturally for them.)

Even if the West's vast manpower and production resources could eventually be brought to bear in sufficient strength to match the conventional forces of the Soviet Union and its Eastern European allies, it could probably not be done all at once. So long as their leaders believe that the United States possesses strategic superiority, most Western governments will tend to rely on it to deter both nuclear and large-scale non-nuclear aggression by the Soviet Union and will probably continue to ignore American exhortations that they accelerate the buildup of their conventional forces. Indeed, if the Soviet Union was to pursue an unaggressive foreign policy in Western Europe and there was no firm evidence of a forthcoming change in Soviet policy, the Western governments might not even recognize that the emergence of a state of strategic parity necessitated accelerated efforts to strengthen their conventional forces. Some of these governments might become concerned about possible leaks in the United States nuclear umbrella only after a new campaign of Soviet threats had been unleashed. Even then, the policies they would adopt to cope with this new situation might not lead to a strengthening of the alliance's conventional military capabilities. Moreover, if most Western governments did adopt a conventional buildup as a substitute for primary reliance on United States strategic superiority to deter a Soviet non-nuclear attack, such a buildup would take time to complete. The West would face a transitional period, possibly

---

[15] Apparently also with but partial success. See Thomas W. Wolfe, *Soviet Strategy at the Crossroads* (Cambridge, Mass.: Harvard University Press, 1964), pp. 139–52.

prolonged, during which countervailing Western conventional forces were not yet in the field and the credibility of United States strategic deterrence of large-scale non-nuclear Soviet aggression was in question.

It is not possible to predict Soviet foreign and military policies during such a transition period. They would be conditioned by a number of interrelated political and military calculations: Soviet assessment of the new opportunities for political gain created by the improved strategic environment, the costs and risks of a renewed political offensive, the availability of alternative strategies and tactics for securing political gains, and so on. Finally, the actual decision would depend on the political character of the Soviet leadership at the time.

In these circumstances, the Soviet leaders might have to make a difficult choice among several alternative policies. They might view the disequilibrium created by the advent of United States–Soviet strategic parity as a transitory phenomenon that would soon be superseded by the development of a military balance on the continent. Whatever unique opportunities for political gain such an environment might offer, they would soon disappear if not exploited. In these perhaps temporary circumstances, a dramatic political or diplomatic success by the Soviet Union could have revolutionary effects on the political and military complexion of Europe. There might be a chance, if the opportunity were seized, to accelerate rapidly a process of historical development that might otherwise take decades to unfold, if it ever did.

Yet such a course of action, involving considerably stronger pressures than the Soviet leaders have yet dared to apply, would entail serious risks. Moreover, if these pressures proved insufficient, the offensive would not only fail to achieve its objectives but might leave the Soviet Union relatively worse off than before. Renewed Soviet threats and pressures might reverse the trend toward gradual, if unspectacular, erosion of the Western alliance. If the renewed offensive failed to rout or paralyze the Western allies, it might have the effect of restoring their unity and firmness of purpose. Consequently, unless the Soviet leaders believed that strategic parity provided excellent conditions for achieving large political gains, they would be unlikely to apply sharp pressures to that end. Conceivably, a series of estimates by the Soviet leaders that the situation was not yet ripe for a renewed offensive against the West could gradually lead, in effect, to abandonment of plans for such an offensive and to a new relationship between the Soviet Union, the United States, and the NATO allies. Alternatively, the Soviet leaders might decide that the necessary conditions of success in a new offensive against the West required not merely the achievement of strategic parity but also credit for having achieved some margin of strategic superiority. How they might seek to gain credit for possessing it and how they might proceed to exploit it are considered in the next chapter.

FIFTEEN

QUEST FOR SUPERIORITY

A SOVIET POLITICAL OFFENSIVE based on claims of strategic superiority is theoretically consistent with actual strategic states of various kinds. Even when the U.S.S.R. was markedly inferior in intercontinental nuclear power, as we have seen, the Soviet leaders claimed to be militarily superior and made such claims the basis of an ambitious political offensive. Of course, something like genuine strategic parity or some real margin of superiority, if either could be achieved, would provide more promising bases for claims of superiority and for corresponding efforts to make gains in the cold war. Although a future Soviet political offensive based on claimed strategic superiority could be launched from any of these positions of relative strength, the prospects of success necessarily depend on which one it is. Moreover, the choice and credibility of the claims to be made will depend largely upon the real military balance. Equally important, the Soviet leaders' willingness to take the actions necessary to compel large concessions by the West and bring success to the offensive depends critically on their actual estimate of the strategic balance. If the gap is too great between their estimate and their claims, even a high degree of success in concealing this discrepancy from the West may not compensate for the self-limitations imposed by the Soviet leaders' awareness of their inferiority. If they have learned from past experience to be cautious in setting such limits, they may be reluctant to initiate a new political offensive based on claims of strategic superiority without first radically improving the Soviet strategic position with respect to the United States. An attempt to do so would certainly encounter serious military and economic obstacles. But if the Soviet leaders were satisfied with less than this, it is questionable that their strategic forces would secure them large political gains.

Clearly, the difficulties the Soviet leaders would face in trying to gain credit for strategic superiority are considerable, and they might prove insuperable. Moreover, the political as well as the economic costs of trying but failing in an ambitious new political offensive based on claims of strategic superiority could be great. Is this, then, an alternative that the Soviet leaders will consider seriously in the next few years? Certainly, a strategic policy in which superiority might play a prominent part cannot be ruled out for the future. Its attractiveness to the Soviet leaders, even when the military situation was not propitious, has already been demonstrated. Such a political strategy deserves our attention if for no other reason than that it indicates what the Soviet leaders may have hoped to achieve by its use in the past. Moreover, future circumstances may sharply increase the likelihood that the Soviet leaders will choose it. Finally, such a strategy is of theoretical interest, as the limiting case of the Soviet political use of strategic power.

Consideration of a future Soviet political strategy based on strategic superiority must necessarily be highly speculative; if it is not to be simply academic, the military foundation postulated can only be strategic superiority of a limited kind. This is because *decisive* strategic superiority, such as would be conferred by a manifestly effective first-strike capability, appears to lie outside the spectrum of Soviet strategic postures that are attainable or that the Soviet Union could gain credit for possessing in the foreseeable future. It is not a question, then, of clear-cut, unequivocal strategic superiority—that is, of the U.S.S.R.'s acquiring (or persuading others that it has acquired) a retaliation-proof strategic force. In all probability, such superiority is no longer obtainable by either side. But short of this there are degrees of superiority that under certain conditions might be achieved by the Soviet Union or that it might be credited with possessing. In purely military terms—that is, in the event of war—the advantages conferred by such lesser forms of superiority might be considered doubtful or marginal by the side possessing them. The question to be considered is whether such militarily ambiguous or marginal superiority in the hands of the Soviet Union might be exploited to yield disproportionately large political gains.

In Western strategic discourse one school of thought holds that, since decisive strategic superiority is no longer attainable, lesser forms of superiority are meaningless (not credible), wasteful ("overkill"), and potentially dangerous (provocative). The Soviet leaders were quick to associate themselves with the views of those in the West who contend that United States strategic superiority ceased to have significant military or political value once the Soviet Union acquired the means to inflict substantial damage on the United States. At the end, Khrushchev, like some Western critics of American defense policy, denied that superiority in "overkill" capacity had any value. "To calculate who can destroy whom several times over is stupid arithmetic," Khrushchev said. "If they destroy you once, what difference does it make if they then destroy you five times more?" [1] It is doubtful, however, that the Soviet leaders would believe such

---

[1] *Pravda*, April 7, 1964.

"superiority" made no difference were the positions of the two sides reversed or made to appear so. There is historical evidence suggesting that the Soviet leaders would value highly the political advantages conferred by ambiguous forms of strategic superiority, even though they fell far short of a manifest capability to strike first without suffering substantial damage in retaliation.

In late 1959, the Soviet leaders began to claim a marginal form of strategic superiority at a time when Western anxieties about the widely predicted "missile gap" had reached a new peak.[2] In the winter months following his meetings with President Eisenhower at Camp David (September, 1959), Khrushchev claimed for the U.S.S.R. a form of strategic superiority such that, if the Soviet Union were attacked, the retaliatory blows of surviving Soviet strategic forces "could literally wipe from the face of the earth the country or countries that attacked" it; the U.S.S.R. would survive, he maintained, though suffering "great losses." He made this differentiation between expected war outcomes for the U.S.S.R. and its opponents most explicit in his speech to the Supreme Soviet on January 14, 1960. Talking of military affairs, he remarked:

Of course, in the event of a new world war all countries would ultimately suffer in one way or another. We, too, would have many losses, but we would survive. Our territory is immense and the population is less concentrated in major industrial centers than in many other countries. The West would suffer incomparably more.[3]

Earlier we termed the strategic capability implied by this claim "a maximum retaliatory damage capability."[4] Possession of such a capability confers some form of superiority if, as Khrushchev asserted in January, 1960, the opponent does not possess a like capability. Evidently, Khrushchev believed that even such a limited form of superiority, if the West could be brought to credit it, could be exploited more profitably than an unequivocal state of parity. This conclusion seems obvious since, in asserting this claim, the Soviet leader accepted certain liabilities that he might have avoided had he chosen instead to claim, as he did later, that the U.S.S.R. had achieved strategic parity and that nuclear war would therefore be a catastrophe for both sides without distinction. The latter claim, precisely because it does not assert an advantage for the claimant, is

---

[2] See chapter v.
[3] *Pravda*, January 15, 1960.
[4] See p. 68.

inherently more credible to the opponent. If Khrushchev had not believed there was greater advantage to be gained from even a doubtful claim of limited superiority than from a claim of parity, he would not needlessly have sacrificed credibility. Moreover, the Soviet interest in the Soviet Communist party's dispute with the Chinese Communists, which was then about to erupt into open polemics, would have been better served by the lesser strategic claim. The Soviet position in the dispute over correct strategy and tactics in conducting the cold war rests on the contention that a policy of comparatively limited risk-taking is enjoined by the mutually destructive consequences of general war.[5]

Having claimed to possess a retaliatory capability superior to the United States first-strike capability, why did Khrushchev not go still farther and claim a first-strike capability? The two considerations just mentioned—concern over the credibility of his claim in the West and over the exigencies of the dispute with Peking—probably set limits beyond which Khrushchev could not go, even in pursuit of the political benefits to be derived from higher forms of strategic superiority. In any case, had Khrushchev then claimed for the U.S.S.R. an effective first-strike capability, this claim would have been disbelieved in the West and at the same time might have provoked even more strenuous defense measures in the United States. It would have provided the Chinese Communists with powerful new ammunition by seeming to confirm their contention that the socialist camp had achieved superiority over the West and hence had acquired the basis for more militant and offensive policies than Khrushchev was then willing to pursue. In addition, Khrushchev may have calculated that particular Soviet policies—such as the fostering in the West of sentiment favorable to Soviet disarmament proposals—would be obstructed by assertions that Soviet leaders believed they had the capability (hence possibly harbored the intention) of initiating general war with the expectation of securing a favorable outcome.

Khrushchev may have wished merely to lay a foundation upon which subsequent claims to possess a higher form of superiority might be built. This would have been consistent with the systematic manner in which Soviet military claims normally expand. If this was his plan, it miscarried. The U-2 affair and related events brought the progres-

---

[5] Three months before claiming that the Soviet Union had surpassed the United States in strategic power, Khrushchev had lectured the Chinese leaders in Peking on "the danger of attempting to test the stability of capitalism by force" (*Pravda*, October 1, 1959).

sion of Soviet strategic claims to a halt; and the exposure of Soviet missile deception in the fall of 1961 forced the Soviet leaders to retreat from claims of superiority to claims of sufficiency.

Since strategic inferiority proved inadequate to support a political offensive based on claims of superiority, it seems unlikely to be tried again. However, what of a future situation in which the U.S.S.R. had achieved a strategic parity with the United States that was acknowledged by United States leaders? Could this improved posture, which is feasible, provide a foundation upon which the Soviet leaders might renew their claims to possess a higher form of strategic superiority? Could the Soviet leaders make credible to the West a claim to such superiority and thus feel free to engage in almost any hostile action against the West short of general war? Moreover, would it be possible on a basis of strategic parity, to make credible even threats of launching a first strike against the United States?

Here it is necessary to amplify the distinction between the political and military effectiveness of a first-strike capability. Its military effectiveness may be measured in terms of the probable retaliatory damage that would be suffered if that capability were actually employed. The classical preventive war strategy in the nuclear age, "the bolt from the blue," requires a highly effective first-strike capability, one that virtually disarms the opponent's strategic forces in an initial surprise blow. Accordingly, to launch a surprise attack requires a high-confidence estimate of the effectiveness of the strategic force to be employed, particularly regarding the upper limits of probable retaliatory damage. Given the tremendous destructive power of thermonuclear weapons, the margin for error is small, and the consequences of miscalculation may be catastrophic. Many observers have therefore concluded that no rational statesman could have sufficient confidence in the paper calculations of his subordinates to launch a premeditated first strike against an opponent armed with large numbers of thermonuclear weapons and delivery vehicles, even if they were numerically inferior to his own and appeared to have serious vulnerabilities that could readily be exploited.[6] Although, in the opinion of others, this conclusion should be qualified, it does recognize what is crucial in deliberations on launching a first strike: the uncertainty of the potential aggressor about the military effectiveness of his strategic forces when employed on such a mission. The defender's uncertainty about the effectiveness of his retaliatory capa-

---

[6] See, for example, the cogent arguments of P. M. S. Blackett, in *Studies of War* (New York: Hill and Wang, 1962), pp. 128–46.

bility is relevant to the extent that the potential aggressor is aware of it. His uncertainty may encourage the aggressor to resolve his own uncertainties in favor of striking. But its relevance is only indirect and derivative.

The situation is otherwise, however, when the political use of strategic force is contemplated. A power's deliberations on employing its first-strike capability politically will be heavily concentrated on the defender's uncertainty about his retaliatory capability. That is to say, an aggressor realizes that the defender's response to a threat, explicit or implied, of having a first strike launched against him in certain contingencies is influenced, perhaps decisively, by his estimate of the military effectiveness of his own retaliatory capability. Thus, the degree of political, as opposed to military, effectiveness of a Soviet first-strike capability would be measured, first of all, in terms of the confidence of the United States in its retaliatory capability. However, the boldness with which the U.S.S.R. might employ the threat of a first strike would necessarily be limited by its confidence in the military effectiveness of its own strategic forces for a first strike. This is true because a contingent threat to launch a first strike, even if an avenue of retreat is left open, in some measure increases the risk of war. Even so, in estimating the risk of provoking a pre-emptive attack by the opponent, the U.S.S.R. would probably be guided less by its expectations of how its strategic forces would perform in a suddenly launched first strike than by its estimate of the United States' belief concerning the Soviet Union's second-strike capability. The risk would probably appear low so long as the United States seemed to credit the U.S.S.R. with a retaliatory capability so strong that there would be only a small inducement for the United States to strike first.

In the era of thermonuclear weapons, uncertainty pervades all military calculations of the strategic balance. But although there is uncertainty on both sides, its effect is not always symmetrical. The successful political employment of strategic power does not require that one's uncertainties be wholly overcome but rather that the relevant uncertainties of the opponent be maximized and the situation so manipulated as to make the outcome of a given confrontation turn on the opponent's uncertainties rather than on one's own.

If elements of Western governments and publics could be made sufficiently uncertain about the military effectiveness of America's second-strike capability, the Soviet Union would thereby gain some of the political advantages of possessing a first-strike capability without actually possessing one. The more uncertain these Western audiences could be made to feel, the greater the range of conditions under which a Soviet first strike might appear credible and the greater would be the West's concern to avoid measures that might realize those conditions. Such a politically usable first-strike capability could provide the Soviet leaders with a foundation for far-reaching political strategies aimed at depriving the West of vital positions while avoiding general war.

To sum up: because the requirements for employing a first-strike capability politically are far less stringent than the requirements for employing such a force militarily, the U.S.S.R. might conceivably hope to satisfy them. Even so, the objective military requirements are not negligible or easily attained. The U.S.S.R might lack the means of satisfying them and, in any case, might be discouraged from making the attempt, particularly if United States defense and foreign policies were deliberately designed to discourage it. This appears to be the situation in the mid-sixties.

The objective military requirements for acquiring a politically exploitable margin of superiority might be lowered if the Soviet leaders could rely on deception to fill the gap between their actual capabilities and those they wished to make credible to their opponents. They have demonstrated over a period of years their readiness to employ such deception, and the large degree of acceptance that the "missile gap" myth gained in the West revealed the special susceptibility of important Western audiences to such Soviet manipulation and their predisposition, for a variety of reasons, to believe the worst regarding Soviet strategic capabilities. The West's views, of course, have varied from group to group. Responsible United States leaders with access to intelligence materials have been less prone to exaggerate Soviet strategic power than various publics in the United States and in allied and neutralist countries. Yet the fact remains that, as a result of deficiencies in information, prevailing beliefs about the character and intentions of the Soviet leaders, and Soviet efforts to manipulate these beliefs, the U.S.S.R. has generally been credited with larger strategic capabilities than it has actually possessed. (The relationship between Soviet strategic claims, Western beliefs about the strategic balance, and "reality" is represented in Figure 1.)

The Soviet leaders did succeed in reducing the politically usable margin of United States strategic superiority. (In terms of the rough graph in Figure 1, the arena of politics was primarily within the bounds of the dotted lines and not between the solid lines below them.) The large margin of real United States superiority, however, served as an insurance factor, preventing exaggerated fears of Soviet strategic power from having calamitous political consequences. If an actual state of strategic parity were to arise in the future, the Soviet leaders would not necessarily be content to adopt such a representation of the strategic balance as their own; on the contrary, if they were accorded parity, they would probably claim some form of superiority.

Of course, the West's experience with the "bomber gap" and the "missile gap," in which Soviet deception and Western self-deception

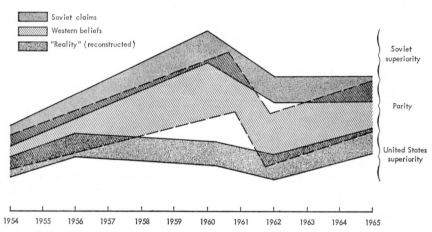

FIG. 1.—The strategic balance, 1954–65: Soviet claims, Western beliefs, and "reality" (reconstructed).

were eventually revealed, may make it much less easy for the Soviet leaders to exploit Western susceptibilities and predispositions for some time. Recent improvements in the effectiveness of Western intelligence capabilities will also make it more difficult to exaggerate future Soviet strategic capabilities (for example, to exploit an "anti-missile missile gap").[7] However, the uncertainties inherent in assessing Soviet strategic capabilities are so great that even substantially improved intelligence could probably not be relied upon to resolve them all with high confidence. Moreover, it is questionable whether the confidence of the most informed circles of the government, even if it were great, could be so persuasively communicated to politically relevant groups in the West and among neutral countries as to

---

[7] According to Secretary McNamara: "The possibility of error [in estimates of Soviet strategic forces] is materially less than it has been at many times in the past, because of the improvement in our intelligence-collection methods, which for obvious reasons I cannot discuss" (*U.S. News & World Report*, April 12, 1965, p. 59).

prevent doubts from arising periodically. And these would be doubts, not about the extent of United States superiority, but about whether the Soviet Union might not be superior.

This situation might change if the powers no longer had to rely solely on unilateral national intelligence-gathering facilities to ensure that no country was engaged in a sudden and clandestine destabilizing arms buildup. One beneficial side-effect of an arms control agreement that provided for international inspection to ensure compliance would be to render ineffective deliberately exaggerated or deceptive military claims as offensive political tools.

In any case, the Soviet acquisition of strategic forces evidently possessing some margin of superiority, or even providing a suitable basis for inducing such a belief in the U.S.S.R.'s opponents, would be a highly uncertain undertaking, both difficult and costly. It may be questioned whether Soviet leaders would undertake such an enterprise just to secure a foundation for ambitious political strategies that might fail for other reasons. Would they not be content with something approaching parity or even with a manifestly inferior though still substantial capability, despite the consequent political limitations? They might well be. We have already suggested some of the conditions under which inferior or roughly equivalent strategic capabilities might be politically acceptable to the Soviet leaders.

Yet a retaliatory capability, even a very powerful one, that manifestly lacks any substantial capacity to limit damage to its possessor's country from the action of the opponent's strategic force, has serious military deficiencies as well as political limitations. A Soviet strategic force possessing only a retaliatory capability, even if it were adequate to deter a deliberate attack by the United States, could not be relied upon to prevent the inadvertent initiation of general war; and such a war could destroy the peoples of the Soviet Union as well as the Soviet state. Soviet military leaders, being professionally preoccupied with the contingency of actually fighting a general war, have on some occasions insisted that nothing less than superior forces can suffice for the Soviet Union.[8] Thus, in addition to providing the Soviet Union with a powerful political instrument, a strategic force that possessed some margin of superiority over that of the United States might also recommend itself to the Soviet leaders as an improved means of

---

[8] See Thomas W. Wolfe, *Soviet Strategy at the Crossroads*, pp. 79–90.

fighting a general war should it occur and of limiting damage to the U.S.S.R. Perhaps, if further strengthened, it might even offer some promise of "victory."

On what kinds of military capabilities might Soviet leaders base future claims of strategic superiority over the United States? Obviously, any answer to this question must be speculative. What follows, therefore, is chiefly meant to illustrate some of the possibilities that might be considered by the Soviet leaders were they to embark on a concerted effort to achieve strategic superiority or the credit for possessing it. The quantitative gap between United States and Soviet intercontinental strike forces is presently so large that the Soviet leaders are unlikely to base a future assertion of strategic superiority on possession of a quantitative edge in current strategic offensive weapon systems. In the mid-sixties, Soviet claims of strategic parity were based, not on claims to possess equal numbers of ICBM's, long-range bombers, and missile-launching submarines but rather on the "sufficiency" of the available force and on its qualitative superiority. Although this could provide a credible basis for claims that the quantitative superiority of an opposing force had been nullified, it could not, without great difficulty, be made the basis of claims to strategic superiority.

A more promising route to a strategic posture that would support claims of strategic superiority over the United States lies through the rapid and extensive exploitation of some major breakthrough or surprise in military technology. Perhaps the most striking and potentially destabilizing breakthrough that can now be anticipated is in the field of antimissile capabilities, for it would reduce the requirement for substantial quantitative superiority in offensive weapons. In addition, opposing offensive weapons that might otherwise remain relatively invulnerable to prelaunch destruction even by a numerically superior attacking force might be made vulnerable to attack while in flight.[9]

At present it is not clear whether it will prove technically feasible to develop and deploy an active ballistic-missile defense system that could achieve a significant rate of attrition or whether in a contest between an improved ballistic-missile defense system and the opponent's improved offensive penetration capabilities the costs for the

---

[9] For a Soviet analysis of the technical potentialities of ABM systems and the strategic implications of their deployment, see N. Talensky, "Anti-Missile Systems and Disarmament," *International Affairs*, 1964, No. 10, pp. 15–19.

defensive side might not prove to be prohibitively disproportionate.[10] It is possible, however, that a moderately effective ballistic-missile defense system, if deployed massively and rapidly, could achieve a militarily and politically significant advantage that might last for several years. Under some future condition of parity, in particular, the strategic balance might be asymmetrically sensitive to technological breakthroughs or surprises, since a politically aggressive power that wished to destabilize the balance could pick and choose among promising new military technologies, concentrate its resources to achieve a rapid peak in a new capability, and thus acquire a temporary advantage suitable for prompt political exploitation.

Moreover, the political effect of a sizable deployment of an antimissile system by the Soviet Union might far exceed its real military value, particularly if no comparable active defense system existed in the West. It might be far easier for the Soviet leaders to claim and demonstrate convincingly that the U.S.S.R. had developed and widely deployed a ballistic-missile defense system than for the West to claim or demonstrate convincingly that the Soviet system deployed would not be effective in actual combat. As Freeman Dyson has written: "Any BMD system is admirably suited for bluffing purposes since nobody will ever know, short of a major war, how good or bad the system really is. It is possible to imagine a successful bluff based on plywood dummies of BMD installations." [11] To feed Western uncertainty regarding the technical efficiency of any Soviet ballistic-missile defense system that might be widely deployed, appropriate demonstrations might be staged. Films of Soviet defensive weapons destroying incoming missiles could be shown, for example. (Several years ago Khrushchev said he had wanted to show delegates at the World Congress on Disarmament in Moscow a documentary film of an antimissile missile in action but was advised by some participants in the Congress that the film might be "misunderstood.") [12]

In addition to demonstrations and disclosures of their active defense capabilities, the Soviet leaders might also find it useful to demonstrate the high accuracy of their ICBM's and, perhaps, their possession of effective carriers of warheads with very high yields, a

---

[10] See the informative article by Freeman J. Dyson, "Defense against Ballistic Missiles," *Bulletin of the Atomic Scientists*, June, 1964, pp. 12–18; and John R. Thomas, "The Role of Missile Defense in Soviet Strategy," *Military Review*, May, 1964, pp. 46–58.

[11] Dyson, *op. cit.*, p. 17.

[12] *Pravda*, July 13, 1962. It was subsequently shown on Soviet television in connection with festivities on V-E day, 1965.

combination of weapon systems that might appear effective even against hardened United States targets. A significant capacity to shelter the Soviet population or to evacuate large urban centers might have to be demonstrated if it appeared that a not insignificant fraction of the United States strategic force was likely to survive Soviet offensive and active defensive operations. These passive defense measures, if extensive, might make it questionable whether a weakened United States retaliatory blow would destroy a large part of the Soviet population.

The types of demonstrations chosen by the Soviet Union would of course depend on the capabilities it actually possessed; however, they would also be influenced by Soviet beliefs about Western intelligence estimates and capabilities. Certainly, the effectiveness of Soviet demonstrations would depend critically upon how Western intelligence evaluated them. Methods that failed to convince intelligence experts, however, might still persuade popular opinion. And in Western societies, at least, the political fears and anxieties of the populace are conveyed to the leaders and affect their policies.

Whether the estimated military effectiveness of forces designed for superiority and the contribution they would be expected to make to Soviet foreign policy would persuade the Soviet leaders to assume the great cost of acquiring them can only be guessed. In the next few years, the U.S.S.R. may strive for real strategic parity, and while it does so, no radical change in the climate of Soviet politics appears likely. It seems doubtful that the Soviet leaders will make a strong bid to achieve a form of strategic superiority despite its appeal as a basis for a new political offensive. What happens in the longer run may depend on new developments in technology, on the politics of the Communist world, and on the West's choice among the alternative strategies open to it in the cold war.

CONCLUSION

We brothers and comrades-in-arms in socialism and communism have a right to ask of the Soviet brothers and comrades: What security have you for the Soviet Union itself against the imperialist danger? Is it not time to check with the greatest strictness on the activities of your chattering, bluffing, treacherous, and Khrushchevite leaders? Khrushchev and his disciples, who are in power at present, not only make false boasts to conceal the abyss, but they give away vital information to the Americans to strip the Soviet Union bare. Soviet brothers, check up a little on these people and see whether the weapons created by your renowned scientists are in safe hands. . . .

The Khrushchevite revisionists have bluffed . . . in international affairs. This is one of their characteristics. It is the way they work. [It] happened in 1956 in the case of Egypt, and later in the case of Berlin, Cuba, and so on. But while the bluff on Egypt had some results at the time, the other revisionist bluffs for Berlin and Cuba failed for a very simple reason: the imperialists had seen the cards held by the Khrushchevite revisionists.

Zeri I Popullit (organ of the Albanian Workers' Party), April 20, 1965

IN THIS ACCOUNT we have examined some of the broadest and most characteristic features of the political use of Soviet strategic power, chiefly as they have been manifested since Stalin's death but also as they may appear in the future. Fundamentally, however, strategic forces are but one instrument of foreign policy; hence, their peacetime use by the Soviet leaders must be understood in the light of overall Soviet foreign policy. Moreover, to be properly understood, the political use of strategic forces must be juxtaposed with other instruments of Soviet foreign policy, such as foreign aid programs and the peace campaign. Is their effectiveness significantly enhanced or impaired, or is it largely unaffected, by the concurrent political use of Soviet strategic forces?

Since the mid-fifties, during a period when the resources available to it were spread rather thin, Soviet foreign policy has been confronted with a series of striking opportunities and dangers. Soviet vulnerability to a United States nuclear attack, regardless of the circumstances in which it might be initiated, was a danger that could not be ignored, and it colored the whole of Soviet foreign policy. At the same time, the West's fear of Soviet nuclear power, especially its concern about the unprecedented Soviet progress in developing intercontinental weapons that could attack the United States, presented Moscow with an opportunity that was hard to pass over. In the underdeveloped areas, there were manifest opportunities for Soviet gains, as Western colonialism waned and numerous nations in Asia and Africa won their independence. Within the Communist camp, however, there was a whole series of dangers: that Soviet leadership of the Communist world might be undermined, that the U.S.S.R. might lose its postwar hegemony in Eastern Europe, and that Communist China might effect a rapid transition from subordinate ally, through dissident equal, to hostile heretic. All of these dangers, of course, were to some extent realized.

Although Soviet foreign policy is somewhat more unified than our own, these dangers and opportunities were probably dealt with piecemeal and not in strict accordance with some grand design. Yet neither could these dangers and prospective gains be isolated from each other. The pursuit of one objective by whatever means were available to the Soviet leaders—foreign economic aid, military assistance, conventional diplomacy, diplomacy within the United Nations, the political use of strategic power—was bound to affect progress toward the others. To take a simple example: economic aid to India worsened Soviet relations with Communist China. This was no less true with respect to the political use of Soviet strategic power. It was impossible to employ nuclear threats against the United States for Soviet ends without encouraging Communist China to press for their use in support of her own demands against the United States. Had Soviet economic resources been more abundant, it might have been possible to use them more freely to compensate for the unwillingness of the Soviet leaders to assume risks on behalf of their clients and allies. Communist China, for example, might have been given increased economic aid to make up for Soviet failure to offer military support for the C.P.R.'s foreign policy objectives. Throughout this period, however, the Soviet leaders used their economic, diplomatic, and military means, which were far inferior to what was required for success, in attempts both to avert major dangers and to exploit major opportunities.

Had the Soviet leaders concentrated on coping with the dangers facing them, they might have had greater success. The threat posed by the United States might have been neutralized by early adoption of a consistent policy of *détente*, such as Malenkov seemed to advocate, combined with a military policy of minimum deterrence that was based on a substantial but limited intercontinental capability against the United States. Conceivably, the threat of dissidence within the camp could have been reduced or at least postponed by concentrating attention on the grievances of the Communist China, avoiding unnecessary slights to its leaders, and granting large economic subsidies and military assistance. The Soviet leaders were enticed, however, by the opportunities that opened before them to neutralize the "reserves" of imperialism in the underdeveloped countries and to win concessions from the main opponent by sharp, though carefully controlled, pressure at vulnerable points.

Whatever the outcome of a conservative policy of coping with dangers and passing over opportunities might have been—whether it would have left the U.S.S.R. in a better or worse situation than the one in which it now finds itself—such a policy would unquestionably have altered radically the history of the cold war in the post-Stalin period. We have only to ask ourselves what the period after 1958 would have been like had the offensive against Berlin not been initiated. Moreover, and this is crucial for our theme, such a conservative policy would have assigned a significantly smaller part to the political use of strategic forces. The political role of these forces was magnified by the high priority assigned to the political offensive and by the need to make the most of the limited means available for excessively ambitious Soviet goals.

Until October, 1964, Soviet strategy in the cold war had for almost a decade originated with Premier Khrushchev and was chiefly executed by him. Yet, as we have seen, he did not create it as a unitary concept; it evolved in accordance with events, as he perceived them. He probably saw the political potential of nuclear weapons early in the post-Stalin period, yet he was also impressed at first by the threat to the security of the U.S.S.R. These two strands in his thinking on world affairs were evident in 1954 and in at least part of 1955. It is hard to know when Khrushchev decided that Soviet security could be assured even when confronted by a greatly preponderant United States strategic force, but it was clearly in the period between mid-1955 and November, 1958, when he initiated the Berlin crisis.

One turning point in his strategic thinking almost certainly was the Geneva summit conference of July, 1955. It not only reassured him about the motive forces of United States policy and the intentions of President Eisenhower; it also demonstrated America responsiveness to Soviet proposals of *détente*. It probably added appreciably to his confidence that he could control the international atmosphere by offering the Western allies relatively small concessions or even by mere gestures. The large, probably unexpected, effect produced on Western leaders at this time by the demonstration that the U.S.S.R. had successfully developed advanced intercontinental bombers may have revealed to Khrushchev something of the West's susceptibility to exaggerated claims of Soviet strategic capabilities. Nevertheless, he made little effort to capitalize on this new insight for several reasons, the most important of which was the incontestable fact of the great United States superiority in strategic bombing forces.

A year later, in the fall of 1956, a critical point was reached in the evolution of Khrushchev's strategic thought. The United States failed to use its strategic preponderance to exploit the critical Soviet vulnerabilities in Eastern Europe that were revealed by the events in Poland and especially in Hungary. This reinforced, perhaps decisively, Khrushchev's growing conviction that the West meant to employ its strategic superiority only defensively and not as a basis for a serious political offensive against the Soviet camp. At the same time, events revolving around the Suez crisis may have encouraged the notion that the emergent Soviet nuclear capability, though far inferior to the American, could be shaped into a potent instrument of Soviet foreign policy, to be employed offensively as well as defensively. The equivocal hint during the crisis that Soviet rockets might be used against France and Great Britain if necessary—although no definite results followed that were clearly attributable to it—probably suggested to Khrushchev the political potentialities of the new weapons and also the tactics he might use for their peacetime employment.

In mid-1957, a conjunction of circumstances made it possible to fit together the major lessons of the previous years and to further the elaboration of a new strategy. Adoption of the new strategy was facilitated at that time by two events: successful development of powerful ICBM rocket engines in advance of the United States, which provided a promising military basis for claims of Soviet strategic superiority, and Khrushchev's virtually coincident advent to supreme power, which established its political basis. By resolving the Stalin succession crisis, Khrushchev was able to provide stable leadership, which was a necessary condition for seriously waging an ambitious political offensive against the West. What was equally important, the adoption of such a strategy was favored both by Khrushchev's political character, boldly vigorous and strongly attracted by the novel, and by his growing conviction, which we have tried to trace, that Soviet strategic forces could be made a potent instrument of Soviet foreign policy.

The first efforts to employ the new political strategy in the fall of 1957 were tentative and inconclusive. In November, 1958, however, Khrushchev undertook a serious test of the new strategy when he personally initiated the Berlin crisis, with results that proved disappointing. By 1962 Khrushchev had discovered that before he could successfully employ Soviet strategic power to make direct and substantial political gains he would have to increase it substantially and make the increase visible to the United States. The Soviet political offensive against Berlin and other targets was held in abeyance while Khrushchev attempted to place missiles in Cuba. The object of this maneuver was not, as in Berlin, to use Soviet strategic power directly to force local concessions but rather to increase Soviet strategic power so that subsequently it could be employed to exact political concessions, in Berlin and elsewhere.

Failure of the Cuban missile venture compelled Khrushchev to reassess the peacetime usefulness of Soviet strategic forces. His decision, as it appears from the events of the next two years, was to downgrade them as an instrument of foreign policy. Not that Khrushchev had ceased to boast of Soviet strategic forces or to threaten the West with them, but they now served less as a positive instrument for eliciting concessions from the West than as a means of neutralizing the West's own strategic forces. This change in a key instrument of Soviet foreign policy affected that policy as a whole as well as the other instruments. It contributed to a policy of lessening tension with the West and to the conclusion of various agreements, most notably the partial nuclear test-ban treaty. Degradation of Soviet strategic power as a political instrument also encouraged the increased use of other means to further the ends of Soviet foreign policy. In the summer of 1964, for example, military aid to such countries as Indonesia was sharply increased, and economic aid was extended on a large scale to Algeria and the United Arab Republic. These expensive new programs were meant to serve a variety of aims, of course, but among them may have been the substitution of other instruments for strategic power, which had been downgraded.

What political use is likely to be made of Soviet strategic power in the coming years by Khrushchev's heirs? It will be recalled that

Khrushchev took three successive positions on the effects of nuclear weapons in the cold war: initially, he viewed nuclear weapons in the hands of the United States as posing an acute threat to the security of the Soviet Union; subsequently, he believed that Soviet strategic nuclear power could be used as a positive instrument for eliciting concessions from the Western allies; finally, he attempted to employ Soviet nuclear power chiefly as a means of neutralizing the American strategic forces. Which of these three positions is likely to provide the basis for Soviet policy now that Khrushchev is gone?

Khrushchev's political character had been formed largely during the course of his long political career, and its salient traits were revealed to the West during the period of his rule. In particular, his understanding of the peacetime use of nuclear force was shaped by his experience over several years, an experience that the West shared with him. We know far less about the political character of Khrushchev's successors. Yet the political character of the leadership can make a difference, at times a decisive difference.

There is a tendency in the West to overlook the fluidity of Soviet policy, to suppose that its lines are set and that they will remain so. This view is questionable. It is therefore worthwhile to consider the views of Khrushchev's predecessor and to contrast them with his own views (and the policies that stemmed from them) in order to indicate why his successors' policies may differ from his own.

Stalin believed in nuclear weapons, contrary to what he said about them publicly. Had this not been so, the U.S.S.R. would not have been so far advanced in the development of ballistic missiles and thermonuclear warheads when he died. As long as he lacked nuclear weapons, Stalin depreciated them, but he showed a healthy respect for the enemy who had them. We do not know what use he would have made of the new weapons once they had entered the Soviet arsenal, but it is unlikely, in view of the political character he revealed over more than three decades, that Stalin would have used them, as Khrushchev did, as the basis for a daring policy of bluff and deception. Stalin probably would have spoken softly and carried a big stick, that is, have procured a sizable operational capability rapidly and used it cautiously on behalf of limited and carefully chosen political ends. Stalin sought his gains in contiguous countries, in order to secure and extend the Soviet borders, rather than at a great distance from the U.S.S.R. We may hazard a guess that had Stalin lived another few years the U.S.S.R. would have adopted a more ambitious program to procure intercontinental delivery vehicles and that the new weapons would have been used as a basis for renewed pressure, say, on Iran and Turkey, instead of being projected politically into Western Europe, North Africa, and Cuba to capitalize on developments there. Khrushchev's political strategy, as we have seen, was quite different. He boasted of Soviet strategic superiority when the U.S.S.R. was grossly inferior, and he tried to project a simulated strategic force to the ends of the earth.

What then of Khrushchev's heirs? How will they use strategic power as an instrument of foreign policy? As we have said, it is hard to know since their political character has not yet been fully revealed. Conceivably, they may prove to be men who, unlike Stalin and Khrushchev, would willingly engage the West at the brink of nuclear war. Although they probably shared Khrushchev's experience of trying to make strategic weapons a coercive instrument in the cold war, we cannot know how they have been affected by this experience. They may have concluded that Khrushchev was "adventuristic" in pursuing large political ends with inadequate nuclear forces or that he simply was inept in employing this novel instrument of foreign policy. In either case, the various policies considered in the previous chapter might still have an attraction for them. On the other hand, they may believe that Khrushchev overestimated the offensive value of strategic forces in peacetime or that he bungled a golden opportunity that will not recur. If so, they may be disinclined to use strategic power as the basis of new political offensives against the West.

The Kremlin might find it expedient to continue to employ strategic threats that seemed to involve little or no risk, since this is an instrument of the cold war that is not yet available to Communist China. Soviet strategic threats are not a promising means of forcing concessions from the West as long as the United States has a preponderance of strategic power, knows it, and knows that the U.S.S.R. knows it. Yet such threats may usefully serve to demonstrate to the Communist world the intensity of Soviet efforts to win new victories for communism and to reassure exposed allies of the U.S.S.R. without risking a serious confrontation with the United States. As Communist China acquires strategic weapons, and with them the capacity to threaten their use in support of other states, the Soviet leaders may find themselves drawn into a contest with the Chinese that will take the form of bidding for the allegiance of adherents and potential adherents through far-reaching strategic commitments.

In the first months of the new regime, Soviet strategic forces retained roughly the same relatively limited role in Soviet foreign policy that they had played in the last years of Khrushchev's rule: that of neutralizing the strategic forces of the United States. This was true even though Soviet involvement in the conflict in Vietnam increased sharply soon after the new leaders assumed power, thus ending Khrushchev's evident disengagement from Southeast Asia. They demonstrated an extreme reluctance to employ strategic threats against the United States in support of their objectives in this area. And since the departure of Khrushchev had not lessened the fundamental antagonism between the Soviet and Chinese Communist parties, they also remained wary of allowing Soviet strategic power to be brought to bear on behalf of Communist China's foreign policies. The Chinese leaders publicly took note of this continuity in Soviet policy and began to castigate Russia's new rulers as Khrushchevite revisionists and capitulationists.[1] For Moscow the question remained: Once Soviet strategic power has been projected into such distant arenas as Cuba and North Africa, can it subsequently be withheld from Communist states that are endangered?

The problem of defending such states was posed with special force after February, 1965, when North Vietnam came under attack by American bombers. The Soviet leaders had repeatedly boasted since the Suez crisis of 1956 that "the imperialists" were deterred by Soviet strategic power from aggression against socialist states and even against formerly colonial countries. They cited a series of encounters to demonstrate this, among them Suez (1956), Hungary (1956), Syria (1957), Iraq (1958), and Cuba (1961). The U.S.S.R. asserted that it was a reliable defender of Communist states and other potential victims of "imperialist aggression," and on this assertion it rested the claim to leadership of the Communist and anticolonial movements. When the United States adopted its policy of bombing North Vietnam, a Communist state, however, and continued to do so with impunity in the following months, this long-standing Soviet claim was discredited.

Since the U.S.S.R. failed to respond to the American bombings by military reprisals, the threshold for Soviet involvement in hostilities against the United States was revealed to be even higher than had been implied by Soviet declaratory policy. This further exposure of the U.S.S.R.'s reluctance to engage in hostilities with the United

---

[1] Joint article published by *People's Daily* and *Red Flag*, March 23, 1965, in *Peking Review*, March 26, 1965, pp. 7–13. See also the Albanian polemic quoted at the head of this chapter.

States has proved politically expensive. It has provided grounds for the Chinese leaders' assertion that Communist states cannot rely upon the Soviet Union to defend them against direct attack by the United States. It remains a question, which has not yet been put to the test, whether an effort by the United States to overthrow a Communist regime would bring certain Soviet military intervention. Were the U.S.S.R. to fail to intervene, the political costs no doubt would be far greater than they have yet been in the case of North Vietnam.

The dangerous developments in North Vietnam may compel the post-Khrushchev leaders to re-examine the strategic choices facing them. So long as the U.S.S.R. remains inferior to the United States in strategic power, can it risk engaging in hostilities with the United States? If not, can the U.S.S.R. maintain its pretensions to be the protector of the Communist and anticolonial worlds? If a posture of strategic inferiority involves rising political costs, the post-Khrushchev leaders may come to re-evaluate the acceptability of the sacrifices required to achieve strategic parity.

Alternatively, the U.S.S.R. may alter its policy toward other Communist states and toward governments and revolutionary movements in non-Communist countries that seek Soviet strategic military backing. The Soviet leaders might reaffirm and even strengthen their undertakings but make the fulfilment of such commitments contingent on their prior approval of moves likely to provoke United States armed intervention. This policy would be in accord with Moscow's warning to Peking that it could not rely on the U.S.S.R. to support with its military power interests peculiar to China.[2] Extended to other quarters, the policy might weaken the Soviet position in the Communist movement and in the underdeveloped world; but until China comes to possess the necessary strategic power to assume the U.S.S.R.'s international responsibilities, Soviet political losses might be kept within acceptable bounds. Moreover, such losses might be more than outweighed in the Soviet view by the reduced risks to Soviet security.

The place of strategic power in Soviet foreign policy, then, will depend on several political factors. It will depend upon the growth of polycentrism in the Communist world and upon the resulting situation in which even small Communist states act independently of Moscow to create the circumstances in which Soviet foreign policy must evolve. It will depend upon the West's will to resist Communist

[2] V. A. Zorin, "Disarmament Problems and Peking's Maneuvers," *Izvestiia*, June 30, 1964.

pressures and on the kinds of action by which that will is given expression. Finally, it will depend upon the political character of Khrushchev's heirs: Brezhnev and Kosygin, in the first instance, and whoever may gain ascendancy in the future.[3]

The interplay of the strategic nuclear balance, exaggerated Soviet claims, uncertain intelligence estimates, and the opposing political goals of the two sides will no doubt continue in the coming years. If the United States, as before, can maintain a sufficient margin of superiority without giving a large stimulus to the arms race, it may hope to deter not only war but also the dangerous employment of Soviet strategic power for political ends. Even this crucial objective, however, cannot be the final goal of United States policy toward the U.S.S.R. Its attainment could set the stage for the deeper accommodation that will be required to bring an end to the cold war itself.

[3] See Myron Rush, *Political Succession in the USSR* (New York: Columbia University Press, 1965).

INDEX